W9-DIR-614

SUPREME COURT WATCH 2001

Highlights of the 1999–2000 Terms
Preview of the 2001–2002 Term

DAVID M. O'BRIEN

UNIVERSITY OF VIRGINIA

W. W. NORTON & COMPANY

New York   London

Copyright © 2002, 2001 by W. W. Norton & Company, Inc.

All rights reserved

Printed in the United States of America

ISBN 0-393-97750-1 (pbk.)

W. W. Norton & Company, Inc., 500 Fifth Avenue, New York, N.Y. 10110
    www.wwnorton.com
W. W. Norton & Company Ltd., Castle House, 75/76 Wells Street,
London W1T 3QT

1 2 3 4 5 6 7 8 9 0

CONTENTS

VOLUME TWO

Chapter 3. *Economic Rights and American Capitalism* 71

C. The "Takings Clause" and Just Compensation *71*

❏ THE DEVELOPMENT OF LAW: Other Important Rulings
on the Takings Clause *71*

Chapter 4. *The Nationalization of the Bill of Rights* 72

B. The Rise and Retreat of the "Due Process Revolution" 72
[*Kansas v. Crane*] 72

❏ THE DEVELOPMENT OF LAW: Rulings on Substantive
and Procedural Due Process *73*

Chapter 5. *Freedom of Expression and Association* 74

A. Judicial Approaches to the First Amendment *74*

(2) Judicial Line Drawing: *Ad Hoc* and Definitional
Balancing *74*
[*Legal Services Corporation v. Velazquez*] *74*
*Board of Regents of the University of Wisconsin System
v. Southworth* 75

B. Obscenity, Pornography, and Offensive Speech *79*
(1) Obscenity and Pornography *79*
[*Los Angeles, California v. Alameda Books, Inc.*] *79*
City of Erie v. Pap's A.M. *79*

(2) Fighting Words and Offensive Speech *85*
[*Apprendi v. New Jersey*] *85*

D. Commercial Speech *86*
Lorillard Tobacco Co. v. Reilly *86*

PREFACE

Supreme Court Watch 2001 examines the changes and decisions made during the Supreme Court's 1999–2000 terms. (In addition, a few of the important rulings that came down at the end of the Court's 1998–1999 term are also included here, because it was impossible to include them in the fourth edition of *Constitutional Law and Politics*.) In addition to highlighting the major constitutional rulings in excerpts from leading cases, I discuss in section-by-section introductions other important decisions and analyze recent developments in various areas of constitutional law. The important cases that the Court has granted review and will decide in its 2001–2002 term are also previewed here. To offer even more information in an efficient format, I have included special boxes titled "The Development of Law" and "Inside the Court."

The favorable reception of and comments received on previous editions of the *Watch* have been gratifying, and I hope that this 2001 edition will further contribute to students' understanding of constitutional law, politics, and history, as well as to their appreciation for how the politics of constitutional interpretation turns on differing interpretations of constitutional politics. I am also most grateful to Ann Marcy, Todd Rankin, and Jane Carter for doing a terrific and expeditious job of copyediting.

D.M.O.
June 28, 2000

VOLUME ONE

2

LAW AND POLITICS IN THE SUPREME COURT: JURISDICTION AND DECISION-MAKING PROCESS

A. JURISDICTION AND JUSTICIABLE CONTROVERSIES

THE DEVELOPMENT OF LAW

Other Important Rulings on Standing

Case	Vote	Ruling
Friends of Earth, Inc. v. Laidlaw Environmental Services, 528 U.S. 167 (2000)	7:2	In an important ruling on citizen suits brought to enforce federal environmental laws, Justice Ginsburg upheld the

right of Friends of Earth, Inc., to sue Laidlaw Environmental Services for failing to comply with the Clean Water Act by impermissibly dumping mercury into a South Carolina river on 489 occasions from 1987 to 1995. Justice Ginsburg held that the group had shown sufficient personal injury from their loss of enjoyment of the river to gain standing to sue, without also having to prove "direct injury" to the river. The test for standing, in Justice Ginsburg's words, is "not injury to the environment but injury to the plaintiff." Moreover, Justice Ginsburg ruled that the fact that fines won under citizen suits go to the federal government, not to the individuals bringing the suits, does not diminish the personal injury at stake or deprive plaintiffs of standing. Joined by Justice Thomas in dissent, Justice Scalia lamented the majority's upholding of standing to bring such citizen suits and for turning "over to private citizens the function of enforcing the law."

| *Alexander. v. Sandoval,* | 5:4 | Writing for the Court, Justice |
| 121 S.Ct. 1511 (2001) | | Scalia held that individuals |

do not have standing to sue in order to enforce compliance with Title VI of the Civil Rights Act, which bars state and local governments from spending federal funds in a discriminatory manner, unless they can show that the *intent* of the institution—a state, school district, hospital, etc.—was to discriminate. Previously, the Department of Justice and federal courts had held that, in most cases, individuals could sue upon showing that the *effect* of a particular practice or policy—hiring or admissions rules, for example—worked to disadvantage minorities and women. As a result, the threshold for standing for private individuals to enforce state and local government compliance with Title VI was raised and the filing of so-called disparite-impact lawsuits limited. Justices Stevens, Souter, Ginsburg, and Breyer dissented.

B. THE COURT'S DOCKET AND SCREENING CASES

The Supreme Court's docket over the last few decades has continued to grow steadily, reaching more than 8,900 cases in the 2000–2001 term. Since the early 1990s, the largest growth has been in unpaid, or *in forma pauperis*, cases, which tend to be filed by prison inmates. (For further discussion, see Vol. 1 or 2, Ch. 2.[1]) In the 2000–2001 term, for instance, 6,651 unpaid cases were filed, compared with only 2,305 paid cases. Over the same period, the Court has steadily cut back on the number of cases granted review. As a result, the Court has been granting only 80 to 90 cases each term, or about 1 percent of its docket.[2]

Although the Rehnquist Court gives plenary consideration to fewer cases, it has not abandoned its responsibility to supervise the lower federal courts. The Court generally takes only cases with nationwide importance, especially to resolve conflicting rulings rendered by lower courts or to reverse decisions of lower federal and state courts. The Court's affirmance and reversal of lower court decisions in its 2000–2001 term is indicated on the next page:

---

[1] References to Vols. 1 and 2 are to the author's two-volume *Constitutional Law and Politics* (Norton, 4th ed., 2000).

[2] For a further discussion, see David M. O'Brien, "The Rehnquist Court's Shrinking Plenary Docket," 81 *Judicature* 58–65 (1997).

The Court's Disposition of Appeals in the 2000 Term

	Affirmed	Reversed or Vacated
First Circuit		1
Second Circuit	5	3
Third Circuit	1	3
Fourth Circuit	3	2
Fifth Circuit	3	3
Sixth Circuit	4	3
Seventh Circuit		5
Eighth Circuit	1	1
Ninth Circuit	4	12
Tenth Circuit		2
Eleventh Circuit	2	3
Federal Circuit		2
District of Columbia Circuit		1
Other Federal Courts		2
State Courts and Other	2	12
*Totals	25	55

* Excludes three cases decided on original jurisdiction or dismissed for lack of jurisdiction.

INSIDE THE COURT

The Business of the Supreme Court in the 2000–2001 Term[*]

Subject of Court Opinions	Summary	Plenary
Admiralty		1
Antitrust		
Bankruptcy		
Bill of Rights (other than rights of accused) and Equal Protection	1	13
Commerce Clause		
1. Constitutionality and construction of federal regulation		1
2. Constitutionality of state regulation		1
Common Law		1
Miscellaneous Statutory Construction	1	22
Due process		
1. Economic interests		2
2. Procedure and rights of accused	2	10
3. Substantive due process (noneconomic)		
Impairment of Contract and Just Compensation		1
International Law, War, and Peace		
Jurisdiction, Procedure, and Practice		12
Land Legislation		
Native Americans		4
Patents, Copyright, and Trademarks		2
Other Suits Against the Government		4
Suits by States		1
Taxation (federal and state)		4
Totals	4	79

[*] Note: The classification of cases is that of the author and necessarily invites differences of opinion as to the dominant issue in some cases. The table includes opinions in cases whether decided summarily or given plenary consideration, but not cases summarily disposed of by simple orders, opinions dissenting from the denial of review, and those dismissing cases as improvidently granted.

H. OPINION DAYS AND COMMUNICATING DECISIONS

In April 2000 the Supreme Court began making its decisions and opinions immediately available on its Web site at http://www.supremecourtus.gov. A link to the site may also be found at the *Supreme Court Watch*'s site at http://www.wwnorton.com/scww/.

INSIDE THE COURT

Opinion Writing during the 2000–2001 Term[*]

Opinions	Majority	Concurring	Dissenting	Separate	Totals
Per Curiam	7				7
Rehnquist	9	2	3		14
Stevens	9	6	12	3	30
O'Connor	9	3	3	1	16
Scalia	8	11	9		28
Kennedy	8	5	1		14
Souter	8	4	6	2	20
Thomas	8	8	4		20
Ginsburg	8	4	4	1	17
Breyer	9	2	12		23
Totals	83	45	54	7	189

[*] Note that Court opinions disposing of two or more companion cases are counted only once here. In addition, this table includes opinions in cases disposed of either summarily or upon plenary consideration, but does not include cases summarily disposed of by simple orders or concurring or dissenting opinions from the denial of *certiorari*.

INSIDE THE COURT

Voting Alignments in the Rehnquist Court, 1986–1999 Terms

	Rehnquist	White	Blackmun	Stevens	O'Connor	Scalia	Kennedy	Souter	Thomas	Brennan	Marshall	Ginsburg	Breyer
Rehnquist	--	80.8	55.2	51.7	81.0	78.6	88.5	67.9	79.6	47.6	46.4	64.6	63.5
White	80.8	--	62.2	60.4	72.5	69.8	75.7	73.5	67.7	52.9	52.9		
Blackmun	55.2	62.2	--	72.0	58.4	49.1	57.6	64.8	44.4	77.4	77.0	68.2	
Stevens	51.7	60.4	72.0	--	56.1	47.1	57.3	68.9	44.3	69.9	71.6	77.1	74.2
O'Connor	81.0	72.5	58.4	56.1	--	71.8	84.7	71.4	72.4	49.4	47.9	66.6	72.0
Scalia	78.6	69.8	49.1	47.1	71.8	--	75.7	61.5	87.6	47.5	45.0	56.3	54.5
Kennedy	88.5	75.7	57.6	57.3	84.7	75.7	--	71.3	73.5	53.7	51.2	67.9	67.2
Souter	67.9	73.5	64.8	68.9	71.4	61.5	71.3	--	58.6		54.6	82.5	82.1
Thomas	79.6	67.7	44.4	44.3	72.4	87.6	73.5	58.6	--			53.8	53.5
Brennan	47.6	52.9	77.4	69.9	49.4	47.5	53.7			--	95.0		
Marshall	46.4	52.9	77.0	71.6	47.9	45.0	51.2	54.6		95.0	--		
Ginsburg	64.6		68.2	77.1	66.6	56.3	67.9	82.5	53.8			--	79.7
Breyer	63.5			74.2	72.0	54.5	67.2	82.1	53.5			79.7	--

Note: The above are average percentages. The percentages for each term are from Table 1 of the *Harvard Law Review*'s annual review of the Supreme Court's term in volumes 101–114 (1988–2000).

4

THE PRESIDENT AS
CHIEF EXECUTIVE
IN DOMESTIC AFFAIRS

C. LEGISLATIVE POWERS IN THE
ADMINISTRATIVE STATE

Reaffirming the so-called *Chevron* doctrine, set forth in *Chevron v. Natural Resources Defense Council*, 467 U.S. 837 (1984) (see Vol. 1, Ch. 4), which states that if a statute is "silent or ambiguous" on a matter, the courts will defer to the executive branch's interpretation, the Court rebuffed the U.S. Food and Drug Administration's (FDA) 1996 decision to claim jurisdiction over tobacco products. Writing for the Court in *Food and Drug Administration v. Brown and Williamson*, 529 U.S. 120 (2000), Justice O'Connor held that Congress, in passing numerous laws governing tobacco products, and the FDA's own prior interpretation of its governing statute made clear Congress's intent to exempt tobacco from the FDA's jurisdiction. Moreover, Justice O'Connor observed that it was impossible for tobacco products to be rendered safe and therefore the FDA would have to ban their sale if it had jurisdiction over them. In dissent, Justice Breyer, joined by Justices Stevens, Souter, and Ginsburg, contended that the FDA could assume jurisdiction over tobacco products without having to ban their sale.

5

CONGRESS:
MEMBERSHIP, IMMUNITIES,
AND INVESTIGATORY POWERS

A. MEMBERSHIP AND IMMUNITIES

In response to the ruling in *U.S. Term Limits, Inc. v. Thorton*, 514
U.S. 779 (1995) (excerpted in Vol. 1, Ch. 5), which struck down Arkansas's
law on term limits for members of Congress, a year later Missouri amended
its state constitution to require that the words "Disregarded Voters' Instruction on Term Limits" be placed on the ballot next to the name of an incumbent who failed to support term limits and who runs for reelection. For
candidates who are not incumbents and who refuse to vow to support term
limits, the law required that the label "Declined to Pledge to Support Term
Limits" be placed next to their names. Donald Gralike, a congressional candidate, challenged the constitutionality of the law. As in *U.S. Term Limits*,
writing for the Court in *Cook v. Gralike*, 531 U.S. 510 (2001), Justice
Stevens struck down Missouri's law for running afoul of Elections Clause
of Article 1, Section 4, by impermissibly attempting to add qualifications
for holding congressional office beyond those specified for members' age,
citizenship, and residency. Chief Justice Rehnquist and Justices Kennedy
and Thomas each filed concurring opinions.

6

CONGRESS: LEGISLATIVE, TAXING, AND SPENDING POWERS

C. FROM THE NEW DEAL CRISIS TO THE ADMINISTRATIVE STATE

In spite of recent rulings curbing congressional power under the Commerce Clause of Article I, in *United States v. Lopez*, 514 U.S. 549 (1995) (excerpted in Vol. 1, Ch. 6), and *Printz v. United States* and *Mack v. United States*, 521 U.S. 898 (1997) (excerpted in Vol. 1, Ch. 7), as well as under Section 5 of the Fourteenth Amendment, in *City of Boerne v. Flores*, 521 U.S. 507 (1997) (excerpted in Vol. 2, Ch. 6), the Court unanimously upheld the Drivers' Privacy Protection Act of 1994 in *Reno v. Condon* (excerpted below). The bare majority striking down other congressional legislation, however, held firm in holding unconstitutional the Violence Against Women Act of 1994, in *United States v. Morrison* (excerpted below).

In a related ruling, *Jones v. United States*, 530 U.S. 1222 (2000), the Court unanimously held that a congressional statute making the offense of arson of property "used in interstate or foreign commerce" a federal crime does not extend to arson of a residential home. Writing for the Court, Justice Ginsburg emphasized that *Lopez* made clear that Congress's power over interstate commerce extends to only noncommercial activities that "significantly affect commerce" and that here, because the statute was ambiguous, it was appropriate for the Court to avoid the constitutional question of whether Congress aimed to reach the arson of homes, which is a paradigmatic common-law state crime, and thereby alter the federal-state balance in the prosecution of crime.

Reno v. Condon
528 U.S. 141, 120 S.Ct. 666 (2000)

Congress enacted the Drivers' Privacy Protection Act of 1994 to protect individuals' privacy and other interests. The law regulates the disclosure of personal information contained in the records of state motor vehicle departments. Specifically, it forbids the disclosure of personal information—name, address, telephone number, identification number, photograph, and medical information—except for certain purposes related, for instance, to driver safety and motor vehicle recalls. The law also regulates the resale of such information by private parties and imposes penalties for violations. South Carolina and some other states regularly sold such information and immediately challenged the constitutionality of the law. Charlie Condon, South Carolina's attorney general, argued that the law violated the Tenth and Eleventh Amendments and was incompatible with principles of federalism. A federal district court agreed and was affirmed by the Court of Appeals for the Fourth Circuit. Attorney General Janet Reno appealed and the Supreme Court granted review.

The appellate court's decision was reversed in a unanimous opinion for the Court delivered by Chief Justice Rehnquist.

Chief Justice REHNQUIST delivered the opinion of the Court.

The Driver's Privacy Protection Act of 1994 (DPPA or Act) regulates the disclosure of personal information contained in the records of state motor vehicle departments (DMVs). We hold that in enacting this statute Congress did not run afoul of the federalism principles enunciated in *New York v. United States*, 505 U.S. 144 (1992), and *Printz v. United States*, 521 U.S. 898 (1997). . . .

The United States asserts that the DPPA is a proper exercise of Congress' authority to regulate interstate commerce under the Commerce Clause. The United States bases its Commerce Clause argument on the fact that the personal, identifying information that the DPPA regulates is a "thin[g] in interstate commerce," and that the sale or release of that information in interstate commerce is therefore a proper subject of congressional regulation. *United States v. Lopez*, 514 U.S. 549 (1995). We agree with the United States' contention. The motor vehicle information which the States have historically sold is used by insurers, manufacturers, direct marketers, and others engaged in interstate commerce to contact drivers with customized solicitations. The information is also used in the stream of interstate commerce by various public and private entities for matters related to interstate motoring. Because drivers' information is, in this context, an article of commerce, its sale or release into the interstate stream of business is sufficient to support congressional regulation. We therefore need not address the Government's alternative argument that the States' individual, intrastate activities in gathering, maintaining, and distributing drivers' personal information has a sufficiently substantial impact on interstate commerce to create a constitutional base for federal legislation.

But the fact that drivers' personal information is, in the context of this case, an article in interstate commerce does not conclusively resolve the constitutionality of the DPPA. In *New York* and *Printz*, we held federal statutes invalid, not because Congress lacked legislative authority over the subject matter, but because those statutes violated the principles of federalism contained in the Tenth Amendment. . . .

We agree with South Carolina's assertion that the DPPA's provisions will require time and effort on the part of state employees, but reject the State's argument that the DPPA violates the principles laid down in either *New York* or *Printz*. We think, instead, that this case is governed by our decision in *South Carolina v. Baker*, 485 U.S. 505 (1988). In *Baker*, we upheld a statute that prohibited States from issuing unregistered bonds because the law "regulate[d] state activities," rather than "seek[ing] to control or influence the manner in which States regulate private parties." We further noted: "The NGA [National Governor's Association] nonetheless contends that Section 310 has commandeered the state legislative and administrative process because many state legislatures had to amend a substantial number of statutes in order to issue bonds in registered form and because state officials had to devote substantial effort to determine how best to implement a registered bond system. Such 'commandeering' is, however, an inevitable consequence of regulating a state activity. Any federal regulation demands compliance. That a State wishing to engage in certain activity must take administrative and sometimes legislative action to comply with federal standards regulating that activity is a commonplace that presents no constitutional defect."

Like the statute at issue in *Baker*, the DPPA does not require the States in their sovereign capacity to regulate their own citizens. The DPPA regulates the States as the owners of databases. It does not require the South Carolina Legislature to enact any laws or regulations, and it does not require state officials to assist in the enforcement of federal statutes regulating private individuals. We accordingly conclude that the DPPA is consistent with the constitutional principles enunciated in *New York* and *Printz*. . . .

The judgment of the Court of Appeals is therefore reversed.

United States v. Morrison
529 U.S. 598, 120 S.Ct. 1740 (2000)

After holding extensive hearings on gender-motivated violence and finding that such violence costs the national economy $3 billion annually, Congress enacted the Violence Against Women Act of 1994, which made violence against women a federal crime and, in Section 13981 of the U.S. Code, created as a remedy a private cause of action for victims to sue their attackers for damages. In 1994, Christy Brozonkala, a first-year student at Virginia Polytechnic Institute and State University, was allegedly raped in her dormitory room by two football players, Antonio Morrison and James Crawford. No criminal charges were filed against the latter, but subsequently Brozonkala sued them for damages under the Violence Against

Women Act. A federal district court, however, concluded that the law was an unconstitutional intrusion on traditional state concerns, and the Court of Appeals for the Fourth Circuit agreed, relying on *United States v. Lopez*, 514 U.S. 549 (1995), and *City of Boerne v. Flores*, 521 U.S. 507 (1997). The U.S. government and Brozonkala appealed, and 36 states joined a brief in support of the law. The Supreme Court granted review.

The decision of the appellate court was affirmed by a five to four vote. Chief Justice Rehnquist delivered the opinion for the Court. Justice Thomas filed a concurring opinion. Justices Souter and Breyer filed dissenting opinions, which were joined by Justices Ginsburg and Stevens.

Chief Justice REHNQUIST delivered the opinion of the Court.

The United States Court of Appeals for the Fourth Circuit, sitting *en banc*, struck down Section 13981 because it concluded that Congress lacked constitutional authority to enact the section's civil remedy. Believing that these cases are controlled by our decisions in *United States v. Lopez*, 514 U.S. 549 (1995), *United States v. Harris*, 106 U.S. 629 (1883), and the *Civil Rights Cases*, 109 U.S. 3 (1883), we affirm. . . .

Every law enacted by Congress must be based on one or more of its powers enumerated in the Constitution. Congress explicitly identified the sources of federal authority on which it relied in enacting Section 13981. It said that a "federal civil rights cause of action" is established "[p]ursuant to the affirmative power of Congress under Section 5 of the Fourteenth Amendment to the Constitution, as well as under Section 8 of Article I of the Constitution." We address Congress' authority to enact this remedy under each of these constitutional provisions in turn. . . .

As we discussed at length in *Lopez*, our interpretation of the Commerce Clause has changed as our Nation has developed. We need not repeat that detailed review of the Commerce Clause's history here; it suffices to say that, in the years since *NLRB v. Jones & Laughlin Steel Corp.*, 301 U.S. 1 (1937), Congress has had considerably greater latitude in regulating conduct and transactions under the Commerce Clause than our previous case law permitted.

As we observed in *Lopez*, modern Commerce Clause jurisprudence has "identified three broad categories of activity that Congress may regulate under its commerce power." "First, Congress may regulate the use of the channels of interstate commerce" (citing *Heart of Atlanta Motel, Inc. v. United States*, 379 U.S. 241, 256 [1964]; *United States v. Darby*, 312 U.S. 100 [1941]). "Second, Congress is empowered to regulate and protect the instrumentalities of interstate commerce, or persons or things in interstate commerce, even though the threat may come only from intrastate activities" (citing *Shreveport Rate Cases*, 234 U.S. 342 [1914]; *Southern R. Co. v. United States*, 222 U.S. 20 [1911]; *Perez* [*v. United States*, 402 U.S. 146 (1971)]). "Finally, Congress' commerce authority includes the power to regulate those activities having a substantial relation to interstate commerce, i.e., those activities that substantially affect interstate commerce" (citing *Jones & Laughlin Steel*).

Petitioners do not contend that these cases fall within either of the first two of these categories of Commerce Clause regulation. They seek to sustain Section 13981 as a regulation of activity that substantially affects interstate commerce. Given Section 13981's focus on gender-motivated violence wherever it occurs (rather than violence directed at the instrumentalities of interstate commerce, interstate markets, or things or persons in interstate commerce), we agree that this is the proper inquiry.

Since *Lopez* most recently canvassed and clarified our case law governing this third category of Commerce Clause regulation, it provides the proper framework for conducting the required analysis of Section 13981. In *Lopez*, we held that the Gun-Free School Zones Act of 1990, 18 U.S.C. Section 922(q)(1)(A), which made it a federal crime to knowingly possess a firearm in a school zone, exceeded Congress' authority under the Commerce Clause. Several significant considerations contributed to our decision.

First, . . . "Where economic activity substantially affects interstate commerce, legislation regulating that activity will be sustained." . . .

The second consideration that we found important . . . was that the statute contained "no express jurisdictional element which might limit its reach to a discrete set of firearm possessions that additionally have an explicit connection with or effect on interstate commerce." Such a jurisdictional element may establish that the enactment is in pursuance of Congress' regulation of interstate commerce.

Third, we noted that neither Section 922(q) "nor its legislative history contain[s] express congressional findings regarding the effects upon interstate commerce of gun possession in a school zone." While "Congress normally is not required to make formal findings as to the substantial burdens that an activity has on interstate commerce," the existence of such findings may "enable us to evaluate the legislative judgment that the activity in question substantially affect[s] interstate commerce, even though no such substantial effect [is] visible to the naked eye."

Finally, our decision in *Lopez* rested in part on the fact that the link between gun possession and a substantial effect on interstate commerce was attenuated. . . . We rejected these "costs of crime" and "national productivity" arguments because they would permit Congress to "regulate not only all violent crime, but all activities that might lead to violent crime, regardless of how tenuously they relate to interstate commerce."

With these principles underlying our Commerce Clause jurisprudence as reference points, the proper resolution of the present cases is clear. Gender-motivated crimes of violence are not, in any sense of the phrase, economic activity. While we need not adopt a categorical rule against aggregating the effects of any non-economic activity in order to decide these cases, thus far in our Nation's history our cases have upheld Commerce Clause regulation of intrastate activity only where that activity is economic in nature.

Like the Gun-Free School Zones Act at issue in *Lopez*, Section 13981 contains no jurisdictional element establishing that the federal cause of action is in pursuance of Congress' power to regulate interstate commerce. Although *Lopez* makes clear that such a jurisdictional element would lend support to the argument that Section 13981 is sufficiently tied to interstate commerce, Congress elected to cast Section 13981's remedy over a wider, and more purely intrastate, body of violent crime.

In contrast with the lack of congressional findings that we faced in *Lopez*, Section 13981 is supported by numerous findings regarding the serious impact that gender-motivated violence has on victims and their families. But the existence of congressional findings is not sufficient, by itself, to sustain the constitutionality of Commerce Clause legislation. As we stated in *Lopez*, "[S]imply because Congress may conclude that a particular activity substantially affects interstate commerce does not necessarily make it so." Rather, "[w]hether particular operations affect interstate commerce sufficiently to come under the constitutional power of Congress to regulate them is ultimately a judicial rather than a legislative question, and can be settled finally only by this Court."

In these cases, Congress' findings are substantially weakened by the fact that they rely so heavily on a method of reasoning that we have already rejected as unworkable if we are to maintain the Constitution's enumeration of powers. Congress found that gender-motivated violence affects interstate commerce "by deterring potential victims from traveling interstate, from engaging in employment in interstate business, and from transacting with business, and in places involved in interstate commerce; by diminishing national productivity, increasing medical and other costs, and decreasing the supply of and the demand for interstate products." Given these findings and petitioners' arguments, the concern that we expressed in *Lopez* that Congress might use the Commerce Clause to completely obliterate the Constitution's distinction between national and local authority seems well founded. . . . If accepted, petitioners' reasoning would allow Congress to regulate any crime as long as the nationwide, aggregated impact of that crime has substantial effects on employment, production, transit, or consumption. Indeed, if Congress may regulate gender-motivated violence, it would be able to regulate murder or any other type of violence since gender-motivated violence, as a subset of all violent crime, is certain to have lesser economic impacts than the larger class of which it is a part. . . .

We accordingly reject the argument that Congress may regulate noneconomic, violent criminal conduct based solely on that conduct's aggregate effect on interstate commerce. The Constitution requires a distinction between what is truly national and what is truly local. In recognizing this fact we preserve one of the few principles that has been consistent since the Clause was adopted. The regulation and punishment of intrastate violence that is not directed at the instrumentalities, channels, or goods involved in interstate commerce has always been the province of the States.

Because we conclude that the Commerce Clause does not provide Congress with authority to enact Section 13981, we address petitioners' alternative argument that the section's civil remedy should be upheld as an exercise of Congress' remedial power under Section 5 of the Fourteenth Amendment.

The principles governing an analysis of congressional legislation under Section 5 are well settled. . . . *City of Boerne v. Flores*, 521 U.S. 507 (1997). Section 5 is "a positive grant of legislative power," *Katzenbach v. Morgan*, 384 U.S. 641 (1966), that includes authority to "prohibit conduct which is not itself unconstitutional and [to] intrud[e] into 'legislative spheres of autonomy previously reserved to the States.'" However, "[a]s broad as the congressional enforcement power is, it is not unlimited." *Oregon v. Mitchell*, 400 U.S. 112 (1970). . . .

As our cases have established, state-sponsored gender discrimination violates equal protection unless it "serves important governmental objectives and the discriminatory means employed" are "substantially related to the achievement of those objectives." *United States v. Virginia*, 518 U.S. 515 (1996). However, the language and purpose of the Fourteenth Amendment place certain limitations on the manner in which Congress may attack discriminatory conduct. These limitations are necessary to prevent the Fourteenth Amendment from obliterating the Framers' carefully crafted balance of power between the States and the National Government. Foremost among these limitations is the time-honored principle that the Fourteenth Amendment, by its very terms, prohibits only state action.

Shortly after the Fourteenth Amendment was adopted, we decided two cases interpreting the Amendment's provisions, *United States v. Harris*, 106 U.S. 629 (1883), and the *Civil Rights Cases*, 109 U.S. 3 (1883). In *Harris*, the Court considered a challenge to Section 2 of the Civil Rights Act of 1871. That section sought to punish "private persons" for "conspiring to deprive any one of the equal protection of the laws enacted by the State." We concluded that this law exceeded Congress' Section 5 power because the law was "directed exclusively against the action of private persons, without reference to the laws of the State, or their administration by her officers."

We reached a similar conclusion in the *Civil Rights Cases*. In those consolidated cases, we held that the public accommodation provisions of the Civil Rights Act of 1875, which applied to purely private conduct, were beyond the scope of the Section 5 enforcement power. . . .

Petitioners alternatively argue that, unlike the situation in the *Civil Rights Cases*, here there has been gender-based disparate treatment by state authorities, whereas in those cases there was no indication of such state action. There is abundant evidence, however, to show that the Congresses that enacted the Civil Rights Acts of 1871 and 1875 had a purpose similar to that of Congress in enacting Section 13981: There were state laws on the books bespeaking equality of treatment, but in the administration of these laws there was discrimination against newly freed slaves. . . .

But even if that distinction were valid, we do not believe it would save Section 13981's civil remedy. For the remedy is simply not "corrective in its character, adapted to counteract and redress the operation of such prohibited [s]tate laws or proceedings of [s]tate officers." *Civil Rights Cases*. Or, as we have phrased it in more recent cases, prophylactic legislation under Section 5 must have a "congruence and proportionality between the injury to be prevented or remedied and the means adopted to that end." *Florida Prepaid Postsecondary Ed. Expense Bd. v. College Savings Bank*, 527 U.S. 627 (1999); *Flores*. Section 13981 is not aimed at proscribing discrimination by officials which the Fourteenth Amendment might not itself proscribe; it is directed not at any State or state actor, but at individuals who have committed criminal acts motivated by gender bias. . . .

[Section 13981] is, therefore, unlike any of the Section 5 remedies that we have previously upheld. For example, in *Katzenbach v. Morgan*, 384 U.S. 641 (1966), Congress prohibited New York from imposing literacy tests as a prerequisite for voting because it found that such a requirement disenfranchised thousands of Puerto Rican immigrants who had been educated in the Spanish language of their home territory. That law, which we upheld, was directed at New York officials who administered the State's election law and prohibited them from using a provision of that law. In *South Carolina v. Katzenbach*, 383 U.S. 301 (1966), Congress imposed voting rights requirements on States that, Congress found, had a history of discriminating against blacks in voting. The remedy was also directed at state officials in those States. . . .

For these reasons, we conclude that Congress' power under Section 5 does not extend to the enactment of Section 13981.

Justice THOMAS, concurring.

The majority opinion correctly applies our decision in *United States v. Lopez* and I join it in full. I write separately only to express my view that the very notion of a "substantial effects" test under the Commerce Clause is inconsistent with the original understanding of Congress' powers and with this Court's early Commerce Clause cases. By continuing to apply this rootless and malleable standard, however circumscribed, the Court has encouraged the Federal Government to persist in its view that the Commerce Clause has virtually no limits. Until this Court replaces its existing Commerce Clause jurisprudence with a standard more consistent with the original understanding, we will continue to see Congress appropriating state police powers under the guise of regulating commerce.

Justice SOUTER, with whom Justice STEVENS, Justice GINSBURG, and Justice BREYER join, dissenting.

Congress has the power to legislate with regard to activity that, in the aggregate, has a substantial effect on interstate commerce. See *Wickard v. Filburn*, 317 U.S. 111 (1942). The fact of such a substantial effect is not an issue for the courts in the first instance, but for the Congress, whose institutional capacity for gathering evidence and taking testimony far exceeds ours. By passing legislation, Congress indicates its conclusion, whether explicitly or not, that facts support its exercise of the commerce power. The business of the courts is to review the congressional assessment, not for soundness but simply for the rationality of concluding that a jurisdictional basis exists in fact. Any explicit findings that Congress chooses to make, though not dispositive of the question of rationality, may advance judicial review by identifying factual authority on which Congress relied.

One obvious difference from *United States v. Lopez* is the mountain of data assembled by Congress here showing the effects of violence against women on interstate commerce. Passage of the Act in 1994 was preceded by four years of hearings, which included testimony from physicians and law professors; from survivors of rape and domestic violence; and from representatives of state law enforcement and private business. The record includes reports on gender bias from task forces in 21 States, and we have the benefit of specific factual findings in the eight separate Reports issued by Congress and its committees over the long course leading to enactment.

With respect to domestic violence, Congress received evidence for the following findings: "Three out of four American women will be victims of violent crimes sometime during their life." "Violence is the leading cause of injuries to women ages 15 to 44." "[A]s many as 50 percent of homeless women and children are fleeing domestic violence." "Since 1974, the assault rate against women has outstripped the rate for men by at least twice for some age groups and far more for others." "[B]attering is the single largest cause of injury to women in the United States." "An estimated 4 million American women are battered each year by their husbands or partners." "Over 1 million women in the United States seek medical assistance each year for injuries sustained [from] their husbands or other partners." "Between 2,000 and 4,000 women die every year from [domestic] abuse." "Partial estimates show that violent crime against women costs this country at least 3 billion—not million, but billion—dollars a year." "[E]stimate[s] suggest that we spend $5 to $10 billion a year on health care, criminal justice, and other social costs of domestic violence."

The evidence as to rape was similarly extensive, supporting these conclusions: "[The incidence of] rape rose four times as fast as the total national crime rate over the past 10 years." "According to one study, close to half a million girls now in high school will be raped before they graduate." "[One hundred twenty-five thousand] college women can expect to be raped during this—or any—year." "[T]hree-quarters of women never go to the movies alone after dark because of the fear of rape and nearly 50 percent do not use public transit alone after dark for the same reason." "[Forty-one] percent of judges surveyed believed that juries give sexual assault victims less credibility than other crime victims." "Less than 1 percent of all [rape] victims have collected damages." "[A]n individual who commits rape has only about 4 chances in 100 of being arrested, prosecuted, and found guilty of any offense." "Almost one-quarter of convicted rapists never go to prison and another quarter received sentences in local jails where the average sentence is 11 months." "[A]lmost 50 percent of rape victims lose their jobs or are forced to quit because of the crime's severity."

Based on the data thus partially summarized, Congress found that "crimes of violence motivated by gender have a substantial adverse effect on interstate commerce, by deterring potential victims from traveling interstate, from engaging in employment in interstate business, and from transacting with business, and in places involved, in interstate commerce[,] 'by diminishing national productivity, increasing medical and other costs, and decreasing the supply of and the demand for interstate products.'"

Congress thereby explicitly stated the predicate for the exercise of its Commerce Clause power. Is its conclusion irrational in view of the data amassed? True, the methodology of particular studies may be challenged, and some of the figures arrived at may be disputed. But the sufficiency of the evidence before Congress to provide a rational basis for the finding cannot seriously be questioned.

Indeed, the legislative record here is far more voluminous than the record compiled by Congress and found sufficient in two prior cases upholding Title II of the Civil Rights Act of 1964 against Commerce Clause challenges. In *Heart of Atlanta Motel, Inc. v. United States*, 379 U.S. 241 (1964), and *Katzenbach v. McClung*, 379 U.S. 294 (1964), the Court referred to evidence showing the consequences of racial discrimination by motels and restaurants on interstate commerce. Congress had relied on compelling anecdotal reports that individual instances of segregation cost thousands to millions of dollars.

While Congress did not, to my knowledge, calculate aggregate dollar values for the nationwide effects of racial discrimination in 1964, in 1994 it did rely on evidence of the harms caused by domestic violence and sexual assault, citing annual costs of $3 billion in 1990, and $5 to $10 billion in 1993. Equally important, though, gender-based violence in the 1990's was shown to operate in a manner similar to racial discrimination in the 1960's in reducing the mobility of employees and their production and consumption of goods shipped in interstate commerce. Like racial discrimination, "[g]ender-based violence bars its most likely targets—women—from full partic[ipation] in the national economy."

If the analogy to the Civil Rights Act of 1964 is not plain enough, one can always look back a bit further. In *Wickard*, we upheld the application of the Agricultural Adjustment Act to the planting and consumption of homegrown wheat. The effect on interstate commerce in that case followed from the possibility that wheat grown at home for personal consumption could either be drawn into the market by rising prices, or relieve its grower of any need to purchase wheat in the market. The Commerce Clause predicate was simply the effect of the production of wheat for home consumption on supply and demand in interstate commerce. Supply and demand for goods in interstate commerce will also be affected by the deaths of 2,000 to 4,000 women annually at the hands of domestic abusers, and by the reduction in the work force by the 100,000 or more rape victims who lose their jobs each year or are forced to quit. Violence against women may be found to affect interstate commerce and affect it substantially.

The Act would have passed muster at any time between *Wickard* in 1942 and *Lopez* in 1995, a period in which the law enjoyed a stable understanding that congressional power under the Commerce Clause, complemented by the authority of the Necessary and Proper Clause, Art. I., Sec. 8, cl. 18, extended to all activity that, when aggregated, has a substantial effect on interstate commerce. As already noted, this understanding was secure even against the turmoil at the passage of the Civil Rights Act of 1964, in the aftermath of which the Court not only reaffirmed the cumulative effects and rational basis features of the substantial effects test, see *Heart of Atlanta*, *McClung*, but declined to limit the commerce power through a formal distinction between legislation focused on "commerce" and statutes addressing "moral and social wrong[s]."

The fact that the Act does not pass muster before the Court today is therefore proof, to a degree that *Lopez* was not, that the Court's nominal adherence to the substantial effects test is merely that. Although a new jurisprudence has not emerged with any distinctness, it is clear that some congressional conclusions about obviously substantial, cumulative effects on commerce are being assigned lesser values than the once-stable doctrine would assign them. These devaluations are accomplished not by any express repudiation of the substantial effects test or its application through the aggregation of individual conduct, but by supplanting rational basis scrutiny with a new criterion of review.

Thus the elusive heart of the majority's analysis in these cases is its statement that Congress's findings of fact are "weakened" by the presence of a disfavored "method of reasoning." This seems to suggest that the "substantial effects" analysis is not a factual enquiry, for Congress in the first instance with subsequent judicial review looking only to the rationality of the congressional conclusion, but one of a rather different sort, dependent upon a uniquely judicial competence.

This new characterization of substantial effects has no support in our cases (the self-fulfilling prophecies of *Lopez* aside), least of all those the majority cites. Perhaps this explains why the majority is not content to rest on its cited precedent but claims a textual justification for moving toward its new system of congressional deference subject to selective discounts. . . .

The premise that the enumeration of powers implies that other powers are withheld is sound; the conclusion that some particular categories of subject matter are therefore presumptively beyond the reach of the commerce power is, however, a *non sequitur*. From the fact that Art. I, Sec. 8, cl. 3 grants an authority limited to regulating commerce, it follows only that Congress may claim no authority under that section to address any subject that does not affect commerce. It does not at all follow that an activity affecting commerce nonetheless falls outside the commerce power, depending on the specific character of the activity, or the authority of a State to regulate it along with Congress. My disagreement with the majority is not, however, confined to logic, for history has shown that categorical exclusions have proven as unworkable in practice as they are unsupportable in theory.

Chief Justice MARSHALL's seminal opinion in *Gibbons v. Ogden*, [9 Wheat 1 (1824)], construed the commerce power from the start with "a breadth never yet exceeded," *Wickard v. Filburn*. In particular, it is worth noting, the Court in *Wickard* did not regard its holding as exceeding the scope of Chief Justice MARSHALL's view of interstate commerce; *Wickard* applied an aggregate effects test to ostensibly domestic, noncommercial farming consistently with Chief Justice MARSHALL's indication that the commerce power may be understood by its exclusion of subjects, among others, "which do not affect other States." This plenary view of the power has either prevailed or been acknowledged by this Court at every stage of our jurisprudence. And it was this understanding, free of categorical qualifications, that prevailed in the period after 1937 through *Lopez*, as summed up by Justice HARLAN: "Of course, the mere fact that Congress has said when particular activity shall be deemed to affect commerce does not preclude further examination by this Court. But where we find that the legislators have a rational basis for finding a chosen regulatory scheme necessary to the protection of commerce, our investigation is at an end." *Maryland v. Wirtz*, 392 U.S. 183 (1968).

Justice HARLAN spoke with the benefit of hindsight, for he had seen the result of rejecting the plenary view, and today's attempt to distinguish between primary activities affecting commerce in terms of the relatively commercial or noncommercial character of the primary conduct proscribed comes with the pedigree of near-tragedy that I outlined in *United States v. Lopez* (dissenting opinion). In the half century following the modern activation of the commerce power with passage of the Interstate Commerce Act in 1887, this Court from time to time created categorical enclaves beyond congressional reach by declaring such activities as "mining," "production," "manufacturing," and union membership to be outside the definition of "commerce" and by limiting application of the effects test to "direct" rather than "indirect" commercial consequences. See, e.g., *United States v. E. C. Knight Co.*, 156 U.S. 1 (1895) (narrowly construing the Sherman Antitrust Act in light of the distinction between "commerce" and "manufacture"); *Hammer v. Dagenhart*, 247 U.S. 251 (1918) (invalidating law prohibiting interstate shipment of goods manufactured with child labor as a regulation of "manufacture"); *A. L. A. Schechter Poultry Corp. v. United States*, 295 U.S. 495 (1935) (invalidating regulation of activities that only "indirectly" affected commerce); *Carter v. Carter Coal Co.*, 298 U.S. 238 (1936) (holding that regulation of unfair labor practices in mining regulated "production," not "commerce").

Since adherence to these formalistically contrived confines of commerce power in large measure provoked the judicial crisis of 1937, one might reasonably have doubted that Members of this Court would ever again toy with a return to the days before *NLRB v. Jones & Laughlin Steel Corp.*, 301 U.S. 1 (1937), which brought the earlier and nearly disastrous experiment to an end. And yet today's decision can only be seen as a step toward recapturing the prior mistakes. . . .

Why is the majority tempted to reject the lesson so painfully learned in 1937? An answer emerges from contrasting *Wickard* with one of the predecessor cases it superseded. It was obvious in *Wickard* that growing wheat for consumption right on the farm was not "commerce" in the common vocabulary, but that did not matter constitutionally so long as the aggregated activity of domestic wheat growing affected commerce substantially. Just a few years before *Wickard*, however, it had certainly been no less obvious that "mining" practices could substantially affect commerce, even though *Carter Coal Co.* had held mining regulation beyond the national commerce power. When we try to fathom the difference between the two cases, it is clear that they did not go in different directions because the *Carter Coal* Court could not understand a causal connection that the *Wickard* Court could grasp; the difference, rather, turned on the fact that the Court in *Carter Coal* had a reason for trying to maintain its categorical, formalistic distinction, while that reason had been abandoned by the time *Wickard* was decided. The reason was laissez-faire economics, the point of which was to keep government interference to a minimum. The Court in *Carter Coal* was still trying to create a laissez-faire world out of the 20th-century economy, and formalistic commercial distinctions were thought to be useful instruments in achieving that object. The Court in *Wickard* knew it could not do any such thing and in the aftermath of the New Deal had long since stopped attempting the impossible. Without the animating economic theory, there was no point in contriving formalisms in a war with Chief Justice MARSHALL's conception of the commerce power.

If we now ask why the formalistic economic/noneconomic distinction might matter today, after its rejection in *Wickard*, the answer is not that the majority fails to see causal connections in an integrated economic world. The answer is that in the minds of the majority there is a new animating theory that makes categorical formalism seem useful again. Just as the old formalism had value in the service of an economic conception, the new one is useful in serving a conception of federalism. It is the instrument by which assertions of national power are to be limited in favor of preserving a supposedly discernible, proper sphere of state autonomy to legislate or refrain from legislating as the individual States see fit. The legitimacy of the Court's current emphasis on the noncommercial nature of regulated activity, then, does not turn on any logic serving the text of the Commerce Clause or on the realism of the majority's view of the national economy. The essential issue is rather the strength of the majority's claim to have a constitutional warrant for its current conception of a federal relationship enforceable by this Court through limits on otherwise plenary commerce power. This conception is the subject of the majority's second categorical discount applied today to the facts bearing on the substantial effects test.

The Court finds it relevant that the statute addresses conduct traditionally subject to state prohibition under domestic criminal law, a fact said to have some heightened significance when the violent conduct in question is not itself aimed directly at interstate commerce or its instrumentalities. Again, history seems to be recycling, for the theory of traditional state concern as grounding a limiting principle has been rejected previously, and more than once. . . .

The objection to reviving traditional state spheres of action as a consideration in commerce analysis, however, not only rests on the portent of incoherence, but is compounded by a further defect just as fundamental. The defect, in essence, is the majority's rejection of the Founders' considered judgment that politics, not judicial review, should mediate between state and national interests as the strength and legislative jurisdiction of the National Government inevitably increased through the expected growth of the national economy. Whereas today's majority takes a leaf from the book of the old judicial economists in saying that the Court should somehow draw the line to keep the federal relationship in a proper balance, Madison, Wilson, and MARSHALL understood the Constitution very differently.

Although Madison had emphasized the conception of a National Government of discrete powers (a conception that a number of the ratifying conventions thought was too indeterminate to protect civil liberties), Madison himself must have sensed the potential scope of some of the powers granted (such as the authority to regulate commerce), for he took care in The Federalist No. 46 to hedge his argument for limited power by explaining the importance of national politics in protecting the States' interests. The National Government "will partake sufficiently of the spirit [of the States], to be disinclined to invade the rights of the individual States, or the prerogatives of their governments." . . .

Politics as the moderator of the congressional employment of the commerce power was the theme many years later in *Wickard*, for after the Court acknowledged the breadth of the *Gibbons* formulation it invoked Chief Justice MARSHALL yet again in adding that "(h)e made emphatic the embracing and penetrating nature of this power by warning that effective restraints on its exercise must proceed from political rather than judicial processes." *Wickard*.

As with "conflicts of economic interest," so with supposed conflicts of sovereign political interests implicated by the Commerce Clause: the Constitution remits them to politics. The point can be put no more clearly than the Court put it the last time it repudiated the notion that some state activities categorically defied the commerce power as understood in accordance with generally accepted concepts. [In *Garcia v. San Antonio Metropolitan Transit Authority*, 469 U.S. 528 (1985), the Court] concluded that "the Framers chose to rely on a federal system in which special restraints on federal power over the States inhered principally in the workings of the National Government itself, rather than in discrete limitations on the objects of federal authority. State sovereign interests, then, are more properly protected by procedural safeguards inherent in the structure of the federal system than by judicially created limitations on federal power." . . .

All of this convinces me that today's ebb of the commerce power rests on error, and at the same time leads me to doubt that the majority's view will prove to be enduring law. There is yet one more reason for doubt. Although we sense the presence of *Carter Coal*, *Schechter*, and [*National League of Cities v.*] *Usery*, [426 U.S. 833 (1976)], once again, the majority embraces them only at arm's-length. Where such decisions once stood for rules, today's opinion points to considerations by which substantial effects are discounted. Cases standing for the sufficiency of substantial effects are not overruled; cases overruled since 1937 are not quite revived. The Court's thinking betokens less clearly a return to the conceptual straitjackets of *Schechter* and *Carter Coal* and *Usery* than to something like the unsteady state of obscenity law between *Redrup v. New York*, 386 U.S. 767 (1967), and *Miller v. California*, 413 U.S. 15 (1973), a period in which the failure to provide a workable definition left this Court to review each case ad hoc. As our predecessors learned then, the practice of such ad hoc review cannot preserve the distinction between the judicial and the legislative, and this Court, in any event, lacks the institutional capacity to maintain such a regime for very long. This one will end when the majority realizes that the conception of the commerce power for which it entertains hopes would inevitably fail the test expressed in Justice HOLMES's statement that "[t]he first call of a theory of law is that it should fit the facts." The facts that cannot be ignored today are the facts of integrated national commerce and a political relationship between States and Nation much affected by their respective treasuries and constitutional modifications adopted by the people. The federalism of some earlier time is no more adequate to account for those facts today than the theory of laissez-faire was able to govern the national economy 70 years ago.

Justice BREYER, with whom Justice STEVENS joins, and with whom Justice SOUTER and Justice GINSBURG join as to Part I-A, dissenting.

The majority holds that the federal commerce power does not extend to such "noneconomic" activities as "noneconomic, violent criminal conduct" that significantly affects interstate commerce only if we "aggregate" the interstate "effect[s]" of individual instances. Justice SOUTER explains why history, precedent, and legal logic militate against the majority's approach. I agree and join his opinion. I add that the majority's holding illustrates the difficulty of finding a workable judicial Commerce Clause touchstone—a set of comprehensible interpretive rules that courts might use to impose some meaningful limit, but not too great a limit, upon the scope of the legislative authority that the Commerce Clause delegates to Congress.

Consider the problems. The "economic/noneconomic" distinction is not easy to apply. Does the local street corner mugger engage in "economic" activity or "noneconomic" activity when he mugs for money? See *Perez v. United States*, 402 U.S. 146 (1971) (aggregating local "loan sharking" instances); *United States v. Lopez*, 514 U.S. 549 (1995) (loan sharking is economic because it consists of "intrastate extortionate credit transactions"). Would evidence that desire for economic domination underlies many brutal crimes against women save the present statute?

The line becomes yet harder to draw given the need for exceptions. The Court itself would permit Congress to aggregate, hence regulate, "noneconomic" activity taking place at economic establishments. See *Heart of Atlanta Motel, Inc. v. United States*, 379 U.S. 241 (1964) (upholding civil rights laws forbidding discrimination at local motels); *Katzenbach v. McClung*, 379 U.S. 294 (1964) (same for restaurants); *Lopez* (recognizing congressional power to aggregate, hence forbid, noneconomically motivated discrimination at public accommodations).

More important, why should we give critical constitutional importance to the economic, or noneconomic, nature of an interstate-commerce-affecting cause? If chemical emanations through indirect environmental change cause identical, severe commercial harm outside a State, why should it matter whether local factories or home fireplaces release them? The Constitution itself refers only to Congress' power to "regulate Commerce . . . among the several States," and to make laws "necessary and proper" to implement that power. The language says nothing about either the local nature, or the economic nature, of an interstate-commerce-affecting cause. . . .

Most important, the Court's complex rules seem unlikely to help secure the very object that they seek, namely, the protection of "areas of traditional state regulation" from federal intrusion. The Court's rules, even if broadly interpreted, are underinclusive. The local pickpocket is no less a traditional subject of state regulation than is the local gender-motivated assault. Regardless, the Court reaffirms, as it should, Congress' well-established and frequently exercised power to enact laws that satisfy a commerce-related jurisdictional prerequisite—for example, that some item relevant to the federally regulated activity has at some time crossed a state line.

And in a world where most everyday products or their component parts cross interstate boundaries, Congress will frequently find it possible to redraft a statute using language that ties the regulation to the interstate movement of some relevant object, thereby regulating local criminal activity or, for that matter, family affairs. Although this possibility does not give the Federal Government the power to regulate everything, it means that any substantive limitation will apply randomly in terms of the interests the majority seeks to protect. How much would be gained, for example, were Congress to reenact the present law in the form of "An Act Forbidding Violence Against Women Perpetrated at Public Accommodations or by Those Who Have Moved in, or through the Use of Items that Have Moved in, Interstate Commerce"? Complex Commerce Clause rules creating fine distinctions that achieve only random results do little to further the important federalist interests that called them into being. That is why modern (pre-*Lopez*) case law rejected them. . . .

For these reasons, as well as those set forth by Justice SOUTER, this statute falls well within Congress's Commerce Clause authority, and I dissent from the Court's contrary conclusion. . . .

7

THE STATES AND AMERICAN FEDERALISM

A. STATES' POWER OVER COMMERCE AND REGULATION

THE DEVELOPMENT OF LAW

Other Rulings on State Regulatory Powers in Alleged Conflict with Federal Legislation

Case	Vote	Ruling
United States v. Locke, 529 U.S. 89 (2000)	9:0	The Court unanimously struck down Washington's navigational regulations as preempt-

ed by the Oil Pollution Act of 1990. Following the oil spill of the Exxon *Valdez* in 1989, both Congress and Washington enacted laws to protect the environment from future oil spills, but the state's regulations were more extensive and stringent than those set forth in federal statutes and international treaties.

Case	Vote	Ruling
Crosby v. National Foreign Trade Council, 530 U.S. 363 (2000)	9:0	The Court invalidated Massachusetts's 1996 law restricting public agencies from contract-

ing with companies that also conduct business with Burma—a repressive Southeast Asian country that changed its name to Myanmar in 1989. Writing for the Court, Justice Souter held that a 1996 federal statute imposing a set of mandatory and conditional sanctions on Burma preempted the state law. The fact that Congress had not expressly preempted state laws on the matter was deemed irrelevant because Massachusetts's law ran contrary to Congress's authorization for the President to set and adjust the nation's policy toward Burma.

Egelhoff v. Egelhoff,	7:2	Writing for the Court , Justice
121 S.Ct. 1322 (2001)		Thomas invalidated a Wash-
		ington statute, providing that

the designation of a spouse as the beneficiary of a nonprobate asset is automatically revoked upon divorce, as preempted by the Employee Retirement
Income Security Act of 1974 (ERISA). Justices Breyer and Stevens dissented.

Lorillard Tobacco v. Reilly,	9:0	Writing for the Court , Justice
121 S.Ct. 2404 (2001)	& 5:4	O'Connor invalidated most of
		Massachusetts's restrictions

on the advertising of tobacco products as preempted by the Federal Cigarette
Labeling and Advertising Act. O'Connor also deemed the restrictions to violate the First Amendment. Justices Souter and Stevens filed separate opinions in part concurring and dissenting, which would have upheld some of the
restrictions over First Amendment objections; Justices Ginsburg and Breyer
joined the latter's opinion.

B. THE TENTH AMENDMENT AND THE STATES

Continuing a recent trend, Chief Justice Rehnquist again commanded
bare majorities for limiting congressional power and buttressing state
authority. In *Florida Prepaid Postsecondary Education Expense Board v.
College Savings Bank*, 527 U.S. 627 (1999), Chief Justice Rehnquist,
joined by Justices Kennedy, O'Connor, Scalia, and Thomas, held that Congress exceeded its powers in abrogating states' sovereign immunity when
enacting the Patent and Plant Variety Protection Remedy Clarification Act.
Relying on the five to four decision in *Seminole Tribe of Florida v. Florida*,
517 U.S. 44 (1996) (excerpted in Vol. 1, Ch. 6), the chief justice ruled that
Congress had exceeded its power under Article I and, drawing on the
Court's analysis and holding in *City of Boerne v. Flores*, 521 U.S. 507 (1997)
(excerpted in Vol. 2, Ch. 6), also ruled that Congress had exceeded its enforcement power under Section 5 of the Fourteenth Amendment. Here, as
in other recent rulings supporting states' rights and limiting congressional
power, Justices Stevens, Souter, Ginsburg, and Breyer dissented.

In another major decision upholding state authority, *Alden v. Maine*
(1999) (excerpted below), Justice Kennedy ruled that the Constitution's
"structure and history" shields states not only from being sued in federal
courts, but also makes them immune from lawsuits filed in state courts that
seek to enforce federal rights against them. Here, Maine's probation officers had sought to enforce a federal right to be paid for overtime work.
Once again, Justices Stevens, Souter, Ginsburg, and Breyer dissented. And

in a related ruling bearing on lawsuits filed against states, the Court held, in *Vermont Agency of Natural Resources v. United States ex rel. Stevens*, 529 U.S. 765 (2000), that a private individual may not bring a suit in federal court on behalf of the U.S. government against a state or state agency under the False Claims Act. Stevens had sued the Vermont Agency of Natural Resources, alleging that it had submitted false claims to the Environmental Protection Agency in connection with federal grants it administers. Writing for the Court, Justice Scalia held that a sovereign state is not a legal "person" subject to suit under the act. Justices Souter and Stevens dissented.

In its 1999–2000 term Chief Justice Rehnquist's bare majority further extended the doctrine in *Seminole Tribe*, *City of Boerne*, and *Alden* in *Kimel v. Florida Board of Regents* (excerpted below). Writing for the Court, Justice O'Connor held that Congress exceeded its powers in abrogating states' sovereign immunity under the Eleventh Amendment in extending the Age Discrimination in Employment Act to state employees and ruled that state employees could not bring suits in federal courts to enforce provisions of the law. Yet again, Justices Stevens, Breyer, Ginsburg, and Souter dissented.

In its 2000–2001 term, the Court further extended its evolving doctrine on states' sovereign immunity under the Eleventh Amendment. In *Board of Trustees of the University of Alabama v. Garrett*, 531 U.S. 356 (2001), a bare majority held that state employees may not sue their state employers under the Americans with Disabilities Act of 1990 (ADA), which prohibits employers from "discriminat[ing] against a qualified individual with a disability" in employment. Writing for the Court, Chief Justice Rehnquist reaffirmed that Congress may abrogate states' Eleventh Amendment immunity when it both unequivocally intends to do so and acts pursuant to its constitutional authority, under *Kimel v. Florida Board of Regents* (2000). While Congress may not base abrogation of state immunity upon its Article I power to regulate interstate commerce, *City of Boerne v. Flores*, 521 U.S. 507 (1997), held that it may do so under Section 5 of the Fourteenth Amendment, which authorizes Congress to enforce the Fourteenth Amendment's protection by enacting "appropriate legislation." The Court has held, however, that disability, like age, is not a protected suspect or quasi-suspect classification under the Fourteenth Amendment; see *City of Cleburne, Texas v. Cleburne Living Center*, 473 U.S. 432 (1985) (discussed in Vol. 2, Ch. 12). Thus, Congress exceeded its enforcement and remedial powers under the Fourteenth Amendment and unconstitutionally abrogated states' sovereign immunity under the Eleventh Amendment. Moreover, Chief Justice Rehnquist concluded that the ADA's legislative history failed to establish that Congress had identified a history and pattern of irrational employment discrimination by states against the disabled. As in *Kimel*, Justices Stevens, Souter, Ginsburg, and Breyer dissented.

Alden v. Maine
527 U.S. 706, 119 S.Ct. 2240 (1999)

The pertinent facts are discussed by Justice Kennedy in his opinion for the Court, affirming the decision of Maine Supreme Judicial Court. The Court's decision was five to four. Justice Souter filed a dissenting opinion, which was joined by Justices Stevens, Ginsburg, and Breyer.

Justice KENNEDY delivered the opinion of the Court.

In 1992, petitioners, a group of probation officers, filed suit against their employer, the State of Maine, in the United States District Court for the District of Maine. The officers alleged the State had violated the overtime provisions of the Fair Labor Standards Act of 1938 (FLSA), and sought compensation and liquidated damages. While the suit was pending, this Court decided *Seminole Tribe of Fla. v. Florida*, 517 U.S. 44 (1996), which made it clear that Congress lacks power under Article I to abrogate the States' sovereign immunity from suits commenced or prosecuted in the federal courts. Upon consideration of *Seminole Tribe*, the District Court dismissed petitioners' action, and the Court of Appeals affirmed. Petitioners then filed the same action in state court. The state trial court dismissed the suit on the basis of sovereign immunity, and the Maine Supreme Judicial Court affirmed. . . .

We hold that the powers delegated to Congress under Article I of the United States Constitution do not include the power to subject nonconsenting States to private suits for damages in state courts. We decide as well that the State of Maine has not consented to suits for overtime pay and liquidated damages under the FLSA. On these premises we affirm the judgment sustaining dismissal of the suit.

The Eleventh Amendment makes explicit reference to the States' immunity from suits "commenced or prosecuted against one of the United States by Citizens of another State, or by Citizens or Subjects of any Foreign State." We have, as a result, sometimes referred to the States' immunity from suit as "Eleventh Amendment immunity." The phrase is convenient shorthand but something of a misnomer, for the sovereign immunity of the States neither derives from nor is limited by the terms of the Eleventh Amendment. Rather, as the Constitution's structure, and its history, and the authoritative interpretations by this Court make clear, the States' immunity from suit is a fundamental aspect of the sovereignty which the States enjoyed before the ratification of the Constitution, and which they retain today (either literally or by virtue of their admission into the Union upon an equal footing with the other States) except as altered by the plan of the Convention or certain constitutional Amendments.

Although the Constitution establishes a National Government with broad, often plenary authority over matters within its recognized competence, the founding document "specifically recognizes the States as sovereign entities."

Seminole Tribe of Fla. Various textual provisions of the Constitution assume the States' continued existence and active participation in the fundamental processes of governance. See *Printz v. United States*, 521 U.S. 898 (1997) (citing Art. III, Sec. 2; Art. IV, Secs. 2–4; Art. V). The limited and enumerated powers granted to the Legislative, Executive, and Judicial Branches of the National Government, moreover, underscore the vital role reserved to the States by the constitutional design. Any doubt regarding the constitutional role of the States as sovereign entities is removed by the Tenth Amendment, which, like the other provisions of the Bill of Rights, was enacted to allay lingering concerns about the extent of the national power. The Amendment confirms the promise implicit in the original document: "The powers not delegated to the United States by the Constitution, nor prohibited by it to the States, are reserved to the States respectively, or to the people."

The federal system established by our Constitution preserves the sovereign status of the States in two ways. First, it reserves to them a substantial portion of the Nation's primary sovereignty, together with the dignity and essential attributes inhering in that status. . . .

Second, even as to matters within the competence of the National Government, the constitutional design secures the founding generation's rejection of "the concept of a central government that would act upon and through the States" in favor of "a system in which the State and Federal Governments would exercise concurrent authority over the people—who were, in Hamilton's words, "the only proper objects of government." *Printz.* In this the founders achieved a deliberate departure from the Articles of Confederation: Experience under the Articles had "exploded on all hands" the "practicality of making laws, with coercive sanctions, for the States as political bodies." . . .

The generation that designed and adopted our federal system considered immunity from private suits central to sovereign dignity. When the Constitution was ratified, it was well established in English law that the Crown could not be sued without consent in its own courts. See *Chisholm v. Georgia*, 2 Dall. 419 (1793) (IREDELL, J., dissenting). . . .

[The Court's decision in *Chisholm v. Georgia* met with wide spread opposition and resulted in the adoption and ratification of the Eleventh Amendment, guaranteeing states' sovereign immunity against lawsuits by citizens of other states.] Each House spent but a single day discussing the Amendment, and the vote in each House was close to unanimous. All attempts to weaken the Amendment were defeated. . . .

It might be argued that the *Chisholm* decision was a correct interpretation of the constitutional design and that the Eleventh Amendment represented a deviation from the original understanding. This, however, seems unsupportable. First, despite the opinion of Justice IREDELL, the majority failed to address either the practice or the understanding that prevailed in the States at the time the Constitution was adopted. Second, even a casual reading of the opinions suggests the majority suspected the decision would be unpopular and surprising. . . .

The text and history of the Eleventh Amendment also suggest that Congress acted not to change but to restore the original constitutional design. Although earlier drafts of the Amendment had been phrased as express limits on the judicial power granted in Article III, the adopted text addressed the proper interpretation of that provision of the original Constitution, see U.S. Const., Amdt. 11

("The Judicial Power of the United States shall not be construed to extend to any suit in law or equity, commenced or prosecuted against one of the United States"). By its terms, then, the Eleventh Amendment did not redefine the federal judicial power but instead overruled the Court. . . .

The Court has been consistent in interpreting the adoption of the Eleventh Amendment as conclusive evidence "that the decision in *Chisholm* was contrary to the well-understood meaning of the Constitution," *Seminole Tribe*, and that the views expressed by Hamilton, Madison, and Marshall during the ratification debates, and by Justice IREDELL in his dissenting opinion in *Chisholm*, reflect the original understanding of the Constitution. In accordance with this understanding, we have recognized a "presumption that no anomalous and unheard-of proceedings or suits were intended to be raised up by the Constitution—anomalous and unheard of when the constitution was adopted." As a consequence, we have looked to "history and experience, and the established order of things," rather than "[a]dhering to the mere letter" of the Eleventh Amendment in determining the scope of the States' constitutional immunity from suit. . . .

[Prior] holdings reflect a settled doctrinal understanding, consistent with the views of the leading advocates of the Constitution's ratification, that sovereign immunity derives not from the Eleventh Amendment but from the structure of the original Constitution itself. The Eleventh Amendment confirmed rather than established sovereign immunity as a constitutional principle; it follows that the scope of the States' immunity from suit is demarcated not by the text of the Amendment alone but by fundamental postulates implicit in the constitutional design. . . .

In this case we must determine whether Congress has the power, under Article I, to subject nonconsenting States to private suits in their own courts. As the foregoing discussion makes clear, the fact that the Eleventh Amendment by its terms limits only "[t]he Judicial power of the United States" does not resolve the question. To rest on the words of the Amendment alone would be to engage in the type of ahistorical literalism we have rejected in interpreting the scope of the States' sovereign immunity since the discredited decision in *Chisholm.*

While the constitutional principle of sovereign immunity does pose a bar to federal jurisdiction over suits against nonconsenting States, this is not the only structural basis of sovereign immunity implicit in the constitutional design. Rather, "[t]here is also the postulate that States of the Union, still possessing attributes of sovereignty, shall be immune from suits, without their consent, save where there has been a surrender of this immunity in the plan of the convention." This separate and distinct structural principle is not directly related to the scope of the judicial power established by Article III, but inheres in the system of federalism established by the Constitution. In exercising its Article I powers Congress may subject the States to private suits in their own courts only if there is "compelling evidence" that the States were required to surrender this power to Congress pursuant to the constitutional design.

Petitioners contend the text of the Constitution and our recent sovereign immunity decisions establish that the States were required to relinquish this portion of their sovereignty. [But, we disagree.] The Constitution, by delegating to Congress the power to establish the supreme law of the land when acting within its enumerated powers, does not foreclose a State from asserting immunity to claims arising under federal law merely because that law derives not from the

State itself but from the national power. A contrary view could not be reconciled with . . . *Employees of Dept. of Public Health and Welfare of Mo. v. Department of Public Health and Welfare of Mo.*, 411 U.S. 279 (1973), which recognized that the FLSA was binding upon Missouri but nevertheless upheld the State's immunity to a private suit to recover under that Act; or with numerous other decisions to the same effect. We reject any contention that substantive federal law by its own force necessarily overrides the sovereign immunity of the States. When a State asserts its immunity to suit, the question is not the primacy of federal law but the implementation of the law in a manner consistent with the constitutional sovereignty of the States. . . .

Whether Congress has authority under Article I to abrogate a State's immunity from suit in its own courts is, then, a question of first impression. In determining whether there is "compelling evidence" that this derogation of the States' sovereignty is "inherent in the constitutional compact," we continue our discussion of history, practice, precedent, and the structure of the Constitution.

We look first to evidence of the original understanding of the Constitution. Petitioners contend that because the ratification debates and the events surrounding the adoption of the Eleventh Amendment focused on the States' immunity from suit in federal courts, the historical record gives no instruction as to the founding generation's intent to preserve the States' immunity from suit in their own courts.

We believe, however, that the founders' silence is best explained by the simple fact that no one, not even the Constitution's most ardent opponents, suggested the document might strip the States of the immunity. In light of the overriding concern regarding the States' war-time debts, together with the well known creativity, foresight, and vivid imagination of the Constitution's opponents, the silence is most instructive. It suggests the sovereign's right to assert immunity from suit in its own courts was a principle so well established that no one conceived it would be altered by the new Constitution. . . .

[W]hile the Eleventh Amendment by its terms addresses only "the Judicial power of the United States," nothing in *Chisholm*, the catalyst for the Amendment, suggested the States were not immune from suits in their own courts. . . .

In light of the language of the Constitution and the historical context, it is quite apparent why neither the ratification debates nor the language of the Eleventh Amendment addressed the States' immunity from suit in their own courts. The concerns voiced at the ratifying conventions, the furor raised by *Chisholm*, and the speed and unanimity with which the Amendment was adopted, moreover, underscore the jealous care with which the founding generation sought to preserve the sovereign immunity of the States. . . .

Our final consideration is whether a congressional power to subject nonconsenting States to private suits in their own courts is consistent with the structure of the Constitution. We look both to the essential principles of federalism and to the special role of the state courts in the constitutional design. . . .

Petitioners contend that immunity from suit in federal court suffices to preserve the dignity of the States. Private suits against nonconsenting States, however, present "the indignity of subjecting a State to the coercive process of judicial tribunals at the instance of private parties," *In re Ayers*, [123 U.S. 443 (1887)], regardless of the forum. Not only must a State defend or default but also it must face the prospect of being thrust, by federal fiat and against its will, into the disfavored status of a debtor, subject to the power of private citizens to levy on its treasury or perhaps even government buildings or property which the State administers on the public's behalf. . . .

A general federal power to authorize private suits for money damages would place unwarranted strain on the States' ability to govern in accordance with the will of their citizens. Today, as at the time of the founding, the allocation of scarce resources among competing needs and interests lies at the heart of the political process. While the judgment creditor of the State may have a legitimate claim for compensation, other important needs and worthwhile ends compete for access to the public fisc. Since all cannot be satisfied in full, it is inevitable that difficult decisions involving the most sensitive and political of judgments must be made. If the principle of representative government is to be preserved to the States, the balance between competing interests must be reached after deliberation by the political process established by the citizens of the State, not by judicial decree mandated by the Federal Government and invoked by the private citizen.

By "split[ting] the atom of sovereignty," the founders established "two orders of government, each with its own direct relationship, its own privity, its own set of mutual rights and obligations to the people who sustain it and are governed by it." *Saenz v. Roe*, 526 U.S. [526 U.S. 489] (1999). When the Federal Government asserts authority over a State's most fundamental political processes, it strikes at the heart of the political accountability so essential to our liberty and republican form of government.

The asserted authority would blur not only the distinct responsibilities of the State and National Governments but also the separate duties of the judicial and political branches of the state governments, displacing "state decisions that 'go to the heart of representative government.'" *Gregory v. Ashcroft*, 501 U.S. 452 (1991). A State is entitled to order the processes of its own governance, assigning to the political branches, rather than the courts, the responsibility for directing the payment of debts. If Congress could displace a State's allocation of governmental power and responsibility, the judicial branch of the State, whose legitimacy derives from fidelity to the law, would be compelled to assume a role not only foreign to its experience but beyond its competence as defined by the very constitution from which its existence derives. . . .

In light of history, practice, precedent, and the structure of the Constitution, we hold that the States retain immunity from private suit in their own courts, an immunity beyond the congressional power to abrogate by Article I legislation.

The constitutional privilege of a State to assert its sovereign immunity in its own courts does not confer upon the State a concomitant right to disregard the Constitution or valid federal law. The States and their officers are bound by obligations imposed by the Constitution and by federal statutes that comport with the constitutional design. We are unwilling to assume the States will refuse to honor the Constitution or obey the binding laws of the United States.

Sovereign immunity, moreover, does not bar all judicial review of state compliance with the Constitution and valid federal law. Rather, certain limits are implicit in the constitutional principle of state sovereign immunity.

The first of these limits is that sovereign immunity bars suits only in the absence of consent. Many States, on their own initiative, have enacted statutes consenting to a wide variety of suits. The rigors of sovereign immunity are thus "mitigated by a sense of justice which has continually expanded by consent the suability of the sovereign." *Great Northern Life Ins. Co. [v. Read*, 322 U.S. 47 (1944)]. Nor, subject to constitutional limitations, does the Federal Government lack the authority or means to seek the States' voluntary consent to private suits. *South Dakota v. Dole*, 483 U.S. 203 (1987).

We have held also that in adopting the Fourteenth Amendment, the people required the States to surrender a portion of the sovereignty that had been preserved to them by the original Constitution, so that Congress may authorize private suits against nonconsenting States pursuant to its Section 5 enforcement power. By imposing explicit limits on the powers of the States and granting Congress the power to enforce them, the Amendment "fundamentally altered the balance of state and federal power struck by the Constitution." *Seminole Tribe*. When Congress enacts appropriate legislation to enforce this Amendment, see *City of Boerne v. Flores*, 521 U.S. 507 (1997), federal interests are paramount, and Congress may assert an authority over the States which would be otherwise unauthorized by the Constitution.

The second important limit to the principle of sovereign immunity is that it bars suits against States but not lesser entities. The immunity does not extend to suits prosecuted against a municipal corporation or other governmental entity which is not an arm of the State. Nor does sovereign immunity bar all suits against state officers. Some suits against state officers are barred by the rule that sovereign immunity is not limited to suits which name the State as a party if the suits are, in fact, against the State. The rule, however, does not bar certain actions against state officers for injunctive or declaratory relief. Compare *Ex parte Young*, 209 U.S. 123 (1908), and *In re Ayers*, supra, with *Seminole Tribe*, supra, and *Edelman v. Jordan*, 415 U.S. 651 (1974). Even a suit for money damages may be prosecuted against a state officer in his individual capacity for unconstitutional or wrongful conduct fairly attributable to the officer himself, so long as the relief is sought not from the state treasury but from the officer personally. . . .

The sole remaining question is whether Maine has waived its immunity. . . . The State, we conclude, has not consented to suit. . . .

[Finally, t]he State of Maine has not questioned Congress' power to prescribe substantive rules of federal law to which it must comply. Despite an initial good-faith disagreement about the requirements of the FLSA, it is conceded by all that the State has altered its conduct so that its compliance with federal law cannot now be questioned. The Solicitor General of the United States has appeared before this Court, however, and asserted that the federal interest in compensating the States' employees for alleged past violations of federal law is so compelling that the sovereign State of Maine must be stripped of its immunity and subjected to suit in its own courts by its own employees. Yet, despite specific statutory authorization, the United States apparently found the same interests insufficient to justify sending even a single attorney to Maine to prosecute this litigation. The difference between a suit by the United States on behalf of the employees and a suit by the employees implicates a rule that the National Government must itself deem the case of sufficient importance to take action against the State; and history, precedent, and the structure of the Constitution make clear that, under the plan of the Convention, the States have consented to suits of the first kind but not of the second. The judgment of the Supreme Judicial Court of Maine is affirmed.

Justice SOUTER, with whom Justice STEVENS, Justice GINSBURG, and Justice BREYER join, dissenting.

In *Seminole Tribe of Fla. v. Florida*, 517 U.S. 44 (1996), a majority of this Court invoked the Eleventh Amendment to declare that the federal judicial power under Article III of the Constitution does not reach a private action against a State, even on a federal question. In the Court's conception, however, the Eleventh Amendment was understood as having been enhanced by a "background principle" of state sovereign immunity (understood as immunity to suit) that operated beyond its limited codification in the Amendment, dealing solely with federal citizen-state diversity jurisdiction. To the *Seminole Tribe* dissenters, of whom I was one, the Court's enhancement of the Amendment was at odds with constitutional history and at war with the conception of divided sovereignty that is the essence of American federalism.

Today's issue arises naturally in the aftermath of the decision in *Seminole Tribe*. . . . In thus complementing its earlier decision, the Court of course confronts the fact that the state forum renders the Eleventh Amendment beside the point, and it has responded by discerning a simpler and more straightforward theory of state sovereign immunity than it found in *Seminole Tribe*: a State's sovereign immunity from all individual suits is a "fundamental aspect" of state sovereignty "confirm[ed]" by the Tenth Amendment. As a consequence, *Seminole Tribe*'s contorted reliance on the Eleventh Amendment and its background was presumably unnecessary; the Tenth would have done the work with an economy that the majority in *Seminole Tribe* would have welcomed. Indeed, if the Court's current reasoning is correct, the Eleventh Amendment itself was unnecessary. Whatever Article III may originally have said about the federal judicial power, the embarrassment to the State of Georgia occasioned by attempts in federal court to enforce the State's war debt could easily have been avoided if only the Court that decided *Chisholm v. Georgia*, 2 Dall. 419 (1793), had understood a State's inherent, Tenth Amendment right to be free of any judicial power, whether the court be state or federal, and whether the cause of action arise under state or federal law.

The sequence of the Court's positions prompts a suspicion of error, and skepticism is confirmed by scrutiny of the Court's efforts to justify its holding. There is no evidence that the Tenth Amendment constitutionalized a concept of sovereign immunity as inherent in the notion of statehood, and no evidence that any concept of inherent sovereign immunity was understood historically to apply when the sovereign sued was not the font of the law. Nor does the Court fare any better with its subsidiary lines of reasoning, that the state-court action is barred by the scheme of American federalism, a result supposedly confirmed by a history largely devoid of precursors to the action considered here. The Court's federalism ignores the accepted authority of Congress to bind States under the FLSA and to provide for enforcement of federal rights in state court. The Court's history simply disparages the capacity of the Constitution to order relationships in a Republic that has changed since the founding.

On each point the Court has raised it is mistaken, and I respectfully dissent from its judgment.

Kimel v. Florida Board of Regents
528 U.S. 62, 120 S.Ct. 631 (2000)

J. Daniel Kimel, Jr., and several other professors and librarians, all over the age of 40, sued the Florida Board of Regents for age discrimination under the Age Discrimination in Employment Act of 1967 (ADEA). That law, as subsequently amended in 1974 to apply to state and local governments, makes it unlawful for an employer "to fail or refuse to hire or discharge any individual or otherwise discriminate against any individual 'because of such individual's age.'" In a separate suit, state employees sued Alabama for age discrimination. The federal district courts' decisions in these cases were consolidated on appeal before the Court of Appeals for the Eleventh Circuit, which held that the ADEA did not abrogate states' sovereign immunity under the Eleventh Amendment and dismissed the suits. That decision was appealed, and the Supreme Court granted review.

The appellate court's decision was affirmed in an opinion delivered by Justice O'Connor. Justice Stevens filed an opinion in part concurring and dissenting, which Justices Breyer, Ginsburg, and Souter joined. Justice Thomas, joined by Justice Kennedy, issued an opinion in part concurring and dissenting.

Justice O'CONNOR delivered the opinion of the Court.

Although today's cases concern suits brought by citizens against their own States, this Court has long "'understood the Eleventh Amendment to stand not so much for what it says, but for the presupposition—which it confirms.'" *Seminole Tribe of Florida v. Florida*, 517 U.S. 44 (1996). Accordingly, for over a century now, we have made clear that the Constitution does not provide for federal jurisdiction over suits against nonconsenting States. Petitioners nevertheless contend that the States of Alabama and Florida must defend the present suits on the merits because Congress abrogated their Eleventh Amendment immunity in the ADEA. To determine whether petitioners are correct, we must resolve two predicate questions: first, whether Congress unequivocally expressed its intent to abrogate that immunity; and second, if it did, whether Congress acted pursuant to a valid grant of constitutional authority.

To determine whether a federal statute properly subjects States to suits by individuals, we apply a "simple but stringent test: 'Congress may abrogate the States' constitutionally secured immunity from suit in federal court only by making its intention unmistakably clear in the language of the statute.'" *Dellmuth v. Muth*, 491 U.S. 223 (1989). We agree with petitioners that the ADEA satisfies that test. . . .

This is not the first time we have considered the constitutional validity of the 1974 extension of the ADEA to state and local governments. In *EEOC v. Wyoming*, 460 U.S. 226 (1983), we held that the ADEA constitutes a valid exercise of Congress' power "[t]o regulate Commerce among the several States," and that the Act did not transgress any external restraints imposed on the commerce power by the Tenth Amendment. Because we found the ADEA valid under Congress' Commerce Clause power, we concluded that it was unnecessary to determine whether the Act also could be supported by Congress' power under Section 5 of the Fourteenth Amendment. Resolution of today's cases requires us to decide that question.

In *Seminole Tribe*, we held that Congress lacks power under Article I to abrogate the States' sovereign immunity. . . . Under our firmly established precedent then, if the ADEA rests solely on Congress' Article I commerce power, the private petitioners in today's cases cannot maintain their suits against their state employers.

Justice STEVENS disputes that well-established precedent again. . . . In *Alden* [*v. Maine*, 527 U.S. 706 (1999)], we explained that, "[a]lthough the sovereign immunity of the States derives at least in part from the common-law tradition, the structure and history of the Constitution make clear that the immunity exists today by constitutional design." For purposes of today's decision, it is sufficient to note that we have on more than one occasion explained the substantial reasons for adhering to that constitutional design. . . . Today we adhere to our holding in *Seminole Tribe*: Congress' powers under Article I of the Constitution do not include the power to subject States to suit at the hands of private individuals.

Section 5 of the Fourteenth Amendment, however, does grant Congress the authority to abrogate the States' sovereign immunity. In *Fitzpatrick v. Bitzer*, 427 U.S. 445 (1976), we recognized that "the Eleventh Amendment, and the principle of state sovereignty which it embodies, are necessarily limited by the enforcement provisions of Section 5 of the Fourteenth Amendment." Accordingly, the private petitioners in these cases may maintain their ADEA suits against the States of Alabama and Florida if, and only if, the ADEA is appropriate legislation under Section 5. . . .

As we recognized most recently in *City of Boerne v. Flores*, 521 U.S. 507 (1997), Section 5 is an affirmative grant of power to Congress. Congress' power "to enforce" the Amendment includes the authority both to remedy and to deter violation of rights guaranteed thereunder by prohibiting a somewhat broader swath of conduct, including that which is not itself forbidden by the Amendment's text.

Nevertheless, we have also recognized that the same language that serves as the basis for the affirmative grant of congressional power also serves to limit that power. For example, Congress cannot "decree the substance of the Fourteenth Amendment's restrictions on the States. It has been given the power 'to enforce,' not the power to determine what constitutes a constitutional violation." The ultimate interpretation and determination of the Fourteenth Amendment's substantive meaning remains the province of the Judicial Branch. In *City of Boerne*, we noted that the determination whether purportedly prophylactic legislation constitutes appropriate remedial legislation, or instead effects a substantive redefinition of the Fourteenth Amendment right at issue, is often difficult. The line between the two is a fine one. Accordingly, recognizing that "Congress must have wide latitude in determining where [that line] lies," we held that "[t]here must be a congruence and proportionality between the injury to be prevented or remedied and the means adopted to that end." . . .

Applying the same "congruence and proportionality" test in these cases, we conclude that the ADEA is not "appropriate legislation" under Section 5 of the

Fourteenth Amendment. Initially, the substantive requirements the ADEA imposes on state and local governments are disproportionate to any unconstitutional conduct that conceivably could be targeted by the Act. We have considered claims of unconstitutional age discrimination under the Equal Protection Clause three times. See *Gregory v. Ashcroft*, 501 U.S. 452 (1991); *Vance v. Bradley*, 440 U.S. 93 (1979); *Massachusetts Bd. of Retirement v. Murgia*, 427 U.S. 307 (1976). In all three cases, we held that the age classifications at issue did not violate the Equal Protection Clause. . . . Older persons, again, unlike those who suffer discrimination on the basis of race or gender, have not been subjected to a " 'history of purposeful unequal treatment.' " Old age also does not define a discrete and insular minority because all persons, if they live out their normal life spans, will experience it. Accordingly, as we recognized in *Murgia, Bradley*, and *Gregory*, age is not a suspect classification under the Equal Protection Clause.

States may discriminate on the basis of age without offending the Fourteenth Amendment if the age classification in question is rationally related to a legitimate state interest. The rationality commanded by the Equal Protection Clause does not require States to match age distinctions and the legitimate interests they serve with razorlike precision. As we have explained, when conducting rational basis review "we will not overturn such [government action] unless the varying treatment of different groups or persons is so unrelated to the achievement of any combination of legitimate purposes that we can only conclude that the [government's] actions were irrational." In contrast, when a State discriminates on the basis of race or gender, we require a tighter fit between the discriminatory means and the legitimate ends they serve. Under the Fourteenth Amendment, a State may rely on age as a proxy for other qualities, abilities, or characteristics that are relevant to the State's legitimate interests. The Constitution does not preclude reliance on such generalizations. That age proves to be an inaccurate proxy in any individual case is irrelevant. Finally, because an age classification is presumptively rational, the individual challenging its constitutionality bears the burden of proving that the "facts on which the classification is apparently based could not reasonably be conceived to be true by the governmental decisionmaker." Our decisions in *Murgia, Bradley*, and *Gregory* illustrate these principles. In all three cases, we held that the States' reliance on broad generalizations with respect to age did not violate the Equal Protection Clause. . . . Judged against the backdrop of our equal protection jurisprudence, it is clear that the ADEA is "so out of proportion to a supposed remedial or preventive object that it cannot be understood as responsive to, or designed to prevent, unconstitutional behavior." *City of Boerne*. . . .

Finally, the United States' argument that Congress found substantial age discrimination in the private sector is beside the point. Congress made no such findings with respect to the States. . . . In light of the indiscriminate scope of the Act's substantive requirements, and the lack of evidence of widespread and unconstitutional age discrimination by the States, we hold that the ADEA is not a valid exercise of Congress' power under Section 5 of the Fourteenth Amendment. The ADEA's purported abrogation of the States' sovereign immunity is accordingly invalid. . . .

Justice STEVENS, with whom Justice SOUTER, Justice GINSBURG, and Justice BREYER join, dissenting in part and concurring in part.

Congress' power to regulate the American economy includes the power to regulate both the public and the private sectors of the labor market. Federal rules outlawing discrimination in the workplace, like the regulation of wages and hours or health and safety standards, may be enforced against public as well as private employers. Congress' power to authorize federal remedies against state agencies that violate federal statutory obligations is coextensive with its power to impose those obligations on the States in the first place. Neither the Eleventh Amendment nor the doctrine of sovereign immunity places any limit on that power. . . . .

The Eleventh Amendment simply does not support the Court's view. As has been stated before, the Amendment only places a textual limitation on the diversity jurisdiction of the federal courts. Because the Amendment is a part of the Constitution, I have never understood how its limitation on the diversity jurisdiction of federal courts defined in Article III could be "abrogated" by an Act of Congress. Here, however, private petitioners did not invoke the federal courts' diversity jurisdiction; they are citizens of the same State as the defendants and they are asserting claims that arise under federal law. Thus, today's decision (relying as it does on *Seminole Tribe*) rests entirely on a novel judicial interpretation of the doctrine of sovereign immunity, which the Court treats as though it were a constitutional precept. It is nevertheless clear to me that if Congress has the power to create the federal rights that these petitioners are asserting, it must also have the power to give the federal courts jurisdiction to remedy violations of those rights, even if it is necessary to "abrogate" the Court's "Eleventh Amendment" version of the common-law defense of sovereign immunity to do so. That is the essence of the Court's holding in *Pennsylvania v. Union Gas Co.*, 491 U.S. 1 (1989).

I remain convinced that *Union Gas* was correctly decided and that the decision of five Justices in *Seminole Tribe* to overrule that case was profoundly misguided. Despite my respect for *stare decisis*, I am unwilling to accept *Seminole Tribe* as controlling precedent. First and foremost, the reasoning of that opinion is so profoundly mistaken and so fundamentally inconsistent with the Framers' conception of the constitutional order that it has forsaken any claim to the usual deference or respect owed to decisions of this Court. . . . Further, *Seminole Tribe* is a case that will unquestionably have serious ramifications in future cases; indeed, it has already had such an effect, as in the Court's decision today and in the equally misguided opinion of *Alden v. Maine* (1999). Further still, the *Seminole Tribe* decision unnecessarily forces the Court to resolve vexing questions of constitutional law respecting Congress' Section 5 authority. Finally, by its own repeated overruling of earlier precedent, the majority has itself discounted the importance of *stare decisis* in this area of the law. The kind of judicial activism manifested in cases like *Seminole Tribe*, *Alden v. Maine*, [and] *Florida Prepaid Postsecondary Ed. Expense Bd. v. College Savings Bank*, [527 U.S. 627] (1999), represents such a radical departure from the proper role of this Court that it should be opposed whenever the opportunity arises.

Accordingly, I respectfully dissent.

8

REPRESENTATIVE GOVERNMENT, VOTING RIGHTS, AND ELECTORAL POLITICS

A. REPRESENTATIVE GOVERNMENT AND THE FRANCHISE

> ### THE DEVELOPMENT OF LAW
>
> ### Other Rulings Interpreting the Voting Rights Act
>
> | Case | Vote | Ruling |
> | --- | --- | --- |
> | *Reno v. Bossier Parish School Board*, 528 U.S. 320 (2000) | 5:4 | Writing for the majority, Justice Scalia ruled that Section 5 of the Voting Rights Act does |
>
> not prohibit Department of Justice (DoJ) preclearance of a redistricting plan adopted with an ostensibly discriminatory but nonretrogressive purpose. The DoJ had objected to Bossier Parish School Board's plan to give all twelve voting districts white majorities, even though about twenty percent of the population is black. The DoJ contended that it could deny preclearance approval because the plan would dilute African American voting strength. But, Justice Scalia rejected that interpretation of the Voting Rights Act in holding that preclearance could be denied only if a redistricting plan would put blacks in a worse position or to prevent "backsliding." That narrower interpretation was deemed by the Court's majority to be justified given "the substantial federalism costs that the preclearance procedure already exacts" from state and local governments. Justices Stevens, Souter, Ginsburg, and Breyer dissented.

B. VOTING RIGHTS AND THE
REAPPORTIONMENT REVOLUTION

Hunt v. Cromartie
121 S.Ct. 1452 (2001)

For the fourth time, the Court reviewed a challenge to the "racial district-ing" of North Carolina's congressional district 12, one of two districts ini-tially drawn in 1992 that contained a majority of African-American voters. Subsequently, as a result of further litigation, the district was again redrawn in 1997 and 1998, and again challenged. The district as drawn in 1992, 1997, and 1998 appeared as follows:

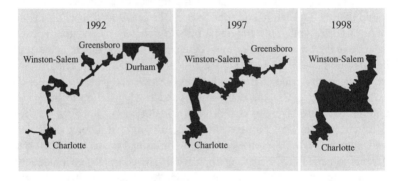

In *Shaw v. Reno*, 509 U.S. 630 (1993) (*Shaw I*) (excerpted in Vol. 1, Ch. 8), the Court held that the legislature had drawn the former district's boun-daries for race-based reasons in violation of the Equal Protection Clause, observing that a violation may exist where the legislature's boundary draw-ing, though "race neutral on its face," nonetheless can be understood only as an effort to "separate voters into different districts on the basis of race," and where the "separation lacks sufficient justification."

In *Shaw v. Hunt*, 517 U.S. 899 (1996) (*Shaw II*) (excerpted in Vol. 1, Ch. 8), the Court reversed a three-judge district court's holding that the 1992 district did not violate the Constitution. The Court deemed the district's "unconventional" snakelike shape, its predominantly African-American racial make-up, and its history to demonstrate a deliberate effort to create an impermissible "majority-black" district.

The Court, then, considered a challenge to a new district as redrawn in 1997, in *Hunt v. Cromartie*, 526 U.S. 541 (1999) (*Hunt I*). A three-judge district court had found the legislature to have again used criteria that were "facially race driven," in violation of the Equal Protection Clause. It based this conclusion upon "uncontroverted material facts" showing that the boundaries created an unusually shaped district; split counties and cities; and placed almost all heavily Democratic-registered, predominantly African-American voting precincts inside the district, while locating some heavily Democratic-registered, predominantly white precincts outside the district. This latter circumstance, the court concluded, showed that the legislature was trying to maximize the new district's African-American voting strength, not the district's Democratic voting strength. That decision, however, was reversed by the Supreme Court in *Hunt I*, upon its finding that the evidence neither by itself nor coupled with the evidence of Democratic registration was sufficient to show the unconstitutional race-based objective that plaintiffs claimed.

On remand, the parties undertook additional discovery, the district was redrawn in 1998, and the three-judge district court again held that the legislature had unconstitutionally drawn the district's boundaries. The court found that the legislature had tried to cure the previous district's constitutional defects, while also drawing a plan to maintain the existing partisan balance in the State's congressional delegation. It noted that to achieve the latter goal, the legislature "drew the new plan (1) to avoid placing two incumbents in the same district and (2) to preserve the partisan core of the existing districts." But the court also found the legislature to have used criteria that were "facially race driven" without any compelling justification for doing so. The court based its conclusion in part upon the district's snakelike shape, the way in which it split cities and towns, and its heavily African-American (47%) voting population. The court also concluded that the legislature drew the boundaries in order "to collect precincts with high racial identification rather than political identification." The state appealed that decision and the Supreme Court granted review.

The district court's decision was reversed. The Court's decision was five to four and its opinion was delivered by Justice Breyer. Justice Thomas filed a dissenting opinion, which Chief Justice Rehnquist and Justices Scalia and Kennedy joined.

Justice BREYER delivered the opinion of the Court.

The issue in this case is evidentiary. We must determine whether there is adequate support for the District Court's key findings, particularly the ultimate finding that the legislature's motive was predominantly racial, not political. In making this determination, we are aware that, under *Shaw I* and later cases, the burden of proof on the plaintiffs (who attack the district) is a "demanding one." *Miller v. Johnson*, 515 U.S. 900 (1995)(O'CONNOR, J., concurring). The Court has specified that those who claim that a legislature has improperly used race as a criterion, in order, for example, to create a majority-minority district, must show at a minimum that the "legislature subordinated traditional race-neutral districting principles . . . to racial considerations." Race must not simply have been "a motivation for the drawing of a majority-minority district," *Bush v. Vera*, 517 U.S. 952 (1996) (O'CONNOR, J., principal opinion), but "the 'predominant factor' motivating the legislature's districting decision," *Cromartie [I]*.

The Court also has made clear that the underlying districting decision is one that ordinarily falls within a legislature's sphere of competence. Hence, the legislature "must have discretion to exercise the political judgment necessary to balance competing interests," and courts must "exercise extraordinary caution in adjudicating claims that a State has drawn district lines on the basis of race." Caution is especially appropriate in this case, where the State has articulated a legitimate political explanation for its districting decision, and the voting population is one in which race and political affiliation are highly correlated. . . .

The critical District Court determination—the matter for which we remanded this litigation—consists of the finding that race rather than politics predominantly explains District 12's 1997 boundaries. That determination rests upon three findings (the district's shape, its splitting of towns and counties, and its high African-American voting population) that we previously found insufficient to support summary judgment. Given the undisputed evidence that racial identification is highly correlated with political affiliation in North Carolina, these facts in and of themselves cannot, as a matter of law, support the District Court's judgment. The District Court rested, however, upon five new subsidiary findings to conclude that District 12's lines are the product of no "mer[e] correlat[ion]," but are instead a result of the predominance of race in the legislature's line-drawing process.

In considering each subsidiary finding, we have given weight to the fact that the District Court was familiar with this litigation, heard the testimony of each witness, and considered all the evidence with care. Nonetheless, we cannot accept the District Court's findings as adequate for reasons which we shall spell out in detail and which we can summarize as follows:

First, the primary evidence upon which the District Court relied for its "race, not politics," conclusion is evidence of voting registration, not voting behavior; and that is precisely the kind of evidence that we said was inadequate the last time this case was before us. Second, the additional evidence to which appellees' expert, Dr. Weber, pointed, and the statements made by Senator Cooper and Gerry Cohen, simply do not provide significant additional support for the District Court's conclusion. Third, the District Court, while not accepting the contrary conclusion of appellants' expert, Dr. Peterson, did not (and as far as the record reveals, could not) reject much of the significant supporting factual information he provided. Fourth, in any event, appellees themselves have provided us with charts summarizing evidence of voting behavior and those charts tend to refute the court's "race not politics" conclusion.

The District Court primarily based its "race, not politics," conclusion upon its finding that "the legislators excluded many heavily-Democratic precincts from District 12, even when those precincts immediately border the Twelfth and would have established a far more compact district." This finding, however—insofar as it differs from the remaining four—rests solely upon evidence that the legislature excluded heavily white precincts with high Democratic Party registration, while including heavily African-American precincts with equivalent, or lower, Democratic Party registration. Indeed, the District Court cites at length figures showing that the legislature included "several precincts with racial compositions of 40 to 100 percent African-American," while excluding certain adjacent precincts "with less than 35 percent African-American population" but which contain between 54% and 76% registered Democrats.

As we said before, the problem with this evidence is that it focuses upon party registration, not upon voting behavior. And we previously found the same evidence inadequate because registration figures do not accurately predict preference at the polls. In part this is because white voters registered as Democrats "cross-over" to vote for a Republican candidate more often than do African-Americans, who register and vote Democratic between 95% and 97% of the time. A legislature trying to secure a safe Democratic seat is interested in Democratic voting behavior. Hence, a legislature may, by placing reliable Democratic precincts within a district without regard to race, end up with a district containing more heavily African-American precincts, but the reasons would be political rather than racial.

Insofar as the District Court relied upon voting registration data, particularly data that were previously before us, it tells us nothing new; and the data do not help answer the question posed when we previously remanded this litigation. . . .

The District Court also relied on two pieces of "direct" evidence of discriminatory intent. The court found that a legislative redistricting leader, Senator Roy Cooper, when testifying before a legislative committee in 1997, had said that the 1997 plan satisfies a "need for 'racial and partisan' balance." The court concluded that the words "racial balance" referred to a 10-to-2 Caucasian/African-American balance in the State's 12-member congressional delegation. Hence, Senator Cooper had admitted that the legislature had drawn the plan with race in mind. . . . We agree that one can read the statement about "racial . . . balance" as the District Court read it—to refer to the current congressional delegation's racial balance. But even as so read, the phrase shows that the legislature considered race, along with other partisan and geographic considerations; and as so read it says little or nothing about whether race played a predominant role comparatively speaking.

The second piece of "direct" evidence relied upon by the District Court is a February 10, 1997, e-mail sent from Gerry Cohen, a legislative staff member responsible for drafting districting plans, to Senator Cooper and Senator Leslie Winner. Cohen wrote: "I have moved Greensboro Black community into the 12th, and now need to take [about] 60,000 out of the 12th. I await your direction on this."

The reference to race—i.e., "Black community"—is obvious. But the e-mail does not discuss the point of the reference. It does not discuss why Greensboro's African-American voters were placed in the 12th District; it does not discuss the political consequences of failing to do so; it is addressed only to two members of the legislature; and it suggests that the legislature paid less attention to race in respect to the 12th District than in respect to the 1st District, where the e-mail provides a far more extensive, detailed discussion of racial percentages. It is less persuasive than the kinds of direct evidence we have found significant in other redistricting cases. Nonetheless, the e-mail offers some support for the District Court's conclusion. . . .

We concede the record contains a modicum of evidence offering support for the District Court's conclusion. That evidence includes the Cohen e-mail, Senator Cooper's reference to "racial balance," and to a minor degree, some aspects of Dr. Weber's testimony. The evidence taken together, however, does not show that racial considerations predominated in the drawing of District 12's boundaries. That is because race in this case correlates closely with political behavior. The basic question is whether the legislature drew District 12's boundaries because of race rather than because of political behavior (coupled with traditional, nonracial districting considerations). It is not, as the dissent contends, whether a legislature may defend its districting decisions based on a "stereotype" about African-American voting behavior. And given the fact that the party attacking the legislature's decision bears the burden of proving that racial considerations are "dominant and controlling," given the "demanding" nature of that burden of proof, and given the sensitivity, the "extraordinary caution," that district courts must show to avoid treading upon legislative prerogatives, the attacking party has not successfully shown that race, rather than politics, predominantly accounts for the result. The record leaves us with the "definite and firm conviction" that the District Court erred in finding to the contrary. And we do not believe that providing appellees a further opportunity to make their "precinct swapping" arguments in the District Court could change this result.

We can put the matter more generally as follows: In a case such as this one where majority-minority districts (or the approximate equivalent) are at issue and where racial identification correlates highly with political affiliation, the party attacking the legislatively drawn boundaries must show at the least that the legislature could have achieved its legitimate political objectives in alternative ways that are comparably consistent with traditional districting principles. That party must also show that those districting alternatives would have brought about significantly greater racial balance. Appellees failed to make any such showing here. We conclude that the District Court's contrary findings are clearly erroneous.

The judgment of the District Court is Reversed.

Justice THOMAS, with whom Chief Justice REHNQUIST, Justice SCALIA, and Justice KENNEDY join, dissenting.

The District Court's conclusion that race was the predominant factor motivating the North Carolina Legislature is a factual finding. See *Hunt v. Cromartie*, 526 U.S. 541 (1999); *Shaw v. Hunt*, 517 U.S. 899 (1996); *Miller v. Johnson*, 515 U.S. 900 (1995). Accordingly, we should not overturn the District Court's determination unless it is clearly erroneous. . . .

Reviewing for clear error, I cannot say that the District Court's view of the evidence was impermissible. First, the court relied on objective measures of compactness, which show that District 12 is the most geographically scattered district in North Carolina, to support its conclusion that the district's design was not dictated by traditional districting concerns. Although this evidence was available when we held that summary judgment was inappropriate, we certainly did not hold that it was irrelevant in determining whether racial gerrymandering occurred. On the contrary, we determined that there was a triable issue of fact. Moreover, although we acknowledged "that a district's unusual shape can give rise to an inference of political motivation," we "doubt[ed] that a bizarre shape equally supports a political inference and a racial one." *Hunt.* As we explained, "[s]ome districts . . . are 'so highly irregular that [they] rationally cannot be understood as anything other than an effort to segregat[e] voters' on the basis of race."

Second, the court relied on the expert opinion of Dr. Weber, who interpreted statistical data to conclude that there were Democratic precincts with low black populations excluded from District 12, which would have created a more compact district had they been included. And contrary to the Court's assertion, Dr. Weber did not merely examine the registration data in reaching his conclusions. Dr. Weber explained that he refocused his analysis on performance. He did so in response to our concerns, when we reversed the District Court's summary judgment finding, that voter registration might not be the best measure of the Democratic nature of a precinct. This fact was not lost on the District Court, which specifically referred to those pages of the record covering Dr. Weber's analysis of performance.

Third, the court credited Dr. Weber's testimony that the districting decisions could not be explained by political motives. In the first instance, I, like the Court, might well have concluded that District 12 was not significantly "safer" than several other districts in North Carolina merely because its Democratic reliability exceeded the optimum by only 3 percent. And I might have concluded that it would make political sense for incumbents to adopt a "the more reliable the better" policy in districting. However, I certainly cannot say that the court's inference from the facts was impermissible.

Fourth, the court discredited the testimony of the State's witness, Dr. Peterson. Again, like the Court, if I were a district court judge, I might have found that Dr. Weber's insistence that one could not ignore the core was unpersuasive. However, even if the core could be ignored, it seems to me that Dr. Weber's testimony—that Dr. Peterson had failed to analyze all of the segments and thus that his analysis was incomplete—reasonably could have supported the court's conclusion.

Finally, the court found that other evidence demonstrated that race was foremost on the legislative agenda: an e-mail from the drafter of the 1992 and 1997 plans to senators in charge of legislative redistricting, the computer capability to draw the district by race, and statements made by Senator Cooper that the legislature was going to be able to avoid Shaw's majority-minority trigger by ending just short of the majority. The e-mail, in combination with the indirect evidence, is evidence ample enough to support the District Court's finding for purposes of clear error review. The drafter of the redistricting plans reported in the bluntest of terms: "I have moved Greensboro Black community into the 12th [District], and now need to take . . . 60,000 out of the 12th [District]." Certainly the District Court was entitled to believe that the drafter was targeting voters and shifting district boundaries purely on the basis of race. The Court tries to belittle the import of this evidence by noting that the e-mail does not discuss why blacks were being targeted. However, the District Court was assigned the task of determining whether, not why, race predominated. As I see it, this inquiry is sufficient to answer the constitutional question because racial gerrymandering offends the Constitution whether the motivation is malicious or benign. It is not a defense that the legislature merely may have drawn the district based on the stereotype that blacks are reliable Democratic voters. And regardless of whether the e-mail tended to show that the legislature was operating under an even stronger racial motivation when it was drawing District 1 than when it was drawing District 12, I am convinced that the District Court permissibly could have accorded great weight to this e-mail as direct evidence of a racial motive. . . .

The only question that this Court should decide is whether the District Court's finding of racial predominance was clearly erroneous. In light of the direct evidence of racial motive and the inferences that may be drawn from the circumstantial evidence, I am satisfied that the District Court's finding was permissible, even if not compelled by the record.

C. CAMPAIGNS AND ELECTIONS

Among several other rulings on campaigns and elections, the Court struck down California's "blanket" primary, under which voters may pick and choose from among candidates of all parties who are listed on a single ballot, in *California Democratic Party v. Jones* (2000) (excerpted below).

More dramatically, in a unique and widely watched ruling that determined the outcome of the 2000 presidential election, a bare majority reversed the Florida supreme court's decision ordering a manual count of state-wide votes in the presidential election and, thus, secured the election of George W. Bush, in *Bush v. Gore* (excerpted below).

In another five to four decision, the Court upheld limitations on political parties' expenditures that are coordinated with candidates in *Federal Election Commission v. Colorado Republican Federal Campaign Committee* (2001) (excerpted below).

THE DEVELOPMENT OF LAW

Other Rulings on Campaign Finance

Case	Vote	Ruling
Nixon v. Shrink Missouri Government PAC, 528 U.S. 377 (2000)	6:3	Reaffirming the basic holding in *Buckley v. Valeo*, 424 U.S. 1 (1976), which upheld a $1,000 cap on donations to

federal candidates over First Amendment objections, the Court upheld Missouri's $1,075 limit on campaign contributions to candidates for state office. Writing for the Court, Justice Souter ruled that the prevention of corruption and the appearance of corruption was a constitutionally sufficient justification for such campaign contribution limits. Justices Kennedy, Scalia, and Thomas dissented, contending that the majority had abandoned "the rigors of our traditional First Amendment structure" and that its ruling would undermine democracy by encouraging the use of "soft money" contributions to political parties, rather than direct contributions to candidates.

THE DEVELOPMENT OF LAW

Other Rulings on Campaigns and Elections

Case	Vote	Ruling
Rice v. Cayetano, 528 U.S. 495 (2000)	7:2	The Court held that the denial of a citizen's right to vote for trustees of the Office of

Hawaiian Affairs (OHA) violates the Fifteenth Amendment for voting rights. The OHA administers programs for two subclasses of Hawaiians: "Hawaiians" and "native Hawaiians"; both trace their ancestry back to 1778. Rice, a Hawaiian citizen who lacked the ancestry to be designated as "Hawaiian," applied to vote in OHA trustee elections but was denied permission and sued. Writing for the Court, Justice Kennedy ruled that the ancestry requirements were a proxy for race and as such were forbidden by the Fifteenth Amendment. Justices Stevens and Ginsburg dissented.

Case	Vote	Ruling
Cook v. Gralike, 531 U.S. 510 (2001)	9:0	In response to the ruling in *U.S. Term Limits, Inc. v. Thornton*, 514 U.S. 779

(1995) (excerpted in Vol. 1, Ch. 5), Missouri amended its state constitution to require that the words "Disregarded Voters' Instruction on Term Limits" be placed on the ballot next to the name of an incumbent who failed to support term limits and who runs for reelection. Concerning candidates who are not incumbents and who refuse to vow to support term limits, the law required that the label "Declined to Pledge to Support Term Limits" be placed next to their names. Writing for the Court, Justice Stevens struck down Missouri's law for running afoul of the Elections Clause of Article 1, Section 4, by impermissibly attempting to add to the qualifications for holding congressional office beyond those specified for members' age, citizenship, and residency.

California Democratic Party v. Jones
530 U.S. 567, 120 S.Ct. 2402 (2000)

Until 1996, California political parties held closed primaries in which only registered voters in a party voted on its nominees. In 1996, however, the state adopted an initiative, Proposition 198, to change to "blanket" primaries, under which all persons eligible, even those not affiliated with a party, may vote for any candidate, regardless of the candidate's political affiliation, and voters may pick and choose among different parties' candidates for various offices listed on the same ballot. Washington and Alaska also have blanket primaries, whereas twenty other states have "open" primaries, allowing voters to decide on election day which party primary they want to participate in; twenty-five states have "closed" primaries.

The California Democratic Party and three other major parties—each of which prohibited persons not affiliated with their party from voting in their primaries—challenged the adoption of blanket primaries as a violation of their First Amendment freedom of association. A federal district court rejected their claim, and its decision was affirmed by the Court of Appeals for the Ninth Circuit, whose decision was granted review by the Supreme Court.

The appellate court's decision was reversed in a seven to two decision, with the opinion for the Court delivered by Justice Scalia. Justice Stevens filed a dissenting opinion, which Justice Ginsburg joined.

Justice SCALIA delivered the opinion of the Court.

This case presents the question whether the State of California may, consistent with the First Amendment to the United States Constitution, use a so-called "blanket" primary to determine a political party's nominee for the general election. . . .

We have recognized, of course, that States have a major role to play in structuring and monitoring the election process, including primaries. We have considered it "too plain for argument," for example, that a State may require parties to use the primary format for selecting their nominees, in order to assure that intraparty competition is resolved in a democratic fashion. *American Party of Tex. v. White*, 415 U.S. 767 (1974).

Similarly, in order to avoid burdening the general election ballot with frivolous candidacies, a State may require parties to demonstrate "a significant modicum of support" before allowing their candidates a place on that ballot. Finally, in order to prevent "party raiding"—a process in which dedicated members of one party formally switch to another party to alter the outcome of that party's primary—a State may require party registration a reasonable period of time before a primary election.

What we have not held, however, is that the processes by which political parties select their nominees are, as respondents would have it, wholly public affairs that States may regulate freely. To the contrary, we have continually stressed that when States regulate parties' internal processes they must act within limits imposed by the Constitution. . . .

Representative democracy in any populous unit of governance is unimaginable without the ability of citizens to band together in promoting among the electorate candidates who espouse their political views. The formation of national political parties was almost concurrent with the formation of the Republic itself. Consistent with this tradition, the Court has recognized that the First Amendment protects "the freedom to join together in furtherance of common political beliefs," which "necessarily presupposes the freedom to identify the people who constitute the association, and to limit the association to those people only." That is to say, a corollary of the right to associate is the right not to associate. "'Freedom of association would prove an empty guarantee if associations could not limit control over their decisions to those who share the interests and persuasions that underlie the association's being.'" [*Democratic Party of United States v. Wisconsin ex rel. La Follette*, 450 U.S. 107 (1981)].

In no area is the political association's right to exclude more important than in the process of selecting its nominee. That process often determines the party's positions on the most significant public policy issues of the day, and even when those positions are predetermined it is the nominee who becomes the party's ambassador to the general electorate in winning it over to the party's views.

Unsurprisingly, our cases vigorously affirm the special place the First Amendment reserves for, and the special protection it accords, the process by which a political party "select[s] a standard bearer who best represents the party's ideologies and preferences." The moment of choosing the party's nominee, we have said, is "the crucial juncture at which the appeal to common principles may be translated into concerted action, and hence to political power in the community." . . .

California's blanket primary violates the principles set forth in these cases. Proposition 198 forces political parties to associate with—to have their nominees, and hence their positions, determined by—those who, at best, have refused to affiliate with the party, and, at worst, have expressly affiliated with a rival. In this respect, it is qualitatively different from a closed primary. Under that system, even when it is made quite easy for a voter to change his party affiliation the day of the primary, and thus, in some sense, to "cross over," at least he must formally become a member of the party; and once he does so, he is limited to voting for candidates of that party.

The evidence in this case demonstrates that under California's blanket primary system, the prospect of having a party's nominee determined by adherents of an opposing party is far from remote—indeed, it is a clear and present danger. For example, in one 1997 survey of California voters 37 percent of Republicans said that they planned to vote in the 1998 Democratic gubernatorial primary, and 20 percent of Democrats said they planned to vote in the 1998 Republican United States Senate primary. . . . The impact of voting by nonparty members is much greater upon minor parties, such as the Libertarian Party and the Peace and Freedom Party. In the first primaries these parties conducted following California's implementation of Proposition 198, the total votes cast for party candidates in some races was more than double the total number of registered party members. . . .

In sum, Proposition 198 forces petitioners to adulterate their candidate-selection process—the "basic function of a political party"—by opening it up to persons wholly unaffiliated with the party. Such forced association has the likely outcome—indeed, in this case the intended outcome—of changing the parties' message. We can think of no heavier burden on a political party's associational freedom. Proposition 198 is therefore unconstitutional unless it is narrowly tailored to serve a compelling state interest. It is to that question which we now turn.

Respondents proffer seven state interests they claim are compelling. Two of them—producing elected officials who better represent the electorate and expanding candidate debate beyond the scope of partisan concerns—are simply circumlocution for producing nominees and nominee positions other than those the parties would choose if left to their own devices. . . .

Respondents' third asserted compelling interest is that the blanket primary is the only way to ensure that disenfranchised persons enjoy the right to an effective vote. By "disenfranchised," respondents do not mean those who cannot vote; they mean simply independents and members of the minority party in "safe" districts. These persons are disenfranchised, according to respondents, because under a closed primary they are unable to participate in what amounts to the determinative election—the majority party's primary; the only way to ensure they have an "effective" vote is to force the party to open its primary to them. This also appears to be nothing more than reformulation of an asserted state interest we have already rejected—recharacterizing nonparty members' keen desire to participate in selection of the party's nominee as "disenfranchisement" if that desire is not fulfilled. . . .

Respondents' remaining four asserted state interests—promoting fairness, affording voters greater choice, increasing voter participation, and protecting privacy—are not, like the others, automatically out of the running; but neither are they, in the circumstances of this case, compelling. That determination is not to be made in the abstract, by asking whether fairness, privacy, etc., are highly significant values; but rather by asking whether the aspect of fairness, privacy, etc., addressed by the law at issue is highly significant. And for all four of these asserted interests, we find it not to be. . . .

Respondents' legitimate state interests and petitioners' First Amendment rights are not inherently incompatible. To the extent they are in this case, the State of California has made them so by forcing political parties to associate with those who do not share their beliefs. And it has done this at the "crucial juncture" at which party members traditionally find their collective voice and select their spokesman. The burden Proposition 198 places on petitioners' rights of political association is both severe and unnecessary. The judgment for the Court of Appeals for the Ninth Circuit is reversed.

Justice STEVENS, with whom Justice GINSBURG joins as to Part I, dissenting.

I

[T]he Court blurs two distinctions that are critical: (1) the distinction between a private organization's right to define itself and its messages, on the one hand, and the State's right to define the obligations of citizens and organizations performing public functions, on the other; and (2) the distinction between laws that abridge participation in the political process and those that encourage such participation.

When a political party defines the organization and composition of its governing units, when it decides what candidates to endorse, and when it decides whether and how to communicate those endorsements to the public, it is engaged in the kind of private expressive associational activity that the First Amendment protects. . . .

I think it clear—though the point has never been decided by this Court—"that a State may require parties to use the primary format for selecting their nominees." The reason a State may impose this significant restriction on a party's associational freedoms is that both the general election and the primary are quintessential forms of state action. It is because the primary is state action that an organization—whether it calls itself a political party or just a "Jaybird" association—may not deny non-Caucasians the right to participate in the selection of its nominees. *Terry v. Adams*, 345 U.S. 461 (1953); *Smith v. Allwright*, 321 U.S. 649 (1944). The Court is quite right in stating that those cases "do not stand for the proposition that party affairs are [wholly] public affairs, free of First Amendment protections." They do, however, stand for the proposition that primary elections, unlike most "party affairs," are state action. The protections that the First Amendment affords to the "internal processes" of a political party do not encompass a right to exclude nonmembers from voting in a state-required, state-financed primary election.

The so-called "right not to associate" that the Court relies upon, then, is simply inapplicable to participation in a state election. A political party, like any other association, may refuse to allow non-members to participate in the party's decisions when it is conducting its own affairs; California's blanket primary system does not infringe this principle. But an election, unlike a convention or caucus, is a public affair. Although it is true that we have extended First Amendment protection to a party's right to invite independents to participate in its primaries, *Tashjian v. Republican Party of Conn.*, 479 U.S. 208 (1986), neither that case nor any other has held or suggested that the "right not to associate" imposes a limit on the State's power to open up its primary elections to all voters eligible to vote in a general election. In my view, while state rules abridging participation in its elections should be closely scrutinized, the First Amendment does not inhibit the State from acting to broaden voter access to state-run, state-financed elections. When a State acts not to limit democratic participation but to expand the ability of individuals to participate in the democratic process, it is acting not as a foe of the First Amendment but as a friend and ally. . . .

In my view, the First Amendment does not mandate that a putatively private association be granted the power to dictate the organizational structure of state-run, state-financed primary elections. It is not this Court's constitutional function to choose between the competing visions of what makes democracy work—party autonomy and discipline versus progressive inclusion of the entire electorate in the process of selecting their public officials—that are held by the litigants in this case. That choice belongs to the people. *U.S. Term Limits, Inc. v. Thornton*, 514 U.S. 779 (1995). . . .

Bush v. Gore
531 U.S. 98 (2000), 121 S.Ct. 525 (2000)

On the night of the presidential election, November 7, 2000, the Democratic candidate, Vice President Albert Gore, won the national popular vote but was locked in a bitter fight with the Republican candidate, Texas Governor George W. Bush, for Florida's 25 electoral votes, which would put either over the required 270 votes of the 528 votes of the Electoral College needed to win. Based on projections, CNN and other news services initially declared Gore and then Bush the winner, but ultimately concluded the election was too close to call. The next day the Florida Division of Elections reported that Bush had received 2,909,135 votes and Gore 2,907,351 votes, a margin of 1,784 for Bush. Because the margin was less than one-half of one percent of the votes cast, an automatic machine recount was conducted, as required under Florida law. The result diminished Bush's lead to 327 votes, so Gore sought manual recounts in three counties, Volusia, Broward, and Miami-Dade Counties, as allowed under Florida's law for *protesting* election results. Palm Beach County subsequently announced that it would manually recount all votes and Bush filed suit in federal district court to bar that recounting. In the meantime, a dispute arose over the deadline for canvassing boards to submit their returns to the Florida secretary of state for certification. The secretary's decision declining to waive a November 14 deadline for certification was challenged in state courts, and the Florida supreme court ruled that the manual recounts should be included in the final vote and extended the certification deadline to November 26. Attorneys for Bush appealed that decision to the U.S. Supreme Court, arguing that the state supreme court had rewritten state election law. Before the Supreme Court heard oral arguments in that case, the secretary of state certified Bush as the winner of the election by 537 votes and Gore filed suit, as provided under Florida law, *contesting* the election.

On Friday, December 1, oral arguments in *Bush v. Palm Beach County Canvassing Board*, 121 S.Ct. 471 (2000), (*Bush I*), were heard, and for the first time an audio recording of the arguments was made available for public broadcasting immediately after the arguments. The following Monday, December 4, the Court unanimously vacated and remanded the Florida Supreme Court's decision extending the certification date. The Court also directed the state supreme court to clarify the basis for its decision—specifically whether its ruling violated the due process clause; Section 5 of the Electoral Count Act of 1887, which provides a "safe harbor" for electoral votes receiving certification by December 12; and Article II of the U.S. Constitution, which provides that "[e]ach state shall appoint, in such Manner as the Legislature thereof may direct" the electors for President and Vice President.

On December 7, the Florida Supreme Court heard oral arguments in Gore's contest of the vote certification and the following day, voting four to three, ordered an immediate manual recount of all votes in the state where no vote for President was machine recorded. That decision was in turn immediately appealed by Bush attorneys to the U.S. Supreme Court, which granted a stay of the state-wide vote recount as well as granted review and set the date for oral arguments the following Monday, December 11, in *Bush v. Gore*. In addition to arguing that the vote recount ran afoul of Article II of the U.S. Constitution and Section 5 of the Electoral Count Act, attorneys for Bush contended that the manual recount was standardless and, thus, violated the Fourteenth Amendment Equal Protection Clause. By contrast, Gore's lawyers claimed that every vote should be counted. The following night at 10 P.M., December 12, the Court handed down its decision, reversing the state supreme court, upon finding that a standardless manual recount violated the equal protection clause but that a remedy—a remedy providing for a recount of votes based on clear standards—was impossible given the December 12 deadline.

The decision of the Court was delivered in a *per curiam* opinion. By a vote of seven to two, with Justices Stevens and Ginsburg dissenting, the state supreme court's decision was held to run afoul of the equal protection clause. By a vote of five to four, the Court held that there was no remedy available. Chief Justice Rehnquist, joined by Justices Scalia and Thomas, filed a concurring opinion. Justices Stevens, Souter, Ginsburg, and Breyer each filed dissenting opinions.

Per Curiam

The petition presents the following questions: whether the Florida Supreme Court established new standards for resolving Presidential election contests, thereby violating Art. II, Sec. 1, cl. 2, of the United States Constitution and failing to comply with [Section 5 of the Electoral Count Act of 1887] and whether the use of standardless manual recounts violates the Equal Protection and Due Process Clauses. With respect to the equal protection question, we find a violation of the Equal Protection Clause. . . .

This case has shown that punch card balloting machines can produce an unfortunate number of ballots which are not punched in a clean, complete way by the voter. After the current counting, it is likely legislative bodies nationwide will examine ways to improve the mechanisms and machinery for voting.

The individual citizen has no federal constitutional right to vote for electors for the President of the United States unless and until the state legislature chooses a statewide election as the means to implement its power to appoint members of the Electoral College. . . . The State, of course, after granting the franchise in the special context of Article II, can take back the power to appoint electors.

The right to vote is protected in more than the initial allocation of the franchise. Equal protection applies as well to the manner of its exercise. Having once granted the right to vote on equal terms, the State may not, by later arbitrary and disparate treatment, value one person's vote over that of another. It must be remembered that "the right of suffrage can be denied by a debasement or dilution of the weight of a citizen's vote just as effectively as by wholly prohibiting the free exercise of the franchise." *Reynolds v. Sims*, 377 U.S. 533 (1964).

The question before us . . . is whether the recount procedures the Florida Supreme Court has adopted are consistent with its obligation to avoid arbitrary and disparate treatment of the members of its electorate.

Much of the controversy seems to revolve around ballot cards designed to be perforated by a stylus but which, either through error or deliberate omission, have not been perforated with sufficient precision for a machine to count them. In some cases a piece of the card—a chad—is hanging, say by two corners. In other cases there is no separation at all, just an indentation.

For purposes of resolving the equal protection challenge, it is not necessary to decide whether the Florida Supreme Court had the authority under the legislative scheme for resolving election disputes to define what a legal vote is and to mandate a manual recount implementing that definition. The recount mechanisms implemented in response to the decisions of the Florida Supreme Court do not satisfy the minimum requirement for non-arbitrary treatment of voters necessary to secure the fundamental right. Florida's basic command for the count of legally cast votes is to consider the "intent of the voter." This is unobjectionable as an abstract proposition and a starting principle. The problem inheres in the absence of specific standards to ensure its equal application. The formulation of uniform rules to determine intent based on these recurring circumstances is practicable and, we conclude, necessary. . . .

The want of those rules here has led to unequal evaluation of ballots in various respects. As seems to have been acknowledged at oral argument, the standards for accepting or rejecting contested ballots might vary not only from county to county but indeed within a single county from one recount team to another. . . .

The State Supreme Court ratified this uneven treatment. It mandated that the recount totals from two counties, Miami-Dade and Palm Beach, be included in the certified total. The court also appeared to hold *sub silentio* that the recount totals from Broward County, which were not completed until after the original November 14 certification by the Secretary of State, were to be considered part of the new certified vote totals even though the county certification was not contested by Vice President Gore. Yet each of the counties used varying standards to determine what was a legal vote. Broward County used a more forgiving standard than Palm Beach County, and uncovered almost three times as many new votes, a result markedly disproportionate to the difference in population between the counties.

In addition, the recounts in these three counties were not limited to so-called undervotes but extended to all of the ballots. The distinction has real consequences. A manual recount of all ballots identifies not only those ballots which show no vote but also those which contain more than one, the so-called overvotes. Neither category will be counted by the machine. This is not a trivial concern. At oral argument, respondents estimated there are as many as 110,000 overvotes statewide. As a result, the citizen whose ballot was not read by a machine because he failed to vote for a candidate in a way readable by a machine may still have his vote counted in a manual recount; on the other hand, the citizen who marks two candidates in a way discernable by the machine will not have the same opportunity to have his vote count, even if a manual examination of the ballot would reveal the requisite indicia of intent. Furthermore, the citizen who marks two candidates, only one of which is discernable by the machine, will have his vote counted even though it should have been read as an invalid ballot. The State Supreme Court's inclusion of vote counts based on these variant standards exemplifies concerns with the remedial processes that were under way.

That brings the analysis to yet a further equal protection problem. The votes certified by the court included a partial total from one county, Miami-Dade. The Florida Supreme Court's decision thus gives no assurance that the recounts included in a final certification must be complete. Indeed, it is respondent's submission that it would be consistent with the rules of the recount procedures to include whatever partial counts are done by the time of final certification, and we interpret the Florida Supreme Court's decision to permit this. This accommodation no doubt results from the truncated contest period established by the Florida Supreme Court in *Bush I*, at respondent's own urging. The press of time does not diminish the constitutional concern. A desire for speed is not a general excuse for ignoring equal protection guarantees.

In addition to these difficulties the actual process by which the votes were to be counted under the Florida Supreme Court's decision raises further concerns. That order did not specify who would recount the ballots. The county canvassing boards were forced to pull together ad hoc teams comprised of judges from various Circuits who had no previous training in handling and interpreting ballots. Furthermore, while others were permitted to observe, they were prohibited from objecting during the recount.

The recount process, in its features here described, is inconsistent with the minimum procedures necessary to protect the fundamental right of each voter in the special instance of a statewide recount under the authority of a single state judicial officer. Our consideration is limited to the present circumstances, for the problem of equal protection in election processes generally presents many complexities. . . .

Upon due consideration of the difficulties identified to this point, it is obvious that the recount cannot be conducted in compliance with the requirements of equal protection and due process without substantial additional work. It would require not only the adoption (after opportunity for argument) of adequate statewide standards for determining what is a legal vote, and practicable procedures to implement them, but also orderly judicial review of any disputed matters that might arise. . . .

The Supreme Court of Florida has said that the legislature intended the State's electors to "participat[e] fully in the federal electoral process," as provided in [Section 5 of the Electoral Count Act]. That statute, in turn, requires that any controversy or contest that is designed to lead to a conclusive selection of electors be completed by December 12. That date is upon us, and there is no recount procedure in place under the State Supreme Court's order that comports with minimal constitutional standards. Because it is evident that any recount seeking to meet the December 12 date will be unconstitutional for the reasons we have discussed, we reverse the judgment of the Supreme Court of Florida ordering a recount to proceed.

Seven Justices of the Court agree that there are constitutional problems with the recount ordered by the Florida Supreme Court that demand a remedy. See SOUTER, J., dissenting; BREYER, J., dissenting. The only disagreement is as to the remedy. Because the Florida Supreme Court has said that the Florida Legislature intended to obtain the safe-harbor benefits of [Section 5] Justice BREYER's proposed remedy—remanding to the Florida Supreme Court for its ordering of a constitutionally proper contest until December 18—contemplates action in violation of the Florida election code, and hence could not be part of an "appropriate" order authorized by [Florida law].

The judgment of the Supreme Court of Florida is reversed, and the case is remanded for further proceedings not inconsistent with this opinion.

Chief Justsice REHNQUIST, with whom Justice SCALIA and Justice THOMAS join, concurring.

We deal here not with an ordinary election, but with an election for the President of the United States. . . . In most cases, comity and respect for federalism compel us to defer to the decisions of state courts on issues of state law. . . . But there are a few exceptional cases in which the Constitution imposes a duty or confers a power on a particular branch of a State's government. This is one of them. Article II, Sec. 1, cl. 2, provides that "[e]ach State shall appoint, in such Manner as the Legislature thereof may direct," electors for President and Vice President. Thus, the text of the election law itself, and not just its interpretation by the courts of the States, takes on independent significance. . . .

If we are to respect the legislature's Article II powers, therefore, we must ensure that postelection state-court actions do not frustrate the legislative desire to attain the "safe harbor" provided by [Section 5 of the Electoral Count Act].

In Florida, the legislature has chosen to hold statewide elections to appoint the State's 25 electors. Importantly, the legislature has delegated the authority to run the elections and to oversee election disputes to the Secretary of State, and to state circuit courts. Isolated sections of the code may well admit of more than one interpretation, but the general coherence of the legislative scheme may not be altered by judicial interpretation so as to wholly change the statutorily provided apportionment of responsibility among these various bodies. . . .

[I]n a Presidential election the clearly expressed intent of the legislature must prevail. And there is no basis for reading the Florida statutes as requiring the counting of improperly marked ballots, as an examination of the Florida Supreme Court's textual analysis shows. We will not parse that analysis here, except to note that the principal provision of the election code on which it relied was . . . entirely irrelevant. The State's Attorney General (who was supporting the Gore challenge) confirmed in oral argument here that never before the present election had a manual recount been conducted on the basis of the contention that "undervotes" should have been examined to determine voter intent. For the court to step away from this established practice, prescribed by the Secretary of State, the state official charged by the legislature with "responsibility to '[o]btain and maintain uniformity in the application, operation, and interpretation of the election laws,'" was to depart from the legislative scheme.

The scope and nature of the remedy ordered by the Florida Supreme Court jeopardizes the "legislative wish" to take advantage of the safe harbor provided by [Section 5]. December 12, 2000, is the last date for a final determination of the Florida electors that will satisfy [Section] 5. Yet in the late afternoon of December 8th—four days before this deadline—the Supreme Court of Florida ordered recounts of tens of thousands of so-called "undervotes" spread through 64 of the State's 67 counties. This was done in a search for elusive—perhaps delusive—certainty as to the exact count of 6 million votes. But no one claims that these ballots have not previously been tabulated; they were initially read by voting machines at the time of the election, and thereafter reread by virtue of Florida's automatic recount provision. No one claims there was any fraud in the election. The Supreme Court of Florida ordered this additional recount under the provision of the election code giving the circuit judge the authority to provide relief that is "appropriate under such circumstances." . . .

Given all these factors, and in light of the legislative intent identified by the Florida Supreme Court to bring Florida within the "safe harbor" provision of [Section] 5, the remedy prescribed by the Supreme Court of Florida cannot be deemed an "appropriate" one as of December 8. It significantly departed from the statutory framework in place on November 7, and authorized open-ended further proceedings which could not be completed by December 12, thereby preventing a final determination by that date.

For these reasons, in addition to those given in the *per curiam*, we would reverse.

Justice STEVENS, with whom Justice GINSBURG and Justice BREYER join, dissenting.

The federal questions that ultimately emerged in this case are not substantial. Article II provides that "[e]ach State shall appoint, in such Manner as the Legislature thereof may direct, a Number of Electors." It does not create state legislatures out of whole cloth, but rather takes them as they come—as creatures born of, and constrained by, their state constitutions. Lest there be any doubt, we stated over 100 years ago in *McPherson v. Blacker*, 146 U.S. 1 (1892), that "[w]hat is forbidden or required to be done by a State" in the Article II context "is forbidden or required of the legislative power under state constitutions as they exist." In the same vein, we also observed that "[t]he [State's] legislative power is the supreme authority except as limited by the constitution of the State." The legislative power in Florida is subject to judicial review pursuant to Article V of the Florida Constitution, and nothing in Article II of the Federal Constitution frees the state legislature from the constraints in the state constitution that created it. . . .

It hardly needs stating that Congress, pursuant to [Section] 5, did not impose any affirmative duties upon the States that their governmental branches could "violate." Rather, [Section] 5 provides a safe harbor for States to select electors in contested elections "by judicial or other methods" established by laws prior to the election day. Section 5, like Article II, assumes the involvement of the state judiciary in interpreting state election laws and resolving election disputes under those laws. Neither [Section] 5 nor Article II grants federal judges any special authority to substitute their views for those of the state judiciary on matters of state law.

Nor are petitioners correct in asserting that the failure of the Florida Supreme Court to specify in detail the precise manner in which the "intent of the voter" is to be determined rises to the level of a constitutional violation. We found such a violation when individual votes within the same State were weighted unequally, see *Reynolds v. Sims*, 377 U.S. 533 (1964), but we have never before called into question the substantive standard by which a State determines that a vote has been legally cast. And there is no reason to think that the guidance provided to the factfinders, specifically the various canvassing boards, by the "intent of the voter" standard is any less sufficient—or will lead to results any less uniform— than, for example, the "beyond a reasonable doubt" standard employed every day by ordinary citizens in courtrooms across this country.

[T]he majority effectively orders the disenfranchisement of an unknown number of voters whose ballots reveal their intent—and are therefore legal votes under state law—but were for some reason rejected by ballot-counting machines. . . .

What must underlie petitioners' entire federal assault on the Florida election procedures is an unstated lack of confidence in the impartiality and capacity of the state judges who would make the critical decisions if the vote count were to proceed. Otherwise, their position is wholly without merit. The endorsement of that position by the majority of this Court can only lend credence to the most cynical appraisal of the work of judges throughout the land. It is confidence in the men and women who administer the judicial system that is the true backbone of the rule of law. Time will one day heal the wound to that confidence that will be inflicted by today's decision. One thing, however, is certain. Although we may never know with complete certainty the identity of the winner of this year's Presidential election, the identity of the loser is perfectly clear. It is the Nation's confidence in the judge as an impartial guardian of the rule of law.

I respectfully dissent.

Justice SOUTER, with whom Justice BREYER joins and with whom Justice STEVENS and Justice GINSBURG join with regard to all but Part C, dissenting

The Court should not have reviewed either *Bush v. Palm Beach County Canvassing Bd.*, or this case, and should not have stopped Florida's attempt to recount all undervote ballots by issuing a stay of the Florida Supreme Court's orders during the period of this review. If this Court had allowed the State to follow the course indicated by the opinions of its own Supreme Court, it is entirely possible that there would ultimately have been no issue requiring our review, and political tension could have worked itself out in the Congress following the procedure provided in [Section 15 of the Electoral Count Act]. The case being before us, however, its resolution by the majority is another erroneous decision. . . .

The [Section] 5 issue is not serious. . . . Conclusiveness requires selection under a legal scheme in place before the election, with results determined at least six days before the date set for casting electoral votes. But no State is required to conform to [Section] 5 if it cannot do that (for whatever reason); the sanction for failing to satisfy the conditions of [Section] 5 is simply loss of what has been called its "safe harbor." And even that determination is to be made, if made anywhere, in the Congress.

The second matter here goes to the State Supreme Court's interpretation of certain terms in the state statute governing election "contests." . . . The issue is whether the judgment of the state supreme court has displaced the state legislature's provisions for election contests: is the law as declared by the court different from the provisions made by the legislature, to which the national Constitution commits responsibility for determining how each State's Presidential electors are chosen? . . .

The starting point for evaluating the claim that the Florida Supreme Court's interpretation effectively re-wrote [Florida law] must be the language of the provision on which Gore relies to show his right to raise this contest: that the previously certified result in Bush's favor was produced by "rejection of a number of legal votes sufficient to change or place in doubt the result of the election." None of the state court's interpretations is unreasonable to the point of displacing the legislative enactment quoted. . . .

In sum, the interpretations by the Florida court raise no substantial question under Article II. . . .

C

It is only on the third issue before us that there is a meritorious argument for relief, as this Court's *Per Curiam* opinion recognizes. . . . Petitioners have raised an equal protection claim (or, alternatively, a due process claim, see generally *Logan v. Zimmerman Brush Co.*, 455 U.S. 422 (1982)), in the charge that unjustifiably disparate standards are applied in different electoral jurisdictions to otherwise identical facts. . . .

In deciding what to do about this, we should take account of the fact that electoral votes are due to be cast in six days. I would therefore remand the case to the courts of Florida with instructions to establish uniform standards for evaluating the several types of ballots that have prompted differing treatments, to be applied within and among counties when passing on such identical ballots in any further recounting (or successive recounting) that the courts might order.

Unlike the majority, I see no warrant for this Court to assume that Florida could not possibly comply with this requirement before the date set for the meeting of electors, December 18. . . .

I respectfully dissent.

Justice GINSBURG, with whom Justice STEVENS joins, and with whom Justice SOUTER and Justice BREYER join as to Part I, dissenting.

I

The extraordinary setting of this case has obscured the ordinary principle that dictates its proper resolution: Federal courts defer to state high courts' interpretations of their state's own law. This principle reflects the core of federalism, on which all agree. The CHIEF JUSTICE's solicitude for the Florida Legislature comes at the expense of the more fundamental solicitude we owe to the legislature's sovereign. Were the other members of this Court as mindful as they generally are of our system of dual sovereignty, they would affirm the judgment of the Florida Supreme Court.

II

I agree with Justice STEVENS that petitioners have not presented a substantial equal protection claim. Ideally, perfection would be the appropriate standard for judging the recount. But we live in an imperfect world, one in which thousands of votes have not been counted. I cannot agree that the recount adopted by the Florida court, flawed as it may be, would yield a result any less fair or precise than the certification that preceded that recount.

Even if there were an equal protection violation, I would agree with Justice STEVENS, Justice SOUTER, and Justice BREYER that the Court's concern about "the December 12 deadline" is misplaced. . . . More fundamentally, the Court's reluctance to let the recount go forward—despite its suggestion that "[t]he search for intent can be confined by specific rules designed to ensure uniform treatment"—ultimately turns on its own judgment about the practical realities of implementing a recount, not the judgment of those much closer to the process. . . .

The Court assumes that time will not permit "orderly judicial review of any disputed matters that might arise." But no one has doubted the good faith and diligence with which Florida election officials, attorneys for all sides of this controversy, and the courts of law have performed their duties. Notably, the Florida Supreme Court has produced two substantial opinions within 29 hours of oral argument. In sum, the Court's conclusion that a constitutionally adequate recount is impractical is a prophecy the Court's own judgment will not allow to be tested. Such an untested prophecy should not decide the Presidency of the United States.

I dissent.

Justice BREYER, with whom Justice STEVENS and Justice GINSBURG join except as to Part I A (1), and with whom Justice SOUTER joins as to Part I, dissenting.

IA(1)

The majority raises three Equal Protection problems with the Florida Supreme Court's recount order: first, the failure to include overvotes in the manual recount; second, the fact that all ballots, rather than simply the undervotes, were recounted in some, but not all, counties; and third, the absence of a uniform, specific standard to guide the recounts. As far as the first issue is concerned, petitioners presented no evidence, to this Court or to any Florida court, that a manual recount of overvotes would identify additional legal votes. The same is true of the second, and, in addition, the majority's reasoning would seem to invalidate any state provision for a manual recount of individual counties in a statewide election.

The majority's third concern does implicate principles of fundamental fairness. The majority concludes that the Equal Protection Clause requires that a manual recount be governed not only by the uniform general standard of the "clear intent of the voter," but also by uniform subsidiary standards (for example, a uniform determination whether indented, but not perforated, "undervotes" should count). . . . I agree that, in these very special circumstances, basic principles of fairness may well have counseled the adoption of a uniform standard to address the problem. In light of the majority's disposition, I need not decide whether, or the extent to which, as a remedial matter, the Constitution would place limits upon the content of the uniform standard.

(2)

Nonetheless, there is no justification for the majority's remedy, which is simply to reverse the lower court and halt the recount entirely. An appropriate remedy would be, instead, to remand this case with instructions that, even at this late date, would permit the Florida Supreme Court to require recounting all undercounted votes in Florida, including those from Broward, Volusia, Palm Beach, and Miami-

Dade Counties, whether or not previously recounted prior to the end of the protest period, and to do so in accordance with a single-uniform substandard. . . .

By halting the manual recount, and thus ensuring that the uncounted legal votes will not be counted under any standard, this Court crafts a remedy out of proportion to the asserted harm. And that remedy harms the very fairness interests the Court is attempting to protect. . . .

II

The decision by both the Constitution's Framers and the 1886 Congress to minimize this Court's role in resolving close federal presidential elections is as wise as it is clear. However awkward or difficult it may be for Congress to resolve difficult electoral disputes, Congress, being a political body, expresses the people's will far more accurately than does an unelected Court. And the people's will is what elections are about.

Moreover, Congress was fully aware of the danger that would arise should it ask judges, unarmed with appropriate legal standards, to resolve a hotly contested Presidential election contest. Just after the 1876 Presidential election, Florida, South Carolina, and Louisiana each sent two slates of electors to Washington. Without these States, Tilden, the Democrat, had 184 electoral votes, one short of the number required to win the Presidency. With those States, Hayes, his Republican opponent, would have had 185. In order to choose between the two slates of electors, Congress decided to appoint an electoral commission composed of five Senators, five Representatives, and five Supreme Court Justices. Initially the Commission was to be evenly divided between Republicans and Democrats, with Justice DAVID DAVIS, an Independent, to possess the decisive vote. However, when at the last minute the Illinois Legislature elected Justice DAVIS to the United States Senate, the final position on the Commission was filled by Supreme Court Justice JOSEPH P. BRADLEY. The Commission divided along partisan lines, and the responsibility to cast the deciding vote fell to Justice BRADLEY. He decided to accept the votes by the Republican electors, and thereby awarded the Presidency to Hayes.

Justice BRADLEY immediately became the subject of vociferous attacks. BRADLEY was accused of accepting bribes, of being captured by railroad interests, and of an eleventh-hour change in position after a night in which his house "was surrounded by the carriages" of Republican partisans and railroad officials.

For present purposes, the relevance of this history lies in the fact that the participation in the work of the electoral commission by five Justices, including Justice BRADLEY, did not lend that process legitimacy. Nor did it assure the public that the process had worked fairly, guided by the law. Rather, it simply embroiled Members of the Court in partisan conflict, thereby undermining respect for the judicial process. And the Congress that later enacted the Electoral Count Act knew it.

This history may help to explain why I think it not only legally wrong, but also most unfortunate, for the Court simply to have terminated the Florida recount. . . . [A]bove all, in this highly politicized matter, the appearance of a split decision runs the risk of undermining the public's confidence in the Court itself. That confidence is a public treasure. . . . It is a vitally necessary ingredient of any successful effort to protect basic liberty and, indeed, the rule of law itself. We run no risk of returning to the days when a President (responding to this Court's efforts to protect the Cherokee Indians) might have said, "JOHN MARSHALL has made his decision; now let him enforce it!" But we do risk a self-inflicted wound—a wound that may harm not just the Court, but the Nation. . . .

I respectfully dissent.

Federal Election Commission v. Colorado Republican Federal Campaign Committee
121 S.Ct. 2351 (2001)

In *Colorado Republican Federal Campaign Committee v. Federal Election Commission (Colorado I)*, 518 U.S. 604 (1996), the Court held that limitations imposed by the Federal Election Commission (FEC) upon the Colorado Republican Federal Campaign Committee were unconstitutional. In doing so, though, the Court limited its holding to campaign expenditures that the party made independently of the candidate and remanded the question of whether political parties are generally immune from limitations on their campaign expenditures and whether limits on parties' expenditures made in coordination with candidates violates the First Amendment guarantee for freedom of speech. Subsequently, a federal district court concluded that parties are immune from such limitations on campaign spending. The Court of Appeals for the Tenth Circuit affirmed and the FEC appealed.

The appellate court was reversed in a five to four decision with Justice Souter delivering the opinion of the Court. Justice Thomas filed a dissenting opinion, which Chief Justice Rehnquist and Justices Scalia and Thomas joined.

Justice SOUTER delivered the opinion of the Court.

We first examined the Federal Election Campaign Act of 1971 in *Buckley v. Valeo*, 424 U.S. 1 (1976) (*per curiam*), where we held that the Act's limitations on contributions to a candidate's election campaign were generally constitutional, but that limitations on election expenditures were not. Later cases have respected this line between contributing and spending. See, e.g., *Nixon v. Shrink Missouri Government PAC*, 528 U.S. 377 (2000); *Colorado I; Federal Election Comm'n v. Massachusetts Citizens for Life, Inc.*, 479 U.S. 238 (1986).

The simplicity of the distinction is qualified, however, by the Act's provision for a functional, not formal, definition of "contribution," which includes "expenditures made by any person in cooperation, consultation, or concert, with, or at the request or suggestion of, a candidate, his authorized political committees, or their agents." Expenditures coordinated with a candidate, that is, are contributions under the Act.

The Federal Election Commission originally took the position that any expenditure by a political party in connection with a particular election for federal office was presumed to be coordinated with the party's candidate.

Colorado I was an as-applied challenge to the Party Expenditure Provision, occasioned by the Commission's enforcement action against the Colorado Republican Federal Campaign Committee (Party) for exceeding the campaign spending limit through its payments for radio advertisements attacking Democratic Congressman and senatorial candidate Timothy Wirth. The Party defended in part with the claim that the party expenditure limitations violated the First Amendment, and the principal opinion in *Colorado I* agreed that the limitations were unconstitutional as applied to the advertising expenditures at issue. . . .

The Party's broader claim remained: that although prior decisions of this Court had upheld the constitutionality of limits on coordinated expenditures by political speakers other than parties, the congressional campaign expenditure limitations on parties themselves are facially unconstitutional, and so are incapable of reaching party spending even when coordinated with a candidate. We remanded that facial challenge, which had not been fully briefed or considered below. On remand the District Court held for the Party, and a divided panel of the Court of Appeals for the Tenth Circuit affirmed. We granted *certiorari* to resolve the question left open by *Colorado I* and we now reverse.

[E]ver since we first reviewed the 1971 Act, we have understood that limits on political expenditures deserve closer scrutiny than restrictions on political contributions. Restraints on expenditures generally curb more expressive and associational activity than limits on contributions do. A further reason for the distinction is that limits on contributions are more clearly justified by a link to political corruption than limits on other kinds of unlimited political spending are (corruption being understood not only as *quid pro quo* agreements, but also as undue influence on an officer holder's judgment, and the appearance of such influence). At least this is so where the spending is not coordinated with a candidate or his campaign.

The First Amendment line between spending and donating is easy to draw when it falls between independent expenditures by individuals or political action committees (PACs) without any candidate's approval (or wink or nod), and contributions in the form of cash gifts to candidates. But facts speak less clearly once the independence of the spending cannot be taken for granted, and money spent by an individual or PAC according to an arrangement with a candidate is therefore harder to classify. . . .

Colorado I addressed the FEC's effort to stretch the functional treatment of coordinated expenditures further than the plain application of the statutory definition. As we said, the FEC argued that parties and candidates are coupled so closely that all of a party's expenditures on an election campaign are coordinated with its candidate; because *Buckley* had treated some coordinated expenditures like contributions and upheld their limitation, the argument went, the Party Expenditure Provision should stand as applied to all party election spending. *Colorado I* held otherwise, however, the principal opinion's view being that some party expenditures could be seen as "independent" for constitutional purposes.

But that still left the question whether the First Amendment allows coordinated election expenditures by parties to be treated functionally as contributions, the way coordinated expenditures by other entities are treated. . . .

The Party's argument that its coordinated spending, like its independent spending, should be left free from restriction under the *Buckley* line of cases boils down to this: because a party's most important speech is aimed at electing candidates and is itself expressed through those candidates, any limit on party support for a candidate imposes a unique First Amendment burden. . . .

Our evaluation of the arguments, however, leads us to reject the Party's claim to suffer a burden unique in any way that should make a categorical difference under the First Amendment. . . .

There are two basic arguments here. The first turns on the relationship of a party to a candidate: a coordinated relationship between them so defines a party that it cannot function as such without coordinated spending, the object of which is a candidate's election. We think political history and political reality belie this argument. The second argument turns on the nature of a party as uniquely able to spend in ways that promote candidate success. We think that this argument is a double-edged sword, and one hardly limited to political parties.

The assertion that the party is so joined at the hip to candidates that most of its spending must necessarily be coordinated spending is a statement at odds with the history of nearly 30 years under the Act. It is well to remember that ever since the Act was amended in 1974, coordinated spending by a party committee in a given race has been limited by the provision challenged here (or its predecessor). It was not until 1996 and the decision in *Colorado I* that any spending was allowed above that amount, and since then only independent spending has been unlimited. As a consequence, the Party's claim that coordinated spending beyond the limit imposed by the Act is essential to its very function as a party amounts implicitly to saying that for almost three decades political parties have not been functional or have been functioning in systematic violation of the law. . . .

There is a different weakness in the seemingly unexceptionable premise that parties are organized for the purpose of electing candidates, so that imposing on the way parties serve that function is uniquely burdensome. The fault here is not so much metaphysics as myopia, a refusal to see how the power of money actually works in the political structure.

When we look directly at a party's function in getting and spending money, it would ignore reality to think that the party role is adequately described by speaking generally of electing particular candidates. The money parties spend comes from contributors with their own personal interests. PACs, for example, are frequent party contributors who "do not pursue the same objectives in electoral politics" that parties do. PACs "are most concerned with advancing their narrow interest[s]" and therefore "provide support to candidates who share their views, regardless of party affiliation." In fact, many PACs naturally express their narrow interests by contributing to both parties during the same electoral cycle, and sometimes even directly to two competing candidates in the same election. Parties are thus necessarily the instruments of some contributors whose object is not to support the party's message or to elect party candidates across the board, but rather to support a specific candidate for the sake of a position on one, narrow issue, or even to support any candidate who will be obliged to the contributors.

Parties thus perform functions more complex than simply electing candidates; whether they like it or not, they act as agents for spending on behalf of those who seek to produce obligated officeholders. It is this party role, which functionally unites parties with other self-interested political actors, that the Party Expenditure Provision targets. This party role, accordingly, provides good reason to view limits on coordinated spending by parties through the same lens applied to such spending by donors, like PACs, that can use parties as conduits for contributions meant to place candidates under obligation.

Insofar as the Party suggests that its strong working relationship with candidates and its unique ability to speak in coordination with them should be taken into account in the First Amendment analysis, we agree. . . . It does not, however, follow from a party's efficiency in getting large sums and spending intelligently that limits on a party's coordinated spending should be scrutinized under an unusually high standard, and in fact any argument from sophistication and power would cut both ways. On the one hand, one can seek the benefit of stricter scrutiny of a law capping party coordinated spending by emphasizing the heavy burden imposed by limiting the most effective mechanism of sophisticated spending. And yet it is exactly this efficiency culminating in coordinated spending that (on the Government's view) places a party in a position to be used to circumvent contribution limits that apply to individuals and PACs, and thereby to exacerbate the threat of corruption and apparent corruption that those contribution limits are aimed at reducing. As a consequence, what the Party calls an unusual burden imposed by regulating its spending is not a simple premise for arguing for tighter scrutiny of limits on a party; it is the premise for a question pointing in the opposite direction. If the coordinated spending of other, less efficient and perhaps less practiced political actors can be limited consistently with the Constitution, why would the Constitution forbid regulation aimed at a party whose very efficiency in channeling benefits to candidates threatens to undermine the contribution (and hence coordinated spending) limits to which those others are unquestionably subject?

The preceding question assumes that parties enjoy a power and experience that sets them apart from other political spenders. But in fact the assumption is too crude. While parties command bigger spending budgets than most individuals, some individuals could easily rival party committees in spending. Rich political activists crop up, and the United States has known its Citizens Kane. Their money speaks loudly, too, and they are therefore burdened by restrictions on its use just as parties are. And yet they are validly subject to coordinated spending limits, *Buckley*, and so are PACs, which may amass bigger treasuries than most party members can spare for politics.

Just as rich donors, media executives, and PACs have the means to speak as loudly as parties do, they would also have the capacity to work effectively in tandem with a candidate, just as a party can do. While a candidate has no way of coordinating spending with every contributor, there is nothing hard about coordinating with someone with a fortune to donate, any more than a candidate would have difficulty in coordinating spending with an inner circle of personal political associates or with his own family. Yet all of them are subject to coordinated spending limits upheld in *Buckley*. . . .

We hold that a party's coordinated expenditures, unlike expenditures truly independent, may be restricted to minimize circumvention of contribution limits. We therefore reject the Party's facial challenge and, accordingly, reverse the judgment of the United States Court of Appeals for the Tenth Circuit.

Justice THOMAS, with whom Justice SCALIA and Justice KENNEDY join, and with whom Chief Justice REHNQUIST joins as to Part II, dissenting.

The Party Expenditure Provision severely limits the amount of money that a national or state committee of a political party can spend in coordination with its own candidate for the Senate or House of Representatives. Because this provision sweeps too broadly, interferes with the party-candidate relationship, and has not been proved necessary to combat corruption, I respectfully dissent.

As an initial matter, I continue to believe that *Buckley v. Valeo*, 424 U.S. 1 (1976) (*per curiam*), should be overruled. . . .

We need not, however, overrule *Buckley* and apply strict scrutiny in order to hold the Party Expenditure Provision unconstitutional. Even under *Buckley*, which described the requisite scrutiny as "exacting" and "rigorous," the regulation cannot pass constitutional muster. . . . By restricting such speech, the Party Expenditure Provision undermines parties' "freedom to discuss candidates and issues," and cannot be reconciled with our campaign finance jurisprudence.

Even if I were to ignore the breadth of the statutory text, and to assume that all coordinated expenditures are functionally equivalent to contributions, I still would strike down the Party Expenditure Provision. The source of the "contribution" at issue is a political party, not an individual or a political committee, as in *Buckley* and *Shrink Missouri*. Restricting contributions by individuals and political committees may, under *Buckley*, entail only a "marginal restriction," but the same cannot be said about limitations on political parties. Political parties and their candidates are "inextricably intertwined" in the conduct of an election. A party nominates its candidate; a candidate often is identified by party affiliation throughout the election and on the ballot; and a party's public image is largely defined by what its candidates say and do. Most importantly, a party's success or failure depends in large part on whether its candidates get elected. Because of this unity of interest, it is natural for a party and its candidate to work together and consult with one another during the course of the election. . . . Thus, the ordinary means for a party to provide support is to make coordinated expenditures. . . .

I am unpersuaded by the Court's attempts to downplay the extent of the burden on political parties' First Amendment rights. First, the Court does not examine the record or the findings of the District Court, but instead relies wholly on the "observ[ations]" of the "political scientists" who happen to have written an *amicus* brief in support of the petitioner. . . . Second, we have never before upheld a limitation on speech simply because speakers have coped with the limitation for 30 years. And finally, if the passage of time were relevant to the constitutional inquiry, I would wonder why the Court adopted a "30-year" rule rather than the possible countervailing "200-year" rule. For nearly 200 years, this country had congressional elections without limitations on coordinated expenditures by political parties. Nowhere does the Court suggest that these elections were not "functional," or that they were marred by corruption. . . .

VOLUME TWO

3

ECONOMIC RIGHTS AND
AMERICAN CAPITALISM

C. THE "TAKINGS CLAUSE" AND
JUST COMPENSATION

THE DEVELOPMENT OF LAW

Other Important Rulings on the Takings Clause

Case	Vote	Ruling
Palazzolo v. Rhode Island 121 S.Ct. 2448 (2001)	6:3	Writing for the Court, Justice Kennedy held that once property owners take title to property that includes land-use restrictions, they have standing to challenge those restrictions, even if the restrictions were imposed years earlier. In the words of Justice Kennedy, the government may not be relieved "of its obligation to defend any action restricting land use, no matter how extreme or unreasonable." Although the ruling invites more challenges to environmental regulations, on the merits the Court reaffirmed that to prevail such challenges must demonstrate that the owner was deprived of all economic value of the land. Justice Ginsburg, joined by Justices Souter and Breyer, dissented, contending that the case was not "ripe" for decision.

4

THE NATIONALIZATION
OF THE
BILL OF RIGHTS

B. THE RISE AND RETREAT
OF THE "DUE PROCESS
REVOLUTION"

In its 2001–2002 term, the Court will revisit the issue of civil commitments and sexual predators. In *Kansas v. Hendricks*, 521 U.S. 346 (1997), a bare majority upheld Kansas's law providing for the involuntary commitment of sexual predators, even after they have served their prison sentences, over due process objections. At issue in *Kansas v. Crane* (No. 00-957) is whether Kansas's civil commitment of an individual as a sexual predator violates due process in the absence of a showing that the individual cannot control his dangerous behavior. Crane was convicted of lewd and lascivious behavior for exposing himself to a tanning salon attendant and was found to be a sexual predator, based on a prior sexual battery conviction. Crane challenged his commitment because the trial court interpreted the ruling in *Hendricks* not to require a showing of volitional impairment that prevented him from controlling his behavior. On appeal, however, that decision was reversed because the appellate court deemed language in the opinion for the Court in *Hendricks* to compel the conclusion that civil commitment of sexual predators is unconstitutional absent a showing that the defendant cannot control his dangerous behavior.

THE DEVELOPMENT OF LAW

Rulings on Substantive and Procedural Due Process

Case	Vote	Ruling
Chicago v. Morales, 527 U.S. 41 (1999)	6:3	In an opinion for the Court, joined only by a plurality, Justice Stevens held that an

ordinance prohibiting "criminal street gang members" from loitering in public places was impermissibly vague in defining "loitering" and, therefore, failed to give citizens adequate notice of what was forbidden. Justices Scalia and Thomas issued dissenting opinions; Chief Justice Rehnquist joined the latter's dissent.

Case	Vote	Ruling
Troxel v. Granville, 530 U.S. 57 (2000)	6:3	Reaffirming that the Fourteenth Amendment has a substantive component provid-

ing "heightened protection against governmental interference with certain fundamental rights and liberty interests," including that of parents to make decisions concerning the care of their children, the Court held that Washington's statute allowing "any person" "at any time" to petition for visitation rights infringed on parents' "fundamental right to rear children." Writing for the Court, Justice O'Connor rejected the claims of grandparents to visitation rights to their deceased son's daughters over the objection of their mother and affirmed her fundamental right to rear her children. Justices Souter and Thomas filed concurring opinions, whereas Justices Stevens, Scalia, and Kennedy each filed dissents.

Case	Vote	Ruling
Cooper Industries, Inc. v. Leatherman Tool Group, Inc., 121 S.Ct. 1678 (2000)	8:1	The Court held that due process requires federal appelate courts to use a *de novo*, rather than an abuse of discretion,

standard when reviewing for "grossly excessive" damage awards. A jury awarded Leatherman Tool Group $50,000 in compensatory damages and $4.5 million in punitive damages for Cooper Industries's unfair competition and false advertising. Writing for the Court, Justice Stevens reasoned that *de novo* review was appropriate because determining whether damages awards are excessive requires courts to determine the reasonableness of the award based on the facts in each case. Justice Ginsburg dissented.

5

FREEDOM OF EXPRESSION
AND ASSOCIATION

A. JUDICIAL APPROACHES TO THE
FIRST AMENDMENT

(2) Judicial Line Drawing: *Ad Hoc* and Definitional Balancing

In *Board of Regents of the University of Wisconsin System v. Southworth*
(excerpted below) the Court unanimously upheld mandatory university
activity fees over the objectiosn of some students that the money was given
to groups and organizations that they deemed offensive and, thus ran afoul
of their First Amendment guarantee for freedom of speech.

In its 2000–2001 term, the Court handed down a decision on a related
controversy in *Legal Services Corporation v. Velazquez*, 531 U.S. 533
(2001). The Legal Services Corporation (LSC) was established in 1974 to
provide the poor with basic legal services by means of grants and assistance from local legal-aid offices. From the outset, Congress restricted the
kinds of advocacy funded, prohibiting the LSC from taking cases involving abortion, for instance, and school desegregation. In 1996, the LSC's
governing statute was further amended to permit LSC lawyers to seek welfare benefits for clients but forbid the lawyers from challenging the constitutionality of changes in federal and state welfare programs. Attorneys for
a woman whose benefits were cut and who had sought aid from the LSC
contended that the restriction was punitive and an unconstitutional restriction under the First Amendment, on the advocacy of particular points of
view. The Court of Appeals for the Second Circuit agreed and its decision
was affirmed by a bare majority of the Court.

Writing for the Court in *Legal Services Corporation v. Velazquez*, Justice
Kennedy distinguished *Rust v. Sullivan*, 500 U.S. 173 (1991) (excerpted
in Vol. 2, Ch. 5), which upheld a restriction on prohibiting doctors employed by federally funded family-planning clinics from discussing abortion
with their patients, and reaffirmed that the *Rust* ban on abortion counseling
amounted to *government* speech, even though it was using private speakers
to communicate its message. By contrast, the LSC program, like that chal-

lenged in *Rosenberger v. Rector and Visitors of the University of Virginia*, 515 U.S. 819 (1995) (excerpted in Vol. 2, Ch. 6), was deemed to facilitate *private speech*, not to promote a governmental message. According to Justice Kennedy, an LSC attorney speaks on behalf of a private, indigent client in seeking welfare benefits, whereas the government's message is delivered by the attorney defending the benefits decision and welfare program. Justices Stevens, Souter, Ginsberg, and Breyer joined that opinion, while Chief Justice Rehnquist and Justices O'Connor, Scalia, and Thomas dissented.

Board of Regents of the University of Wisconsin System v. Southworth
529 U.S. 217, 120 S.Ct. 1346 (2000)

The pertinent facts are discussed by Justice Kennedy in his opinion for a unanimous Court. Justice Souter, with whom Justices Stevens and Breyer joined, filed a concurring opinion.

Justice KENNEDY delivered the opinion of the Court.

Respondents are a group of students at the University of Wisconsin. They brought a First Amendment challenge to a mandatory student activity fee imposed by petitioner Board of Regents of the University of Wisconsin and used in part by the University to support student organizations engaging in political or ideological speech. Respondents object to the speech and expression of some of the student organizations. Relying upon our precedents which protect members of unions and bar associations from being required to pay fees used for speech the members find objectionable, both the District Court and the Court of Appeals invalidated the University's student fee program. The University contends that its mandatory student activity fee and the speech which it supports are appropriate to further its educational mission.

We reverse. The First Amendment permits a public university to charge its students an activity fee used to fund a program to facilitate extracurricular student speech if the program is viewpoint neutral. We do not sustain, however, the student referendum mechanism of the University's program, which appears to permit the exaction of fees in violation of the viewpoint neutrality principle. . . .

It seems that since its founding the University has required full-time students enrolled at its Madison campus to pay a nonrefundable activity fee. The fee is segregated from the University's tuition charge. Once collected, the activity fees are deposited by the University into the accounts of the State of Wisconsin. The fees are drawn upon by the University to support various campus services and extracurricular student activities. In the University's view, the activity fees "enhance the educational experience" of its students by "promot[ing] extracurricular activities," "stimulating advocacy and debate on diverse points of view," enabling "participa[tion] in political activity," "promot[ing] student participa[tion] in campus administrative activity," and providing "opportunities to develop social skills," all consistent with the University's mission.

The board of regents classifies the segregated fee into allocable and nonallocable portions. The nonallocable portion approximates 80% of the total fee and covers expenses such as student health services, intramural sports, debt service, and the upkeep and operations of the student union facilities. Respondents did not challenge the purposes to which the University commits the nonallocable portion of the segregated fee.

The allocable portion of the fee supports extracurricular endeavors pursued by the University's registered student organizations or RSO's. To qualify for RSO status students must organize as a not-for-profit group, limit membership primarily to students, and agree to undertake activities related to student life on campus. During the 1995–1996 school year, 623 groups had RSO status on the Madison campus.

RSO's may obtain a portion of the allocable fees in one of three ways. Most do so by seeking funding from the Student Government Activity Fund (SGAF), administered by the ASM [Associated Students of Madison]. SGAF moneys may be issued to support an RSO's operations and events, as well as travel expenses "central to the purpose of the organization." As an alternative, an RSO can apply for funding from the General Student Services Fund (GSSF), administered through the ASM's finance committee. These RSO's included a campus tutoring center, the student radio station, a student environmental group, a gay and bisexual student center, a community legal office, an AIDS support network, a campus women's center, and the Wisconsin Student Public Interest Research Group (WISPIRG). The University acknowledges that, in addition to providing campus services (e.g., tutoring and counseling), the GSSF-funded RSO's engage in political and ideological expression.

A student referendum provides a third means for an RSO to obtain funding. While the record is sparse on this feature of the University's program, the parties inform us that the student body can vote either to approve or to disapprove an assessment for a particular RSO. . . .

It is inevitable that government will adopt and pursue programs and policies within its constitutional powers but which nevertheless are contrary to the profound beliefs and sincere convictions of some of its citizens. The government, as a general rule, may support valid programs and policies by taxes or other exactions binding on protesting parties. Within this broader principle it seems inevitable that funds raised by the government will be spent for speech and other expression to advocate and defend its own policies. See, e.g., *Rust v. Sullivan*, 500 U.S. 173 (1991). The case we decide here, however, does not raise the issue of the government's right, or, to be more specific, the state-controlled University's right, to use its own funds to advance a particular message. The University's whole justification for fostering the challenged expression is that it springs from the initiative of the students, who alone give it purpose and content in the course of their extracurricular endeavors.

The University having disclaimed that the speech is its own, we do not reach the question whether traditional political controls to ensure responsible government action would be sufficient to overcome First Amendment objections and to allow the challenged program under the principle that the government can speak for itself. If the challenged speech here were financed by tuition dollars and the University and its officials were responsible for its content, the case might be evaluated on the premise that the government itself is the speaker. That is not the case before us.

The University of Wisconsin exacts the fee at issue for the sole purpose of facilitating the free and open exchange of ideas by, and among, its students. We conclude the objecting students may insist upon certain safeguards with respect to the expressive activities which they are required to support. Our public forum cases are instructive here by close analogy. This is true even though the student activities fund is not a public forum in the traditional sense of the term and despite the circumstance that those cases most often involve a demand for access, not a claim to be exempt from supporting speech. The standard of viewpoint neutrality found in the public forum cases provides the standard we find controlling. We decide that the viewpoint neutrality requirement of the University program is in general sufficient to protect the rights of the objecting students. The student referendum aspect of the program for funding speech and expressive activities, however, appears to be inconsistent with the viewpoint neutrality requirement.

We must begin by recognizing that the complaining students are being required to pay fees which are subsidies for speech they find objectionable, even offensive. The *Abhood* and *Keller* cases, then, provide the beginning point for our analysis. *Abhood v. Detroit Bd. of Ed.*, 431 U.S. 209 (1977); *Keller v. State Bar of Cal.*, 496 U.S. 1 (1990). While those precedents identify the interests of the protesting students, the means of implementing First Amendment protections adopted in those decisions are neither applicable nor workable in the context of extracurricular student speech at a university.

In *Abhood,* some nonunion public school teachers challenged an agreement requiring them, as a condition of their employment, to pay a service fee equal in amount to union dues. The objecting teachers alleged that the union's use of their fees to engage in political speech violated their freedom of association guaranteed by the First and Fourteenth Amendments. The Court agreed and held that any objecting teacher could "prevent the Union's spending a part of their required service fees to contribute to political candidates and to express political views unrelated to its duties as exclusive bargaining representative." The principles outlined in *Abhood* provided the foundation for our later decision in *Keller.* There we held that lawyers admitted to practice in California could be required to join a state bar association and to fund activities "germane" to the association's mission of "regulating the legal profession and improving the quality of legal services." The lawyers could not, however, be required to fund the bar association's own political expression.

[However, t]he speech the University seeks to encourage in the program before us is distinguished not by discernible limits but by its vast, unexplored bounds. To insist upon asking what speech is germane would be contrary to the very goal the University seeks to pursue. It is not for the Court to say what is or is not germane to the ideas to be pursued in an institution of higher learning.

Just as the vast extent of permitted expression makes the test of germane speech inappropriate for intervention, so too does it underscore the high potential for intrusion on the First Amendment rights of the objecting students. It is all but inevitable that the fees will result in subsidies to speech which some students find objectionable and offensive to their personal beliefs. If the standard of germane speech is inapplicable, then, it might be argued the remedy is to allow each student to list those causes which he or she will or will not support. If a university decided that its students' First Amendment interests were better protected by some type of optional or refund system it would be free to do so. We decline to impose a system of that sort as a constitutional requirement, however. The restriction could be so disruptive and expensive that the program to support extracurricular speech would be ineffective. The First Amendment does not require the University to put the program at risk. . . .

The University must provide some protection to its students' First Amendment interests, however. The proper measure, and the principal standard of protection for objecting students, we conclude, is the requirement of viewpoint neutrality in the allocation of funding support. Viewpoint neutrality was the obligation to which we gave substance in *Rosenberger v. Rector and Visitors of Univ. of Va.*, 515 U.S. 819 (1995). There the University of Virginia feared that any association with a student newspaper advancing religious viewpoints would violate the Establishment Clause. We rejected the argument, holding that the school's adherence to a rule of viewpoint neutrality in administering its student fee program would prevent "any mistaken impression that the student newspapers speak for the University." . . . There is symmetry then in our holding here and in *Rosenberger*: Viewpoint neutrality is the justification for requiring the student to pay the fee in the first instance and for ensuring the integrity of the program's operation once the funds have been collected. We conclude that the University of Wisconsin may sustain the extracurricular dimensions of its programs by using mandatory student fees with viewpoint neutrality as the operational principle.

The parties have stipulated that the program the University has developed to stimulate extracurricular student expression respects the principle of viewpoint neutrality. If the stipulation is to continue to control the case, the University's program in its basic structure must be found consistent with the First Amendment. . . .

It remains to discuss the referendum aspect of the University's program. While the record is not well developed on the point, it appears that by majority vote of the student body a given RSO may be funded or defunded. It is unclear to us what protection, if any, there is for viewpoint neutrality in this part of the process. To the extent the referendum substitutes majority determinations for viewpoint neutrality it would undermine the constitutional protection the program requires. The whole theory of viewpoint neutrality is that minority views are treated with the same respect as are majority views. Access to a public forum, for instance, does not depend upon majoritarian consent. That principle is controlling here. A remand is necessary and appropriate to resolve this point; and the case in all events must be reexamined in light of the principles we have discussed.

Justice SOUTER, with whom Justice STEVENS and Justice BREYER join, concurring in the judgment.

The majority today validates the University's student activity fee after recognizing a new category of First Amendment interests and a new standard of viewpoint neutrality protection. I agree that the University's scheme is permissible, but do not believe that the Court should take the occasion to impose a cast-iron viewpoint neutrality requirement to uphold it. Instead, I would hold that the First Amendment interest claimed by the student respondents (hereinafter Southworth) here is simply insufficient to merit protection by anything more than the viewpoint neutrality already accorded by the University, and I would go no further.

B. OBSCENITY, PORNOGRAPHY, AND OFFENSIVE SPEECH

(1) Obscenity and Pornography

For the second time in a decade, the Court addressed the issue of First Amendment protection for nude dancing. In a 1991 five to four decision in *Barnes v. Glen Theatre, Inc.*, 501 U.S. 560 (1991) (in Vol. 2, Ch. 5), the Court upheld a state law banning public nudity as applied to totally nude dancing. That decision prompted the city of Erie, Pennsylvania, to enact a similar ordinance, which was upheld in *City of Erie v. Pap's A.M.* (excerpted below).

In its 2001–2002 term, the Court will revisit the issue of First Amendment protection for adult entertainment businesses, in *Los Angeles, California v. Alameda Books, Inc.* (No. 00-799). At issue is the constitutionality of a 1983 city ordinance prohibiting the operation of more than one adult entertainment business in the same building. In 1995, a city inspector found Alameda Books in violation of the ordinance for operating both an adult bookstore and an adult arcade. But, a federal district court issued a permanent injunction against the enforcement of the ordinance. And the Court of Appeals for the Ninth Circuit affirmed that decision, relying on *Renton v. Playtime Theatres, Inc.*, 475 U.S. 41 (1986), upon finding that the city had failed to show any harmful secondary effects, such as prostitution, associated with the businesses and concluded that the ordinance was not narrowly tailored to serve a significant government interest and to survive a First Amendment challenge.

City of Erie v. Pap's A.M.
529 U.S. 277, 120 S.Ct. 1382 (2000)

Following the Supreme Court's ruling in *Barnes v. Glen Theatre, Inc.*, 501 U.S. 560 (1991), that Indiana's law against public nudity could apply to nude dancing in adult clubs and require dancers to wear G-strings and pasties instead of dancing totally nude, the city of Erie, Pennsylvania, enacted an ordinance making it an offense to appear in public in a "state of nudity." Two days after the law went into effect, Pap's A.M., the owner of Kandyland, a club that featured totally nude dancing, sought an injunction against the enforcement of the law. The trial court granted an injunction upon finding the ordinance unconstitutional, but an appellate court reversed. Subsequently, the Pennsylvania Supreme Court overruled that decision, holding that nude dancing was expressive conduct protected by the First Amendment. The state supreme court noted that that was the view of eight members of the Supreme Court in *Barnes*, counting four members in the majority and the four dissenters. But, it also concluded that *Barnes* provided no clear precedent because the Court's decision was five to four and its plurality opinion fragmented the justices with four separate and conflicting opinions. Erie appealed and the Supreme Court granted review.

The Court reversed, and its decision was seven-and-a-half to two-and-a-half. Justice O'Connor delivered the opinion for the Court. Justice Scalia, joined by Justice Thomas, filed a concurring opinion. Justice Souter filed a separate opinion, concurring and dissenting in part. Justice Stevens filed a dissent, which Justice Ginsburg joined.

Justice O'CONNOR announced the judgment of the Court, delivered the opinion of the Court with respect to Parts I and II, and delivered an opinion with respect to Parts III and IV, in which Chief Justice REHNQUIST, Justice KENNEDY, and Justice BREYER join.

III

Being "in a state of nudity" is not an inherently expressive condition. As we explained in *Barnes* [*v. Glen Theatre, Inc.*, 501 U.S. 560 (1991)], however, nude dancing of the type at issue here is expressive conduct, although we think that it falls only within the outer ambit of the First Amendment's protection.

To determine what level of scrutiny applies to the ordinance at issue here, we must decide "whether the State's regulation is related to the suppression of expression." *Texas v. Johnson*, 491 U.S. 397 (1989). If the governmental purpose in enacting the regulation is unrelated to the suppression of expression, then the regulation need only satisfy the "less stringent" standard from [*United States v.*] *O'Brien* [391 U.S. 367 (1968)] for evaluating restrictions on symbolic speech. If the government interest is related to the content of the expression, however, then the regulation falls outside the scope of the *O'Brien* test and must be justified under a more demanding standard.

In *Barnes*, we analyzed an almost identical statute, holding that Indiana's public nudity ban did not violate the First Amendment, although no five Members of the Court agreed on a single rationale for that conclusion. We now clarify that government restrictions on public nudity such as the ordinance at issue here should be evaluated under the framework set forth in *O'Brien* for content-neutral restrictions on symbolic speech.

The ordinance here, like the statute in *Barnes*, is on its face a general prohibition on public nudity. By its terms, the ordinance regulates conduct alone. It does not target nudity that contains an erotic message; rather, it bans all public nudity, regardless of whether that nudity is accompanied by expressive activity. . . .

As Justice SOUTER noted in *Barnes*, "on its face, the governmental interest in combating prostitution and other criminal activity is not at all inherently related to expression." In that sense, this case is similar to *O'Brien*. *O'Brien* burned his draft registration card as a public statement of his antiwar views, and he was convicted under a statute making it a crime to knowingly mutilate or destroy such a card. This Court rejected his claim that the statute violated his

First Amendment rights, reasoning that the law punished him for the "noncommunicative impact of his conduct, and for nothing else." . . . So too here, the ordinance prohibiting public nudity is aimed at combating crime and other negative secondary effects caused by the presence of adult entertainment establishments like Kandyland and not at suppressing the erotic message conveyed by this type of nude dancing. Put another way, the ordinance does not attempt to regulate the primary effects of the expression, i.e., the effect on the audience of watching nude erotic dancing, but rather the secondary effects, such as the impacts on public health, safety, and welfare, which we have previously recognized are "caused by the presence of even one such" establishment. *Renton v. Playtime Theatres, Inc.*, 475 U.S. 41 (1986). . . .

[E]ven if Erie's public nudity ban has some minimal effect on the erotic message by muting that portion of the expression that occurs when the last stitch is dropped, the dancers at Kandyland and other such establishments are free to perform wearing pasties and G-strings. Any effect on the overall expression is *de minimis*. . . .

We conclude that Erie's asserted interest in combating the negative secondary effects associated with adult entertainment establishments like Kandyland is unrelated to the suppression of the erotic message conveyed by nude dancing. The ordinance prohibiting public nudity is therefore valid if it satisfies the four-factor test from *O'Brien* for evaluating restrictions on symbolic speech.

IV

Applying that standard here, we conclude that Erie's ordinance is justified under *O'Brien*. The first factor of the *O'Brien* test is whether the government regulation is within the constitutional power of the government to enact. Here, Erie's efforts to protect public health and safety are clearly within the city's police powers. The second factor is whether the regulation furthers an important or substantial government interest. The asserted interests of regulating conduct through a public nudity ban and of combating the harmful secondary effects associated with nude dancing are undeniably important. And in terms of demonstrating that such secondary effects pose a threat, the city need not "conduct new studies or produce evidence independent of that already generated by other cities" to demonstrate the problem of secondary effects, "so long as whatever evidence the city relies upon is reasonably believed to be relevant to the problem that the city addresses." *Renton v. Playtime Theatres, Inc.* Because the nude dancing at Kandyland is of the same character as the adult entertainment at issue in *Renton, Young v. American Mini Theatres, Inc.*, 427 U.S. 50 (1976), and *California v. LaRue*, 409 U.S. 109 (1972), it was reasonable for Erie to conclude that such nude dancing was likely to produce the same secondary effects. . . .

In any event, Erie also relied on its own findings. The preamble to the ordinance states that "the Council of the City of Erie has, at various times over more than a century, expressed its findings that certain lewd, immoral activities carried on in public places for profit are highly detrimental to the public health, safety and welfare, and lead to the debasement of both women and men, promote violence, public intoxication, prostitution and other serious criminal activity." The city council members, familiar with commercial downtown Erie, are the individuals who would likely have had first-hand knowledge of what took place at and around nude dancing establishments in Erie, and can make particularized, expert judgments about the resulting harmful secondary effects. Here, Kandyland has had ample opportunity to contest the council's findings about secondary effects—before the council itself, throughout the state proceedings, and before this Court. Yet to this day, Kandyland has never challenged the city council's findings or cast any specific doubt on the validity of those findings. . . .

The ordinance also satisfies *O'Brien's* third factor, that the government interest is unrelated to the suppression of free expression. The fourth and final *O'Brien* factor—that the restriction is no greater than is essential to the furtherance of the government interest—is satisfied as well. The ordinance regulates conduct, and any incidental impact on the expressive element of nude dancing is *di minimis.* The requirement that dancers wear pasties and G-strings is a minimal restriction in furtherance of the asserted government interests, and the restriction leaves ample capacity to convey the dancer's erotic message. Justice SOUTER points out that zoning is an alternative means of addressing this problem. It is far from clear, however, that zoning imposes less of a burden on expression than the minimal requirement implemented here. In any event, since this is a content-neutral restriction, least restrictive means analysis is not required.

We hold, therefore, that Erie's ordinance is a content-neutral regulation that is valid under *O'Brien.* Accordingly, the judgment of the Pennsylvania Supreme Court is reversed, and the case is remanded for further proceedings not inconsistent with this opinion.

Justice SCALIA, with whom Justice THOMAS joins, concurring in the judgment.

I agree that the decision of the Pennsylvania Supreme Court must be reversed, but disagree with the mode of analysis the Court has applied.

The city of Erie self-consciously modeled its ordinance on the public nudity statute we upheld against constitutional challenge in *Barnes v. Glen Theatre, Inc.,* calculating (one would have supposed reasonably) that the courts of Pennsylvania would consider themselves bound by our judgment on a question of federal constitutional law. In *Barnes,* I voted to uphold the challenged Indiana statute "not because it survives some lower level of First Amendment scrutiny, but because, as a general law regulating conduct and not specifically directed at expression, it is not subject to First Amendment scrutiny at all." Erie's ordinance, too, by its terms prohibits not merely nude dancing, but the act—irrespective of whether it is engaged in for expressive purposes—of going nude in public. The facts that a preamble to the ordinance explains that its purpose, in part, is to "limi[t] a recent increase in nude live entertainment," that city councilmembers in supporting the ordinance commented to that effect, and that the ordinance includes in the definition of nudity the exposure of devices simulating that condition, neither make the law any less general in its reach nor demonstrate that what the municipal authorities really find objectionable is expression rather than public nakedness. As far as appears (and as seems overwhelmingly likely), the preamble, the council members' comments, and the chosen definition of the prohibited conduct simply reflect the fact that Erie had recently been having a public nudity problem not with streakers, sunbathers or hot-dog vendors, but with lap dancers. . . .

Moreover, even were I to conclude that the city of Erie had specifically singled out the activity of nude dancing, I still would not find that this regulation violated the First Amendment unless I could be persuaded (as on this record I cannot) that it was the communicative character of nude dancing that prompted the ban. When conduct other than speech itself is regulated, it is my view that the First Amendment is violated only "[w]here the government prohibits conduct precisely because of its communicative attributes." Here, even if one hypothesizes that the city's object was to suppress only nude dancing, that would not establish an intent to suppress what (if anything) nude dancing communicates. I do not feel the need, as the Court does, to identify some "secondary effects" associated with nude dancing that the city could properly seek to eliminate. (I am highly skeptical, to tell the truth, that the addition of pasties and G-strings will at all reduce the tendency of establishments such as Kandyland to attract crime and prostitution, and hence to foster sexually transmitted disease.) The traditional power of government to foster good morals (bonos mores), and the acceptability of the traditional judgment (if Erie wishes to endorse it) that nude public dancing itself is immoral, have not been repealed by the First Amendment.

Justice SOUTER, concurring in part and dissenting in part.

Erie's stated interest in combating the secondary effects associated with nude dancing establishments is an interest unrelated to the suppression of expression under *United States v. O'Brien*, and the city's regulation is thus properly considered under the *O'Brien* standards. I do not believe, however, that the current record allows us to say that the city has made a sufficient evidentiary showing to sustain its regulation, and I would therefore vacate the decision of the Pennsylvania Supreme Court and remand the case for further proceedings. . . .

[T]he record before us today is deficient in its failure to reveal any evidence on which Erie may have relied, either for the seriousness of the threatened harm or for the efficacy of its chosen remedy. The plurality does the best it can with the materials to hand, but the pickings are slim. . . .

There is one point, however, on which an evidentiary record is not quite so hard to find, but it hurts, not helps, the city. The final *O'Brien* requirement is that the incidental speech restriction be shown to be no greater than essential to achieve the government's legitimate purpose. To deal with this issue, we have to ask what basis there is to think that the city would be unsuccessful in countering any secondary effects by the significantly lesser restriction of zoning to control the location of nude dancing, thus allowing for efficient law enforcement, restricting effects on property values, and limiting exposure of the public. The record shows that for 23 years there has been a zoning ordinance on the books to regulate the location of establishments like Kandyland, but the city has not enforced it. One councilor remarked that "I think there's one of the problems. The ordinances are on the books and not enforced. Now this takes place. You really didn't need any other ordinances." Another commented, "I felt very, very strongly, and I feel just as strongly right now, that this is a zoning matter." Even on the plurality's view of the evidentiary burden, this hurdle to the application of *O'Brien* requires an evidentiary response.

The record suggests that Erie simply did not try to create a record of the sort we have held necessary in other cases, and the suggestion is confirmed by the course of this litigation. The evidentiary question was never decided (or, apparently, argued) below, nor was the issue fairly joined before this Court. . . .

Accordingly, although I join with the plurality in adopting the *O'Brien* test, I respectfully dissent from the Court's disposition of the case.

Justice STEVENS, with whom Justice GINSBURG joins, dissenting.

Far more important than the question whether nude dancing is entitled to the protection of the First Amendment are the dramatic changes in legal doctrine that the Court endorses today. Until now, the "secondary effects" of commercial enterprises featuring indecent entertainment have justified only the regulation of their location. For the first time, the Court has now held that such effects may justify the total suppression of protected speech. Indeed, the plurality opinion concludes that admittedly trivial advancements of a State's interests may provide the basis for censorship. The Court's commendable attempt to replace the fractured decision in *Barnes v. Glen Theatre, Inc.*, with a single coherent rationale is strikingly unsuccessful; it is supported neither by precedent nor by persuasive reasoning.

The Court relies on the so-called "secondary effects" test to defend the ordinance. The present use of that rationale, however, finds no support whatsoever in our precedents. Never before have we approved the use of that doctrine to justify a total ban on protected First Amendment expression. On the contrary, we have been quite clear that the doctrine would not support that end.

In *Young v. American Mini Theatres, Inc.*, 427 U.S. 50 (1976), we upheld a Detroit zoning ordinance that placed special restrictions on the location of motion picture theaters that exhibited "adult" movies. The "secondary effects" of the adult theaters on the neighborhoods where they were located—lower property values and increases in crime (especially prostitution) to name a few—justified the burden imposed by the ordinance. Essential to our holding, however, was the fact that the ordinance was "nothing more than a limitation on the place where adult films may be exhibited" and did not limit the size of the market in such speech.

In *Renton v. Playtime Theatres, Inc.*, 475 U.S. 41 (1986), we upheld a similar ordinance, again finding that the "secondary effects of such theaters on the surrounding community" justified a restrictive zoning law. We noted, however, that "[t]he Renton ordinance, like the one in *American Mini Theatres*, does not ban adult theaters altogether," but merely "circumscribe[s] their choice as to location." Indeed, in both *Renton* and *American Mini Theatres*, the zoning ordinances were analyzed as mere "time, place, and manner" regulations. Because time, place, and manner regulations must "leave open ample alternative channels for communication of information," *Ward v. Rock Against Racism*, 491 U.S. 781 (1989), a total ban would necessarily fail that test. . . .

The reason we have limited our secondary effects cases to zoning and declined to extend their reasoning to total bans is clear and straightforward: A dispersal that simply limits the places where speech may occur is a minimal imposition whereas a total ban is the most exacting of restrictions. The State's interest in fighting presumed secondary effects is sufficiently strong to justify the former, but far too weak to support the latter, more severe burden. . . . The fact that this censorship may have a laudable ulterior purpose cannot mean that censorship is not censorship. For these reasons, the Court's holding rejects the explicit reasoning in *American Mini Theatres* and *Renton*. . . .

The Court's mishandling of our secondary effects cases is not limited to its approval of a total ban. It compounds that error by dramatically reducing the degree to which the State's interest must be furthered by the restriction imposed on speech, and by ignoring the critical difference between secondary effects caused by speech and the incidental effects on speech that may be caused by a regulation of conduct.

In what can most delicately be characterized as an enormous understatement, the plurality concedes that "requiring dancers to wear pasties and G-strings may not greatly reduce these secondary effects." To believe that the mandatory addition of pasties and a G-string will have any kind of noticeable impact on secondary effects requires nothing short of a titanic surrender to the implausible. . . .

Of course, the line between governmental interests aimed at conduct and unrelated to speech, on the one hand, and interests arising out of the effects of the speech, on the other, may be somewhat imprecise in some cases. In this case, however, we need not wrestle with any such difficulty because Erie has expressly justified its ordinance with reference to secondary effects. Indeed, if Erie's concern with the effects of the message were unrelated to the message itself, it is strange that the only means used to combat those effects is the suppression of the message. For these reasons, the Court's argument that "this case is similar to *O'Brien*" is quite wrong. . . . The Court cannot have its cake and eat it too—either Erie's ordinance was not aimed at speech and the Court may attempt to justify the regulation under the incidental burdens test, or Erie has aimed its law at the secondary effects of speech, and the Court can try to justify the law under that doctrine. But it cannot conflate the two with the expectation that Erie's interests aimed at secondary effects will be rendered unrelated to speech by virtue of this doctrinal polyglot. . . .

The censorial purpose of Erie's ordinance precludes reliance on the judgment in *Barnes* as sufficient support for the Court's holding today. Several differences between the Erie ordinance and the statute at issue in *Barnes* belie the Court's assertion that the two laws are "almost identical." . . . To begin with, the preamble to Erie's ordinance candidly articulates its agenda, declaring: "Council specifically wishes to adopt the concept of Public Indecency prohibited by the laws of the State of Indiana, which was approved by the U.S. Supreme Court in *Barnes v. Glen Theatre Inc.*, for the purpose of limiting a recent increase in nude live entertainment within the City." . . .

It is clear beyond a shadow of a doubt that the Erie ordinance was a response to a more specific concern than nudity in general, namely, nude dancing of the sort found in Kandyland. Given that the Court has not even tried to defend the ordinance's total ban on the ground that its censorship of protected speech might be justified by an overriding state interest, it should conclude that the ordinance is patently invalid. For these reasons, as well as the reasons set forth in Justice WHITE's dissent in *Barnes*, I respectfully dissent.

(2) Fighting Words and Offensive Speech

In *Wisconsin v. Mitchell*, 508 U.S. 476 (1993) (see Vol. 2, Ch. 5), the Court upheld "hate speech" laws that permit enhanced prison sentences for those convicted of crimes who intentionally selected their victims because of their "race, religion, color, disability, sexual orientation, national origin or ancestry." In *Apprendi v. New Jersey*, 530 U.S. 466 (2000), however, the

Court struck down New Jersey's law permitting judges to hand down longer sentences for "hate crimes" based on the "preponderance of evidence" standard. A bare majority ruled that enhanced sentences may only be imposed by a jury and on the basis of the strict "beyond a reasonable doubt" standard. Writing for the Court, Justice Stevens observed that, "other than the fact of prior conviction, any fact that increases the penalty for a crime beyond the prescribed statutory maximum must be submitted to a jury, and proved beyond a reasonable doubt." Writing for dissenting Chief Justice Rehnquist and Justices Breyer and Kennedy, Justice O'Connor criticized the majority for calling into question determinate sentencing and warned that its ruling could "unleash a flood of petitions by convicted defendants seeking to invalidate their sentences."

D. COMMERCIAL SPEECH

In *Lorillard Tobacco Co. v. Reilly* (2001) (excerpted below), the Court struck down Massachusetts's restrictions on the advertising of tobacco products, while upholding its regulations on the sale of those products.

Lorillard Tobacco Co. v. Reilly
121 S.Ct. 2404 (2001)

In 1999, Massachusetts enacted comprehensive regulations on the advertising and sale of tobacco products, which in turn were challenged by Lorillard Tobacco Company and other tobacco producers and retailers who contended that the regulations were preempted by federal law and violated the First Amendment. Among the regulations, outdoor advertising was restricted, effecting a ban on advertising within a 1,000-foot radius of any public playground or school, and the indoor display of tobacco products was restricted. A federal district court upheld the regulations, and the Court of Appeals for the First Circuit concluded that the regulations were not preempted by federal law and did not violate the First Amendment.

The lower court's decision was reversed and affirmed in part by a five to four vote of different justices. In Justice O'Connor's opinion for the Court, Parts I, II–C, and II–D were joined unanimously; Parts III–A, III–C, and III–D were joined by Chief Justice Rehnquist and Justices Scalia, Kennedy, Souter, and Thomas; Part III–B–1 was joined by Chief Justice Rehnquist and Justices Stevens, Souter, Ginsburg, and Breyer; and Parts II–A, II–B, III–B–2, and IV were joined by Chief Justice Rehnquist and Justices Scalia, Kennedy, and Thomas. Justice Kennedy filed an opinion concurring in part and concurring in the judgment, in which Justice Scalia joined. Justice Thomas filed an opinion concurring in part and concurring in the judgment. Justice Souter filed an opinion concurring in part and dissenting in part. Justice Stevens filed an opinion concurring in part and dissenting in part, which Justices Ginsburg and Breyer joined, and in Part I of which Justice Souter joined.

Justice O'CONNOR delivered the opinion of the Court.

II

Before reaching the First Amendment issues, we must decide to what extent federal law preempts the Attorney General's regulations. The cigarette petitioners contend that the [Federal Cigarette Labeling and Advertising Act] FCLAA preempts the [Massachusetts] Attorney General's cigarette advertising regulations. . . .

A

In the FCLAA, Congress has crafted a comprehensive federal scheme governing the advertising and promotion of cigarettes. The FCLAA's pre-emption provision provides:

"(b) State regulations

"No requirement or prohibition based on smoking and health shall be imposed under State law with respect to the advertising or promotion of any cigarettes the packages of which are labeled in conformity with the provisions of this chapter."

The FCLAA's preemption provision does not cover smokeless tobacco or cigars. . . .

In the preemption provision, Congress unequivocally precludes the requirement of any additional statements on cigarette packages beyond those provided in Section 1333. Congress further precludes States or localities from imposing any requirement or prohibition based on smoking and health with respect to the advertising and promotion of cigarettes. . . .

[W]e fail to see how the FCLAA and its preemption provision permit a distinction between the specific concern about minors and cigarette advertising and the more general concern about smoking and health in cigarette advertising, especially in light of the fact that Congress crafted a legislative solution for those very concerns. We also conclude that a distinction between state regulation of the location as opposed to the content of cigarette advertising has no foundation in the text of the preemption provision. Congress preempted state cigarette advertising regulations like the Attorney General's because they would upset federal legislative choices to require specific warnings and to impose the ban on cigarette advertising in electronic media in order to address concerns about smoking and health. Accordingly, we hold that the Attorney General's outdoor and point-of-sale advertising regulations targeting cigarettes are preempted by the FCLAA.

C

Although the FCLAA prevents States and localities from imposing special requirements or prohibitions "based on smoking and health" "with respect to the advertising or promotion" of cigarettes, that language still leaves significant power in the hands of States to impose generally applicable zoning regulations and to regulate conduct.

For instance, the FCLAA does not restrict a State or locality's ability to enact generally applicable zoning restrictions. . . . The FCLAA also does not foreclose all state regulation of conduct as it relates to the sale or use of cigarettes. The FCLAA's preemption provision explicitly governs state regulations of "advertising or promotion." Accordingly, the FCLAA does not preempt state laws prohibiting cigarette sales to minors. . . .

III

By its terms, the FCLAA's preemption provision only applies to cigarettes. Accordingly, we must evaluate the smokeless tobacco and cigar petitioners' First Amendment challenges to the State's outdoor and point-of-sale advertising regulations. . . .

A

For over 25 years, the Court has recognized that commercial speech does not fall outside the purview of the First Amendment. See, e.g., *Virginia Bd. of Pharmacy* [*v. Virginia Citizens Consumer Council, Inc.*, 425 U.S. 748 (1976)]. Instead, the Court has afforded commercial speech a measure of First Amendment protection "'commensurate'" with its position in relation to other constitutionally guaranteed expression. In recognition of the "distinction between speech proposing a commercial transaction, which occurs in an area traditionally subject to government regulation, and other varieties of speech," *Central Hudson* [*Gas & Electric Corp. v. Public Service Commission of New York*, 447 U.S. 557 (1980)], we developed a framework for analyzing regulations of commercial speech that is "substantially similar" to the test for time, place, and manner restrictions. The analysis contains four elements: "At the outset, we must determine whether the expression is protected by the First Amendment. For commercial speech to come within that provision, it at least must concern lawful activity and not be misleading. Next, we ask whether the asserted governmental interest is substantial. If both inquiries yield positive answers, we must determine whether the regulation directly advances the governmental interest asserted, and whether it is not more extensive than is necessary to serve that interest."

Only the last two steps of *Central Hudson*'s four-part analysis are at issue here. The Attorney General has assumed for purposes of summary judgment that petitioners' speech is entitled to First Amendment protection. With respect to the second step, none of the petitioners contests the importance of the State's interest in preventing the use of tobacco products by minors.

The third step of *Central Hudson* concerns the relationship between the harm that underlies the State's interest and the means identified by the State to advance that interest. . . .

We do not, however, require that "empirical data come . . . accompanied by a surfeit of background information. . . . [W]e have permitted litigants to justify speech restrictions by reference to studies and anecdotes pertaining to different locales altogether, or even, in a case applying strict scrutiny, to justify restrictions based solely on history, consensus, and 'simple common sense.'"

The last step of the *Central Hudson* analysis "complements" the third step, "asking whether the speech restriction is not more extensive than necessary to serve the interests that support it." We have made it clear that "the least restrictive means" is not the standard; instead, the case law requires a reasonable "'fit between the legislature's ends and the means chosen to accomplish those ends, . . . a means narrowly tailored to achieve the desired objective.'" Focusing on the third and fourth steps of the *Central Hudson* analysis, we first address the outdoor advertising and point-of-sale advertising regulations for smokeless tobacco and cigars. We then address the sales practices regulations for all tobacco products.

B

The outdoor advertising regulations prohibit smokeless tobacco or cigar advertising within a 1,000-foot radius of a school or playground. . . .

2

Whatever the strength of the Attorney General's evidence to justify the outdoor advertising regulations, however, we conclude that the regulations do not satisfy the fourth step of the *Central Hudson* analysis. The final step of the *Central Hudson* analysis, the "critical inquiry in this case," requires a reasonable fit between the means and ends of the regulatory scheme. The Attorney General's regulations do not meet this standard. The broad sweep of the regulations indicates that the Attorney General did not "carefully calculat[e] the costs and benefits associated with the burden on speech imposed" by the regulations. *Cincinnati v. Discovery Network, Inc.*, 507 U.S. 410 (1993).

The outdoor advertising regulations prohibit any smokeless tobacco or cigar advertising within 1,000 feet of schools or playgrounds. . . . The substantial geographical reach of the Attorney General's outdoor advertising regulations is compounded by other factors. "Outdoor" advertising includes not only advertising located outside an establishment, but also advertising inside a store if that advertising is visible from outside the store. The regulations restrict advertisements of any size and the term advertisement also includes oral statements.

In some geographical areas, these regulations would constitute nearly a complete ban on the communication of truthful information about smokeless tobacco and cigars to adult consumers. The breadth and scope of the regulations, and the process by which the Attorney General adopted the regulations, do not demonstrate a careful calculation of the speech interests involved.

First, the Attorney General did not seem to consider the impact of the 1,000-foot restriction on commercial speech in major metropolitan areas. The Attorney General apparently selected the 1,000-foot distance based on the FDA's decision to impose an identical 1,000-foot restriction when it attempted to regulate cigarette and smokeless tobacco advertising. But the FDA's 1,000-foot regulation was not an adequate basis for the Attorney General to tailor the Massachusetts regulations. The degree to which speech is suppressed—or alternative avenues for speech remain available—under a particular regulatory scheme tends to be case specific. And a case specific analysis makes sense, for although a State or locality may have common interests and concerns about underage smoking and the effects of tobacco advertisements, the impact of a restriction on speech will undoubtedly vary from place to place. The FDA's regulations would have had widely disparate effects nationwide. Even in Massachusetts, the effect of the Attorney General's speech regulations will vary based on whether a locale is rural, suburban, or urban. The uniformly broad sweep of the geographical limitation demonstrates a lack of tailoring.

In addition, the range of communications restricted seems unduly broad. For instance, it is not clear from the regulatory scheme why a ban on oral communications is necessary to further the State's interest. Apparently that restriction means that a retailer is unable to answer inquiries about its tobacco products if that communication occurs outdoors. Similarly, a ban on all signs of any size seems ill suited to target the problem of highly visible billboards, as opposed to smaller signs. . . .

We conclude that the Attorney General has failed to show that the outdoor advertising regulations for smokeless tobacco and cigars are not more extensive than necessary to advance the State's substantial interest in preventing underage tobacco use. . . .

C

Massachusetts has also restricted indoor, point-of-sale advertising for smokeless tobacco and cigars. Advertising cannot be "placed lower than five feet from the floor of any retail establishment which is located within a one thousand foot radius of" any school or playground. . . .

We conclude that the point-of-sale advertising regulations fail both the third and fourth steps of the *Central Hudson* analysis. A regulation cannot be sustained if it "provides only ineffective or remote support for the government's purpose," or if there is "little chance" that the restriction will advance the State's goal. . . .

D

The Attorney General also promulgated a number of regulations that restrict sales practices by cigarette, smokeless tobacco, and cigar manufacturers and retailers. Among other restrictions, the regulations bar the use of self-service displays and require that tobacco products be placed out of the reach of all consumers in a location accessible only to salespersons. . . .

Assuming that petitioners have a cognizable speech interest in a particular means of displaying their products, *Cincinnati v. Discovery Network, Inc.*, 507 U.S. 410 (1993) (distribution of a magazine through newsracks), these regulations withstand First Amendment scrutiny.

Massachusetts' sales practices provisions regulate conduct that may have a communicative component, but Massachusetts seeks to regulate the placement of tobacco products for reasons unrelated to the communication of ideas. We conclude that the State has demonstrated a substantial interest in preventing access to tobacco products by minors and has adopted an appropriately narrow means of advancing that interest.

Unattended displays of tobacco products present an opportunity for access without the proper age verification required by law. Thus, the State prohibits self-service and other displays that would allow an individual to obtain tobacco products without direct contact with a salesperson. It is clear that the regulations leave open ample channels of communication. The regulations do not significantly impede adult access to tobacco products. Moreover, retailers have other means of exercising any cognizable speech interest in the presentation of their products. We presume that vendors may place empty tobacco packaging on open display, and display actual tobacco products so long as that display is only accessible to sales personnel. . . .

We conclude that the sales practices regulations withstand First Amendment scrutiny. The means chosen by the State are narrowly tailored to prevent access to tobacco products by minors, are unrelated to expression, and leave open alternative avenues for vendors to convey information about products and for would-be customers to inspect products before purchase. . . .

IV

To the extent that federal law and the First Amendment do not prohibit state action, States and localities remain free to combat the problem of underage tobacco use by appropriate means. The judgment of the United States Court of Appeals for the First Circuit is therefore affirmed in part and reversed in part, and the cases are remanded for further proceedings consistent with this opinion.

Justice THOMAS, concurring in part and concurring in the judgment.

I join the opinion of the Court (with the exception of Part III–B–1) because I agree that the Massachusetts cigarette advertising regulations are preempted by the Federal Cigarette Labeling and Advertising Act. I also agree with the Court's disposition of the First Amendment challenges to the other regulations at issue here, and I share the Court's view that the regulations fail even the intermediate scrutiny of *Central Hudson Gas & Elec. Corp. v. Public Serv. Comm'n of N.Y.*, 447 U.S. 557 (1980). At the same time, I continue to believe that when the government seeks to restrict truthful speech in order to suppress the ideas it conveys, strict scrutiny is appropriate, whether or not the speech in question may be characterized as "commercial." See *44 Liquormart, Inc. v. Rhode Island*, 517 U.S. 484 (1996) (THOMAS, J., concurring in part and concurring in judgment). I would subject all of the advertising restrictions to strict scrutiny and would hold that they violate the First Amendment. . . .

Justice STEVENS, with whom Justice GINSBURG and Justice BREYER join, and with whom Justice SOUTER joins as to Part I, concurring in part, concurring in the judgment in part, and dissenting in part.

Because I strongly disagree with the Court's conclusion that the Federal Cigarette Labeling and Advertising Act of 1965 (FCLAA or Act) precludes States and localities from regulating the location of cigarette advertising, I dissent from Parts II–A and II–B of the Court's opinion. On the First Amendment questions, I agree with the Court both that the outdoor advertising restrictions imposed by Massachusetts serve legitimate and important state interests and that the record does not indicate that the measures were properly tailored to serve those interests. Because the present record does not enable us to adjudicate the merits of those claims on summary judgment, I would vacate the decision upholding those restrictions and remand for trial on the constitutionality of the outdoor advertising regulations. Finally, because I do not believe that either the point-of-sale advertising restrictions or the sales practice restrictions implicate significant First Amendment concerns, I would uphold them in their entirety. . . .

II

On the First Amendment issues raised by petitioners, my disagreements with the majority are less significant. I would, however, reach different dispositions as to the 1,000-foot rule and the height restrictions for indoor advertising, and my evaluation of the sales practice restrictions differs from the Court's.

The 1,000-Foot Rule

Such statutes may be invalid for two different reasons. First, the means chosen may be insufficiently related to the ends they purportedly serve. See, e.g., *Rubin v. Coors Brewing Co.*, 514 U.S. 476 (1995) (striking a statute prohibiting beer labels from displaying alcohol content because the provision did not significantly forward the government's interest in the health, safety, and welfare of its citizens). Alternatively, the statute may be so broadly drawn that, while effectively achieving its ends, it unduly restricts communications that are unrelated to its policy aims. See, e.g., *United States v. Playboy Entertainment Group, Inc.*, 529 U.S. 803 (2000) (striking a statute intended to protect children from indecent television broadcasts, in part because it constituted "a significant restriction of communication between speakers and willing adult listeners"). The second difficulty is most frequently encountered when government adopts measures for the protection of children that impose substantial restrictions on the ability of adults to communicate with one another. See, e.g., *Playboy Entertainment Group, Inc.*; *Reno v. American Civil Liberties Union*, 521 U.S. 844 (1997).

To my mind, the 1,000-foot rule does not present a tailoring problem of the first type. For reasons cogently explained in our prior opinions and in the opinion of the Court, we may fairly assume that advertising stimulates consumption and, therefore, that regulations limiting advertising will facilitate efforts to stem consumption. Furthermore, if the government's intention is to limit consumption by a particular segment of the community—in this case, minors—it is appropriate, indeed necessary, to tailor advertising restrictions to the areas where that segment of the community congregates—in this case, the area surrounding schools and playgrounds.

However, I share the majority's concern as to whether the 1,000-foot rule unduly restricts the ability of cigarette manufacturers to convey lawful information to adult consumers. This, of course, is a question of line-drawing. While a ban on all communications about a given subject would be the most effective way to prevent children from exposure to such material, the state cannot by fiat reduce the level of discourse to that which is "fit for children." *Butler v. Michigan,* 352 U.S. 380 (1957).

Finding the appropriate balance is no easy matter. Though many factors plausibly enter the equation when calculating whether a child-directed location restriction goes too far in regulating adult speech, one crucial question is whether the regulatory scheme leaves available sufficient "alternative avenues of communication." *Renton v. Playtime Theatres, Inc.,* 475 U.S. 41 (1986). Because I do not think the record contains sufficient information to enable us to answer that question, I would vacate the award of summary judgment upholding the 1,000-foot rule and remand for trial on that issue. . . .

The Sales Practice and Indoor Advertising Restrictions

After addressing petitioners' challenge to the sales practice restrictions imposed by the Massachusetts statute, the Court concluded that these provisions did not violate the First Amendment. I concur in that judgment, but write separately on this issue to make two brief points.

First, I agree with the District Court and the Court of Appeals that the sales practice restrictions are best analyzed as regulating conduct, not speech. . . . This Court has long recognized the need to differentiate between legislation that targets expression and legislation that targets conduct for legitimate non-speech-related reasons but imposes an incidental burden on expression. However difficult that line may be to draw, it seems clear to me that laws requiring that stores maintain items behind counters and prohibiting self-service displays fall squarely on the conduct side of the line. . . .

Second, though I admit the question is closer, I would, for similar reasons, uphold the regulation limiting tobacco advertising in certain retail establishments to the space five feet or more above the floor. When viewed in isolation, this provision appears to target speech. . . . Nonetheless, I am ultimately persuaded that the provision is unobjectionable because it is little more than an adjunct to the other sales practice restrictions. . . . I would accord the Commonwealth some latitude in imposing restrictions that can have only the slightest impact on the ability of adults to purchase a poisonous product and may save some children from taking the first step on the road to addiction.

THE DEVELOPMENT OF LAW

Other Important Rulings on Commercial Speech
and the First Amendment

Case	Vote	Ruling
Greater New Orleans Broadcasting Association v. United States, 527 U.S. 173 (1999)	9:0	In *United States v. Edge Broadcasting Co.*, 509 U.S. 418 (1993) (see Vol. 2, Ch. 5), the Court upheld the applica-

tion of a section of the Communications Act of 1934, forbidding the broadcasting of advertisements for gambling, to bar a radio station in North Carolina, where lotteries are illegal, from broadcasting advertisements for Virginia's lotteries. Here, however, the Court held that the prohibition infringed on First Amendment interests as applied to radio and television broadcasts for private casino gambling in Louisiana, where gambling is legal. Writing for the Court, Justice Stevens emphasized that federal law regulating gambling advertisements is inconsistent and crosscutting. Among the numerous exceptions to the Communications Act's ban on broadcasts for gambling, for instance, Congress in 1975 exempted the broadcasting of advertisements for state-run lotteries and in 1988 exempted the broadcasting of advertisements for gambling operations run by Native American tribes. Because of these exemptions to, and the incoherence of, federal law governing the broadcasting of advertisements for gambling, Justice Stevens held that the government failed to satisfy the four-factor test for regulating commercial speech laid down in *Central Hudson Gas & Electric Corp. v. Public Service Commission of New York,* 447 U.S. 557 (1980) (see Vol. 2, Ch. 5), and reversed the appellate court's decision. Chief Justice Rehnquist and Justice Thomas issued separate concurring opinions.

Los Angeles Police Department v.	7:2	Writing for the Court, Chief
United Reporting Publishing		Justice Rehnquist upheld a
Corporation, 528 U.S. 32 (1999)		California law that permits

police departments to give journalists, scholars, and others access to arrest records, but forbids their release to companies who would use the information for commercial purposes; the law was enacted to safeguard the privacy of arrestees and victims and to protect them from solicitations from lawyers and other businesses, as well as from potential stalkers. The law was challenged by United Reporting Publishing Corporation, which collects the names and addresses of people who have been arrested and sells the information to lawyers, insurance companies, and other businesses. It contended that the law ran afoul of the First Amendment's protection for commercial speech and unconstitutionally discriminated between commercial and noncommercial speech. The U.S. Court of Appeals for the Ninth Circuit agreed. In reversing the appellate court's decision, however, Chief Justice Rehnquist ruled that the dispute was less about free speech concerns than about access to and control over governmental records and information. However, dissenting Justices Stevens and Kennedy countered that the law unconstitutionally discriminated between those who may and may not obtain the names and addresses of arrestees and victims.

United States v. United Foods,	6:3	Writing for the Court, Justice
121 S.Ct. 2334 (2001)		Kennedy struck down a 1990
		federal statute mandating that

mushroom handlers pay an assessment that was used to fund advertisements promoting the sale of mushrooms. In holding that the law violates the First Amendment, the Court distinguished *Glickman v. Wileman Brothers & Elliott, Inc.,* 521 U.S. 457 (1997), upholding the constitutionality of a series of agricultural marketing orders that required producers of certain California fruits to pay a fee used for product advertising. In *Glickman,* according to Justice Kennedy, the mandated fee was part of a larger regulatory marketing scheme, whereas here the forced subsidy for generic advertising was not part of a larger economic regulatory scheme and, thus, ran afoul of the First Amendment protection for commercial speech, relying on *Abhood v. Detroit Board of Education*, 431 U.S. 209 (1977). Justice Breyer filed a dissenting opinion, which Justices Ginsburg and O'Connor joined, rejecting the majority's view that the absence of marketplace regulations makes a critical First Amendment difference and would have upheld the requirement as an economic regulation without significant restrictions on protected freedom of expression.

E. FREEDOM OF THE PRESS

In its 2000–2001 term, the Court further underscored the First Amendment's protection and outweighing of interests in personal privacy and law enforcement. At issue in *Bartnicki v. Vopper*, 121 S.Ct. 1753 (2001), was the reach of federal and state wiretapping laws aimed at preventing people from intercepting private communications versus the First Amendment's protection for the dissemination of information. The case stemmed from heated contract negotiations between a teachers union and a school board, when the union's president, on her cell phone, angrily told the union's chief negotiator that if the school board members did not accept its offer, the teachers were going to "blow off the front porches" of their homes. An opponent of the union said that he found a recording of that conversation in his mailbox and turned it over to a local radio station, which broadcast it. Writing for the Court, Justice Stevens held that the First Amendment protected lawfully obtained information even when the original source acquired the information through unlawful means. In balancing the government's interests, in deterring unlawful wiretapping, and in protecting the privacy of personal communications, against the communication of matters of public importance and against criticisms of public officials, Justice Stevens concluded that the government's interests were not so great as to override the First Amendment's protection for the dissemination of information lawfully obtained, even though the original acquisition of the information was unlawful. Chief Justice Rehnquist and Justices Scalia and Thomas dissented.

F. REGULATING THE BROADCAST AND CABLE MEDIA, AND THE INTERNET

The Telecommunications Act of 1996 required, in part, cable television operators providing channels "primarily dedicated to sexually-oriented programming" to either fully scramble those channels or limit their transmission to late night hours between 10 P.M. and 6 A.M., when children viewers are unlikely. Scrambling proved imprecise, however, and audio or visual portions of the programs often could be heard or viewed in what is known as "signal bleed." As a result, a majority of the cable operators adopted the "time channeling" approach, which in turn meant that, for two-thirds of the day, no viewers in their service areas could watch sexually oriented programming. That practice was challenged by Playboy Entertainment Group as a content-based restriction in violation of the First Amendment. Writing for the Court, in *United States v. Playboy Entertainment Group, Inc.*, 529 U.S. 803 (2000), Justice Kennedy ruled that that section of the Telecommunications Act could not survive strict scrutiny because it was content-based and therefore had to advance a compelling governmental interest in the least restrictive way. Here, Justice Kennedy emphasized the key difference between broadcast television and cable television: Cable television may block unwanted channels on a household-by-household basis, and therefore time channeling on cable television sweeps too broadly. Moreover, he noted that the district court found the government had failed to establish how widespread and serious the problem of signal bleed was for cable viewers. Chief Justice Rehnquist and Justices Breyer, O'Connor, and Scalia dissented.

In its 2001–2002 term, the Court will consider a challenge to the constitutionality of the Child Online Protection Act (COPA) in *Ashcroft v. American Civil Liberties Union* (No. 00-1293). The COPA prohibits transmitting on the Internet any communication for commercial purposes that includes material harmful to minors. The American Civil Liberties Union (ACLU) challenged the COPA's constitutionality and a federal district court granted the ACLU's request for a preliminary injunction against the enforcement of the law. The attorney general appealed and the Third Circuit Court of Appeals affirmed, holding that the COPA ran afoul of the First Amendment. The appellate court reasoned that COPA's "community standards" test was probably invalid because it would essentially require every Internet communication to abide by the standards of the most restrictive community, since the relevant "community" for the purposes of the Internet is geographically expansive. Furthermore, Internet publishers are unable to escape the act's overbreadth, because they cannot restrict access to their sites based on the geographical location of Internet users visiting their sites.

H. SYMBOLIC SPEECH AND SPEECH-PLUS-CONDUCT

Returning to the issue of restrictions on antiabortion protesters, dealt with previously in *Madsen v. Women's Health Center*, 512 U.S. 735 (1994), and *Schenck v. Pro-Choice Network of Western New York*, 519 U.S. 357 (1997), the Court upheld Colorado's law making it unlawful for a person within 100 feet of a health care facility's entrance to "knowingly approach" within eight feet another person, without permission, in order to pass out leaflets or engage in oral protest. Writing for the Court, in *Hill v. Colorado*, 530 U.S. 703 (2000), Justice Stevens found the statute to be a "narrowly tailored" time, place, and manner regulation, under *Ward v. Rock Against Racism*, 491 U.S. 781 (1989). Justice Scalia, along with Justices Kennedy and Thomas, dissented.

In its 2001–2002 term, the justices will review an appeal challenging a regulation requiring permits for political rallies held in public forums, in *Thomas v. Chicago Park District* (No. 00-1249). At issue is whether Chicago's ordinance requiring permits for rallies in city parks, a public forum, is unconstitutionally vague and a prior restraint on free speech. The Court of Appeals for the Seventh Circuit rejected the arguments of the petitioners, who held rallies in city parks to advocate the repeal of laws criminalizing the sale of marijuana. In concluding that the regulation was constitutional, the appellate court found that the ordinance was content neutral and not unduly vague, and that it provided for meaningful judicial review of permit denials, in spite of the petitioners' insistence on an opportunity for both oral submissions to the park authority and an expedited review process.

I. FREEDOM OF ASSOCIATION

In its 1999–2000 term the Court handed down two important rulings on freedom of association. In *California Democratic Party v. Jones* (excerpted above in Vol. 1, Ch. 8), the Court struck down California's law permitting "blanket" primaries as a violation of political parties' freedom of association. And in *Boy Scouts of America v. Dale* (excerpted below) a bare majority ruled that the Boy Scouts may exclude homosexuals.

Boy Scouts of America v. Dale
530 U.S. 640, 120 S.Ct. 2446 (2000)

Founded in 1910, the Boy Scouts of America is a federally chartered corporation that, as of 1992, included more than 4 million youths and 1 million adults as active members in more than 44,000 Boy Scout troops throughout the country. In 1991 the New Jersey legislature amended its Law Against Discrimination (LAD) to include protection from discrimination based on "affectional or sexual orientation." Subsequently, the Boy Scouts revoked James Dale's Boy Scout Adult membership, upon learning that he was a homosexual, and he sued the Boy Scouts for violating the provisions of LAD.

In 1978, at the age of eight, James Dale joined a Cub Scout Pack and remained a member until 1981, when he became a member of a Boy Scout

Troop. He remained a youth member until he reached age 18 in 1988. During that time he earned more than 25 merit badges. In 1989 he sought and received adult membership and became an Assistant Scoutmaster, a position that he held for about a year and a half. About that time, he left home to attend Rutgers University and, while at college, acknowledged for the first time that he was gay. Shortly thereafter Dale became co-president of the Rutgers University Lesbian/Gay Alliance. Then, in July 1990, while attending a seminar on the health needs of lesbian and gay teenagers, Dale was interviewed by the *Star-Ledger*, which subsequently published an article that included Dale's photograph and identified him as the "co-president of the Rutgers University Lesbian/Gay Alliance." Later that month, Dale received from the Boy Scouts a letter revoking his membership and asking him to "sever any relations [he] may have with the Boy Scouts of America." Dale appealed unsuccessfully, and finally, in 1992, he filed a lawsuit in state court against the Boy Scouts of America for discriminating against him in violation of LAD.

The trial court concluded that Dale was "a sexually active homosexual" and the Boy Scouts had always excluded "active homosexual[s]." The court also ruled that the provisions of LAD did not apply to the Boy Scouts because it was not a "public accommodation." A state appellate court reversed and remanded upon concluding that the Boy Scouts was a "public accommodation." The state supreme court affirmed that decision, and the Boy Scouts appealed to the Supreme Court, which granted review.

The decision of the state supreme court was reversed in a five to four decision, and the opinion for the Court was delivered by Chief Justice Rehnquist. Justices Stevens and Souter each filed dissenting opinions, and were joined by Justices Ginsburg and Breyer.

Chief Justice REHNQUIST delivered the opinion of the Court.

In *Roberts v. United States Jaycees*, 468 U.S. 609 (1984), we observed that "implicit in the right to engage in activities protected by the First Amendment" is "a corresponding right to associate with others in pursuit of a wide variety of political, social, economic, educational, religious, and cultural ends." This right is crucial in preventing the majority from imposing its views on groups that would rather express other, perhaps unpopular, ideas. Government actions that may unconstitutionally burden this freedom may take many forms, one of which is "intrusion into the internal structure or affairs of an association" like a "regulation that forces the group to accept members it does not desire." Forcing a group to accept certain members may impair the ability of the group to express those views, and only those views, that it intends to express. Thus, "[f]reedom of association plainly presupposes a freedom not to associate."

The forced inclusion of an unwanted person in a group infringes the group's freedom of expressive association if the presence of that person affects in a significant way the group's ability to advocate public or private viewpoints. *New York State Club Assn., Inc. v. City of New York*, 487 U.S. 1 (1988). But the freedom of expressive association, like many freedoms, is not absolute. We have held that the freedom could be overridden "by regulations adopted to serve compelling state interests, unrelated to the suppression of ideas, that cannot be achieved through means significantly less restrictive of associational freedoms." *Roberts.*

To determine whether a group is protected by the First Amendment's expressive associational right, we must determine whether the group engages in "expressive association." The First Amendment's protection of expressive association is not reserved for advocacy groups. But to come within its ambit, a group must engage in some form of expression, whether it be public or private.

Because this is a First Amendment case where the ultimate conclusions of law are virtually inseparable from findings of fact, we are obligated to independently review the factual record to ensure that the state court's judgment does not unlawfully intrude on free expression. The record reveals the following. The Boy Scouts is a private, nonprofit organization. According to its mission statement: "It is the mission of the Boy Scouts of America to serve others by helping to instill values in young people and, in other ways, to prepare them to make ethical choices over their lifetime in achieving their full potential." "The values we strive to instill are based on those found in the Scout Oath and Law." . . .

Thus, the general mission of the Boy Scouts is clear: "[T]o instill values in young people." The Boy Scouts seeks to instill these values by having its adult leaders spend time with the youth members, instructing and engaging them in activities like camping, archery, and fishing. During the time spent with the youth members, the scoutmasters and assistant scoutmasters inculcate them with the Boy Scouts' values—both expressly and by example. It seems indisputable that an association that seeks to transmit such a system of values engages in expressive activity.

Given that the Boy Scouts engages in expressive activity, we must determine whether the forced inclusion of Dale as an assistant scoutmaster would significantly affect the Boy Scouts' ability to advocate public or private viewpoints. This inquiry necessarily requires us first to explore, to a limited extent, the nature of the Boy Scouts' view of homosexuality.

The values the Boy Scouts seeks to instill are "based on" those listed in the Scout Oath and Law. The Boy Scouts explains that the Scout Oath and Law provide "a positive moral code for living; they are a list of do's rather than don'ts." The Boy Scouts asserts that homosexual conduct is inconsistent with the values embodied in the Scout Oath and Law, particularly with the values represented by the terms "morally straight" and "clean."

Obviously, the Scout Oath and Law do not expressly mention sexuality or sexual orientation. And the terms "morally straight" and "clean" are by no means self-defining. Different people would attribute to those terms very different meanings. For example, some people may believe that engaging in homosexual conduct is not at odds with being "morally straight" and "clean." And others may believe that engaging in homosexual conduct is contrary to being "morally straight" and "clean." The Boy Scouts says it falls within the latter category. . . .

The Boy Scouts asserts that it "teach[es] that homosexual conduct is not morally straight," Brief for Petitioners, and that it does "not want to promote homosexual conduct as a legitimate form of behavior." We accept the Boy Scouts' assertion. We need not inquire further to determine the nature of the Boy Scouts' expression with respect to homosexuality. . . .

The Boy Scouts publicly expressed its views with respect to homosexual conduct by its assertions in prior litigation. For example, throughout a California case with similar facts filed in the early 1980's, the Boy Scouts consistently asserted the same position with respect to homosexuality that it asserts today. We cannot doubt that the Boy Scouts sincerely holds this view.

We must then determine whether Dale's presence as an assistant scoutmaster would significantly burden the Boy Scouts' desire to not "promote homosexual conduct as a legitimate form of behavior." As we give deference to an association's assertions regarding the nature of its expression, we must also give deference to an association's view of what would impair its expression. That is not to say that an expressive association can erect a shield against antidiscrimination laws simply by asserting that mere acceptance of a member from a particular group would impair its message. But here Dale, by his own admission, is one of a group of gay Scouts who have "become leaders in their community and are open and honest about their sexual orientation." Dale was the copresident of a gay and lesbian organization at college and remains a gay rights activist. Dale's presence in the Boy Scouts would, at the very least, force the organization to send a message, both to the youth members and the world, that the Boy Scouts accepts homosexual conduct as a legitimate form of behavior.

Hurley [*v. Irish-American Gay, Lesbian, and Bisexual Group of Boston*, 515 U.S. 557 (1995)], is illustrative on this point. There we considered whether the application of Massachusetts' public accommodations law to require the organizers of a private St. Patrick's Day parade to include among the marchers an Irish-American gay, lesbian, and bisexual group, GLIB, violated the parade organizers' First Amendment rights. We noted that the parade organizers did not wish to exclude the GLIB members because of their sexual orientations, but because they wanted to march behind a GLIB banner. We observed: "[A] contingent marching behind the organization's banner would at least bear witness to the fact that some Irish are gay, lesbian, or bisexual, and the presence of the organized marchers would suggest their view that people of their sexual orientations have as much claim to unqualified social acceptance as heterosexuals. The parade's organizers may not believe these facts about Irish sexuality to be so, or they may object to unqualified social acceptance of gays and lesbians or have some other reason for wishing to keep GLIB's message out of the parade. But whatever the reason, it boils down to the choice of a speaker not to propound a particular point of view, and that choice is presumed to lie beyond the government's power to control." Here, we have found that the Boy Scouts believes that homosexual conduct is inconsistent with the values it seeks to instill in its youth members; it will not "promote homosexual conduct as a legitimate form of behavior." As the presence of GLIB in Boston's St. Patrick's Day parade would have interfered with the parade organizers' choice not to propound a particular point of view, the presence of Dale as an assistant scoutmaster would just as surely interfere with the Boy Scout's choice not to propound a point of view contrary to its beliefs. . . .

Having determined that the Boy Scouts is an expressive association and that the forced inclusion of Dale would significantly affect its expression, we inquire whether the application of New Jersey's public accommodations law to require that the Boy Scouts accept Dale as an assistant scoutmaster runs afoul of the Scouts' freedom of expressive association. We conclude that it does.

State public accommodations laws were originally enacted to prevent discrimination in traditional places of public accommodation—like inns and trains.

Many on the list are what one would expect to be places where the public is invited. For example, the statute includes as places of public accommodation taverns, restaurants, retail shops, and public libraries. But the statute also includes places that often may not carry with them open invitations to the public, like summer camps and roof gardens. In this case, the New Jersey Supreme Court went a step further and applied its public accommodations law to a private entity without even attempting to tie the term "place" to a physical location. As the definition of "public accommodation" has expanded from clearly commercial entities, such as restaurants, bars, and hotels, to membership organizations such as the Boy Scouts, the potential for conflict between state public accommodations laws and the First Amendment rights of organizations has increased.

We recognized in cases such as *Roberts* and *Duarte* that States have a compelling interest in eliminating discrimination against women in public accommodations. But in each of these cases we went on to conclude that the enforcement of these statutes would not materially interfere with the ideas that the organization sought to express. In *Roberts*, we said "[i]ndeed, the Jaycees has failed to demonstrate any serious burden on the male members' freedom of expressive association." We thereupon concluded in each of these cases that the organizations' First Amendment rights were not violated by the application of the States' public accommodations laws.

In *Hurley*, we said that public accommodations laws "are well within the State's usual power to enact when a legislature has reason to believe that a given group is the target of discrimination, and they do not, as a general matter, violate the First or Fourteenth Amendments." But we went on to note that in that case "the Massachusetts [public accommodations] law has been applied in a peculiar way" because "any contingent of protected individuals with a message would have the right to participate in petitioners' speech, so that the communication produced by the private organizers would be shaped by all those protected by the law who wish to join in with some expressive demonstration of their own." And in the associational freedom cases such as *Roberts*, *Duarte*, and *New York State Club Assn.*, after finding a compelling state interest, the Court went on to examine whether or not the application of the state law would impose any "serious burden" on the organization's rights of expressive association. So in these cases, the associational interest in freedom of expression has been set on one side of the scale, and the State's interest on the other. . . .

The judgment of the New Jersey Supreme Court is reversed, and the cause remanded for further proceedings not inconsistent with this opinion.

Justice STEVENS, with whom Justice SOUTER, Justice GINSBURG, and Justice BREYER join, dissenting.

The majority holds that New Jersey's law violates BSA's right to associate and its right to free speech. But that law does not "impos[e] any serious burdens" on BSA's "collective effort on behalf of [its] shared goals," *Roberts v. United States Jaycees*, 468 U.S. 609 (1984), nor does it force BSA to communicate any message that it does not wish to endorse. New Jersey's law, therefore, abridges no constitutional right of the Boy Scouts. . . .

In light of BSA's self-proclaimed ecumenism, furthermore, it is even more difficult to discern any shared goals or common moral stance on homosexuality.

Insofar as religious matters are concerned, BSA's bylaws state that it is "absolutely nonsectarian in its attitude toward religious training." "The BSA does not define what constitutes duty to God or the practice of religion. This is the responsibility of parents and religious leaders." In fact, many diverse religious organizations sponsor local Boy Scout troops. Because a number of religious groups do not view homosexuality as immoral or wrong and reject discrimination against homosexuals, it is exceedingly difficult to believe that BSA nonetheless adopts a single particular religious or moral philosophy when it comes to sexual orientation. This is especially so in light of the fact that Scouts are advised to seek guidance on sexual matters from their religious leaders (and Scoutmasters are told to refer Scouts to them); BSA surely is aware that some religions do not teach that homosexuality is wrong.

The Court seeks to fill the void by pointing to a statement of "policies and procedures relating to homosexuality and Scouting" signed by BSA's President and Chief Scout Executive in 1978 and addressed to the members of the Executive Committee of the national organization. [However, four] aspects of the 1978 policy statement are relevant to the proper disposition of this case. First, at most this letter simply adopts an exclusionary membership policy. But simply adopting such a policy has never been considered sufficient, by itself, to prevail on a right to associate claim.

Second, the 1978 policy was never publicly expressed—unlike, for example, the Scout's duty to be "obedient." It was an internal memorandum, never circulated beyond the few members of BSA's Executive Committee. It remained, in effect, a secret Boy Scouts policy. Far from claiming any intent to express an idea that would be burdened by the presence of homosexuals, BSA's public posture—to the world and to the Scouts themselves—remained what it had always been: one of tolerance, welcoming all classes of boys and young men. In this respect, BSA's claim is even weaker than those we have rejected in the past.

Third, it is apparent that the draftsmen of the policy statement foresaw the possibility that laws against discrimination might one day be amended to protect homosexuals from employment discrimination. Their statement clearly provided that, in the event such a law conflicted with their policy, a Scout's duty to be "obedient" and "obe[y] the laws," even if "he thinks [the laws] are unfair" would prevail in such a contingency. In 1978, however, BSA apparently did not consider it to be a serious possibility that a State might one day characterize the Scouts as a "place of public accommodation" with a duty to open its membership to all qualified individuals. The portions of the statement dealing with membership simply assume that membership in the Scouts is a "privilege" that BSA is free to grant or to withhold. The statement does not address the question whether the publicly proclaimed duty to obey the law should prevail over the private discriminatory policy if, and when, a conflict between the two should arise—as it now has in New Jersey. At the very least, then, the statement reflects no unequivocal view on homosexuality. Indeed, the statement suggests that an appropriate way for BSA to preserve its unpublished exclusionary policy would include an open and forthright attempt to seek an amendment of New Jersey's statute.

Fourth, the 1978 statement simply says that homosexuality is not "appropriate." It makes no effort to connect that statement to a shared goal or expressive activity of the Boy Scouts. Whatever values BSA seeks to instill in Scouts, the idea that homosexuality is not "appropriate" appears entirely unconnected to, and is mentioned nowhere in, the myriad of publicly declared values and creeds of the BSA. That idea does not appear to be among any of the principles actually taught to Scouts. Rather, the 1978 policy appears to be no more than a private statement of a few BSA executives that the organization wishes to exclude gays—and that wish has nothing to do with any expression BSA actually engages in.

The majority also relies on four other policy statements that were issued between 1991 and 1993. All of them were written and issued after BSA revoked Dale's membership. Accordingly, they have little, if any, relevance to the legal question before this Court. In any event, they do not bolster BSA's claim. . . .

It is clear, then, that nothing in these policy statements supports BSA's claim. The only policy written before the revocation of Dale's membership was an equivocal, undisclosed statement that evidences no connection between the group's discriminatory intentions and its expressive interests. The later policies demonstrate a brief—though ultimately abandoned—attempt to tie BSA's exclusion to its expression, but other than a single sentence, BSA fails to show that it ever taught Scouts that homosexuality is not "morally straight" or "clean," or that such a view was part of the group's collective efforts to foster a belief. Furthermore, BSA's policy statements fail to establish any clear, consistent, and unequivocal position on homosexuality. . . .

BSA's claim finds no support in our cases. We have recognized "a right to associate for the purpose of engaging in those activities protected by the First Amendment—speech, assembly, petition for the redress of grievances, and the exercise of religion." *Roberts*. And we have acknowledged that "when the State interferes with individuals' selection of those with whom they wish to join in a common endeavor, freedom of association may be implicated." But "[t]he right to associate for expressive purposes is not absolute"; rather, "the nature and degree of constitutional protection afforded freedom of association may vary depending on the extent to which the constitutionally protected liberty is at stake in a given case." Indeed, the right to associate does not mean "that in every setting in which individuals exercise some discrimination in choosing associates, their selective process of inclusion and exclusion is protected by the Constitution." *New York State Club Assn., Inc. v. City of New York*, 487 U.S. 1 (1988). For example, we have routinely and easily rejected assertions of this right by expressive organizations with discriminatory membership policies, such as private schools, law firms, and labor organizations. In fact, until today, we have never once found a claimed right to associate in the selection of members to prevail in the face of a State's antidiscrimination law. To the contrary, we have squarely held that a State's antidiscrimination law does not violate a group's right to associate simply because the law conflicts with that group's exclusionary membership policy.

In *Roberts v. United States Jaycees*, 468 U.S. 609 (1984), we addressed just such a conflict. The Jaycees was a nonprofit membership organization "designed to inculcate in the individual membership . . . a spirit of genuine Americanism and civic interest, and . . . to provide an avenue for intelligent participation by young men in the affairs of their community." The organization was divided into local chapters, described as "young men's organization[s]," in which regular membership was restricted to males between the ages of 18 and 35. But Minnesota's Human Rights Act, which applied to the Jaycees, made it unlawful to "deny any person the full and equal enjoyment of a place of public accommodation because of sex." The Jaycees, however, claimed that applying the law to it violated its right to associate—in particular its right to maintain its selective membership policy.

We rejected that claim. Cautioning that the right to associate is not "absolute," we held that "[i]nfringements on that right may be justified by regulations adopted to serve compelling state interests, unrelated to the suppression of ideas, that cannot be achieved through means significantly less restrictive of associational freedoms." We found the State's purpose of eliminating discrimination is a compelling state interest that is unrelated to the suppression of ideas. We also held that Minnesota's law is the least restrictive means of achieving that interest. The Jaycees had "failed to demonstrate that the Act imposes any serious burdens on the male members' freedom of expressive association." Though the Jaycees had "taken public positions on a number of diverse issues, [and] regularly engage in a variety of activities worthy of constitutional protection under the First Amendment," there was "no basis in the record for concluding that admission of women as full voting members will impede the organization's ability to engage in these protected activities or to disseminate its preferred views." "The Act," we held, "requires no change in the Jaycees' creed of promoting the interest of young men, and it imposes no restrictions on the organization's ability to exclude individuals with ideologies or philosophies different from those of its existing members."

We took a similar approach in *Board of Directors of Rotary Int'l v. Rotary Club of Duarte*, 481 U.S. 537 (1987). . . .

Several principles are made perfectly clear by *Jaycees* and *Rotary Club*. First, to prevail on a claim of expressive association in the face of a State's antidiscrimination law, it is not enough simply to engage in some kind of expressive activity. Both the Jaycees and the Rotary Club engaged in expressive activity protected by the First Amendment, yet that fact was not dispositive. Second, it is not enough to adopt an openly avowed exclusionary membership policy. Both the Jaycees and the Rotary Club did that as well. Third, it is not sufficient merely to articulate some connection between the group's expressive activities and its exclusionary policy. The Rotary Club, for example, justified its male-only membership policy by pointing to the "aspect of fellowship that is enjoyed by the [exclusively] male membership" and by claiming that only with an exclusively male membership could it "operate effectively" in foreign countries.

Rather, in *Jaycees*, we asked whether Minnesota's Human Rights Law requiring the admission of women "impose[d] any serious burdens" on the group's "collective effort on behalf of [its] shared goals." Notwithstanding the group's obvious publicly stated exclusionary policy, we did not view the inclusion of women as a "serious burden" on the Jaycees' ability to engage in the protected speech of its choice. . . .The relevant question is whether the mere inclusion of the person at issue would "impose any serious burden," "affect in any significant way," or be "a substantial restraint upon" the organization's "shared goals," "basic goals," or "collective effort to foster beliefs." Accordingly, it is necessary to examine what, exactly, are BSA's shared goals and the degree to which its expressive activities would be burdened, affected, or restrained by including homosexuals.

The evidence before this Court makes it exceptionally clear that BSA has, at most, simply adopted an exclusionary membership policy and has no shared goal of disapproving of homosexuality. BSA's mission statement and federal charter say nothing on the matter; its official membership policy is silent; its Scout Oath and Law—and accompanying definitions—are devoid of any view on the topic;

its guidance for Scouts and Scoutmasters on sexuality declare that such matters are "not construed to be Scouting's proper area," but are the province of a Scout's parents and pastor; and BSA's posture respecting religion tolerates a wide variety of views on the issue of homosexuality. Moreover, there is simply no evidence that BSA otherwise teaches anything in this area, or that it instructs Scouts on matters involving homosexuality in ways not conveyed in the Boy Scout or Scoutmaster Handbooks. In short, Boy Scouts of America is simply silent on homosexuality. There is no shared goal or collective effort to foster a belief about homosexuality at all—let alone one that is significantly burdened by admitting homosexuals. . . .

Equally important is BSA's failure to adopt any clear position on homosexuality. BSA's temporary, though ultimately abandoned, view that homosexuality is incompatible with being "morally straight" and "clean" is a far cry from the clear, unequivocal statement necessary to prevail on its claim. Despite the solitary sentences in the 1991 and 1992 policies, the group continued to disclaim any single religious or moral position as a general matter and actively eschewed teaching any lesson on sexuality. It also continued to define "morally straight" and "clean" in the Boy Scout and Scoutmaster Handbooks without any reference to homosexuality. As noted earlier, nothing in our cases suggests that a group can prevail on a right to expressive association if it, effectively, speaks out of both sides of its mouth. A State's antidiscrimination law does not impose a "serious burden" or a "substantial restraint" upon the group's "shared goals" if the group itself is unable to identify its own stance with any clarity.

The majority . . . finds that BSA in fact "teach[es] that homosexual conduct is not morally straight." This conclusion, remarkably, rests entirely on statements in BSA's briefs. . . . This is an astounding view of the law. I am unaware of any previous instance in which our analysis of the scope of a constitutional right was determined by looking at what a litigant asserts in his or her brief and inquiring no further. It is even more astonishing in the First Amendment area, because, as the majority itself acknowledges, "we are obligated to independently review the factual record." It is an odd form of independent review that consists of deferring entirely to whatever a litigant claims. But the majority insists that our inquiry must be "limited," because "it is not the role of the courts to reject a group's expressed values because they disagree with those values or find them internally inconsistent."

But nothing in our cases calls for this Court to do any such thing. An organization can adopt the message of its choice, and it is not this Court's place to disagree with it. But we must inquire whether the group is, in fact, expressing a message (whatever it may be) and whether that message (if one is expressed) is significantly affected by a State's antidiscrimination law. More critically, that inquiry requires our independent analysis, rather than deference to a group's litigating posture. . . .

The majority's argument relies exclusively on *Hurley v. Irish-American Gay, Lesbian and Bisexual Group of Boston, Inc.*, 515 U.S. 557 (1995). In that case, petitioners John Hurley and the South Boston Allied War Veterans Council ran a privately operated St. Patrick's Day parade. Respondent, an organization known as "GLIB," represented a contingent of gays, lesbians, and bisexuals who sought to march in the petitioners' parade "as a way to express pride in their Irish heritage as openly gay, lesbian, and bisexual individuals." When the parade organizers refused GLIB's admission, GLIB brought suit under Massachusetts' antidiscrimination law. That statute, like New Jersey's law, prohibited discrimination on account of sexual orientation in any place of public accommodation, which the state courts interpreted to include the parade. Petitioners argued that forcing them to include GLIB in their parade would violate their free speech rights.

We agreed. We first pointed out that the St. Patrick's Day parade—like most every parade—is an inherently expressive undertaking. Next, we reaffirmed that the government may not compel anyone to proclaim a belief with which he or she disagrees. We then found that GLIB's marching in the parade would be an expressive act suggesting the view "that people of their sexual orientations have as much claim to unqualified social acceptance as heterosexuals." Finally, we held that GLIB's participation in the parade "would likely be perceived" as the parade organizers' own speech—or at least as a view which they approved—because of a parade organizer's customary control over who marches in the parade. Though *Hurley* has a superficial similarity to the present case, a close inspection reveals a wide gulf between that case and the one before us today. . . .

Dale's inclusion in the Boy Scouts is nothing like the case in *Hurley*. His participation sends no cognizable message to the Scouts or to the world. Unlike GLIB, Dale did not carry a banner or a sign; he did not distribute any fact sheet; and he expressed no intent to send any message. If there is any kind of message being sent, then, it is by the mere act of joining the Boy Scouts. Such an act does not constitute an instance of symbolic speech under the First Amendment. . . .

Furthermore, it is not likely that BSA would be understood to send any message, either to Scouts or to the world, simply by admitting someone as a member. Over the years, BSA has generously welcomed over 87 million young Americans into its ranks. In 1992 over one million adults were active BSA members. The notion that an organization of that size and enormous prestige implicitly endorses the views that each of those adults may express in a non-Scouting context is simply mind boggling. . . .

Unfavorable opinions about homosexuals "have ancient roots." *Bowers v. Hardwick*, 478 U.S. 186 (1986). Like equally atavistic opinions about certain racial groups, those roots have been nourished by sectarian doctrine. Over the years, however, interaction with real people, rather than mere adherence to traditional ways of thinking about members of unfamiliar classes, have modified those opinions. A few examples: The American Psychiatric Association's and the American Psychological Association's removal of "homosexuality" from their lists of mental disorders; a move toward greater understanding within some religious communities; Justice BLACKMUN's classic opinion in *Bowers*; Georgia's invalidation of the statute upheld in *Bowers*; and New Jersey's enactment of the provision at issue in this case.

That such prejudices are still prevalent and that they have caused serious and tangible harm to countless members of the class New Jersey seeks to protect are established matters of fact that neither the Boy Scouts nor the Court disputes. That harm can only be aggravated by the creation of a constitutional shield for a policy that is itself the product of a habitual way of thinking about strangers. As Justice BRANDEIS so wisely advised, "we must be ever on our guard, lest we erect our prejudices into legal principles."

If we would guide by the light of reason, we must let our minds be bold. I respectfully dissent.

6

FREEDOM FROM
AND OF RELIGION

A. THE (DIS)ESTABLISHMENT OF RELIGION

In *Santa Fe Independent School District v. Doe* (excerpted below), the Court extended its ruling in *Lee v. Weisman*, 505 U.S. 577 (1992) (excerpted in Vol. 2, Ch. 6), holding that school-sponsored prayer at graduation ceremonies violates the First Amendment, to invalidate school-sponsored, student-led prayers at football games. However, overruling two precedents in *Mitchell v. Helms* (excerpted below), the Court upheld public school districts' loan of computer software and hardware, as well as other forms of aid, to private religious schools. And in *Good News Club v. Milford Central School* (2001) (excerpted below), the Court held that a public school may not deny religious groups access to its facilities for after-school meetings, on the ground that to do so would violate the First Amendment (dis)Establishment Clause. Instead, when a school opens its facilities as a limited public forum to groups for meetings, the denial of access by religious groups constitutes viewpoint discrimination and violates their First Amendment right to freedom of speech. In both cases, Justice Thomas delivered the opinion of the Court and Justices Stevens, Souter, and Ginsburg dissented.

Santa Fe Independent School District v. Doe
530 U.S. 290, 120 S.Ct. 2266 (2000)

Before 1995, at the Santa Fe High School in Texas, an elected student counsel chaplain delivered a prayer over the public address system before each varsity football game. When that practice, along with student-led prayers at graduation ceremonies, was challenged for violating the First Amendment (dis)establishment clause, the school district adopted a new policy—initially entitled "Prayer at Football Games"—permitting, but not requiring, prayer initiated and led by students at all home games. Under this policy, students held two elections: one to determine whether prayers should be delivered before football games and, if so, a second to select the spokesperson to deliver them. A federal district court issued an order, relying on the holding in *Lee v. Weisman*, 505 U.S. 577 (1992), that benedictions at high school graduation ceremonies run afoul of the First Amendment, to preclude student-led prayers at both graduation ceremonies and football games. However, the school district modified its policy to omit the word *prayer* in the title of its policy, referring instead to *messages, statements,* and *invocations.* When that decision was appealed, the Court of Appeals for the Fifth Circuit concluded that the district's policy violated the First Amendment. The school district appealed to the Supreme Court, which granted review.

The appellate court's decision was affirmed by a six to three vote, and Justice Stevens delivered the opinion for the Court. Chief Justice Rehnquist filed a dissenting opinion, joined by Justices Scalia and Thomas.

Justice STEVENS delivered the opinion of the Court.

In *Lee v. Weisman*, 505 U.S. 577 (1992), we held that a prayer delivered by a rabbi at a middle school graduation ceremony violated that Clause. Although this case involves student prayer at a different type of school function, our analysis is properly guided by the principles that we endorsed in *Lee*.

In this case the District first argues that "there is a crucial difference between government speech endorsing religion, which the Establishment Clause forbids, and private speech endorsing religion, which the Free Speech and Free Exercise Clauses protect." *Board of Ed. of Westside Community Schools (Dist. 66) v. Mergens*, 496 U.S. 226 (1990). We certainly agree with that distinction, but we are not persuaded that the pregame invocations should be regarded as "private speech."

These invocations are authorized by a government policy and take place on government property at government-sponsored school-related events. Of course, not every message delivered under such circumstances is the government's own. We have held, for example, that an individual's contribution to a government-created forum was not government speech. See *Rosenberger v. Rector and Visitors of Univ. of Va.*, 515 U.S. 819 (1995). [But, here] the school allows only one student, the same student for the entire season, to give the invocation. The statement or invocation, moreover, is subject to particular regulations that confine the content and topic of the student's message.

Granting only one student access to the stage at a time does not, of course, necessarily preclude a finding that a school has created a limited public forum. Here, however, Santa Fe's student election system ensures that only those messages deemed "appropriate" under the District's policy may be delivered. That is, the majoritarian process implemented by the District guarantees, by definition, that minority candidates will never prevail and that their views will be effectively silenced.

Recently, in *Board of Regents of Univ. of Wis. System v. Southworth*, [529 U.S. 217] (2000), we explained why student elections that determine, by majority vote, which expressive activities shall receive or not receive school benefits are constitutionally problematic. . . . Like the student referendum for funding in *Southworth*, this student election does nothing to protect minority views but rather places the students who hold such views at the mercy of the majority. Because "fundamental rights may not be submitted to vote[,] they depend on the outcome of no elections," *West Virginia Bd. of Ed. v. Barnette*, 319 U.S. 624 (1943), the District's elections are insufficient safeguards of diverse student speech. . . .

Moreover, the District has failed to divorce itself from the religious content in the invocations. . . . The decision whether to deliver a message is first made by majority vote of the entire student body, followed by a choice of the speaker in a separate, similar majority election. Even though the particular words used by the speaker are not determined by those votes, the policy mandates that the "statement or invocation" be "consistent with the goals and purposes of this policy," which are "to solemnize the event, to promote good sportsmanship and student safety, and to establish the appropriate environment for the competition."

In addition to involving the school in the selection of the speaker, the policy, by its terms, invites and encourages religious messages. The policy itself states that the purpose of the message is "to solemnize the event." A religious message is the most obvious method of solemnizing an event. Moreover, the requirements that the message "promote good citizenship" and "establish the appropriate environment for competition" further narrow the types of message deemed appropriate, suggesting that a solemn, yet nonreligious, message, such as commentary on United States foreign policy, would be prohibited. Indeed, the only type of message that is expressly endorsed in the text is an "invocation"—a term that primarily describes an appeal for divine assistance. In fact, as used in the past at Santa Fe High School, an "invocation" has always entailed a focused religious message. Thus, the expressed purposes of the policy encourage the selection of a religious message, and that is precisely how the students understand the policy. The results of the elections described in the parties' stipulation make it clear that the students understood that the central question before them was whether prayer should be a part of the pregame ceremony.

The actual or perceived endorsement of the message, moreover, is established by factors beyond just the text of the policy. Once the student speaker is selected and the message composed, the invocation is then delivered to a large audience assembled as part of a regularly scheduled, school-sponsored function conducted on school property. The message is broadcast over the school's public address system, which remains subject to the control of school officials. It is fair to assume that the pregame ceremony is clothed in the traditional indicia of school sporting events, which generally include not just the team, but also cheerleaders and band members dressed in uniforms sporting the school name and mascot. The school's name is likely written in large print across the field and on banners and flags. The crowd will certainly include many who display the school colors and insignia on their school T-shirts, jackets, or hats and who may also be waving signs displaying the school name. It is in a setting such as this that "[t]he board has chosen to permit" the elected student to rise and give the "statement or invocation."

In this context the members of the listening audience must perceive the pregame message as a public expression of the views of the majority of the student body delivered with the approval of the school administration. In cases involving state participation in a religious activity, one of the relevant questions is "whether an objective observer, acquainted with the text, legislative history, and implementation of the statute, would perceive it as a state endorsement of prayer in public schools." *Wallace* [*v. Jaffree*, 472 U.S. 38 (1985)]. Regardless of the listener's support for, or objection to, the message, an objective Santa Fe High School student will unquestionably perceive the inevitable pregame prayer as stamped with her school's seal of approval.

The District next argues that its football policy is distinguishable from the graduation prayer in *Lee* because it does not coerce students to participate in religious observances. Its argument has two parts: first, that there is no impermissible government coercion because the pregame messages are the product of student choices; and second, that there is really no coercion at all because attendance at an extracurricular event, unlike a graduation ceremony, is voluntary.

The reasons just discussed explaining why the alleged "circuit-breaker" mechanism of the dual elections and student speaker do not turn public speech into private speech also demonstrate why these mechanisms do not insulate the school from the coercive element of the final message. In fact, this aspect of the District's argument exposes anew the concerns that are created by the majoritarian election system. The parties' stipulation clearly states that the issue resolved in the first election was "whether a student would deliver prayer at varsity football games," and the controversy in this case demonstrates that the views of the students are not unanimous on that issue.

One of the purposes served by the Establishment Clause is to remove debate over this kind of issue from governmental supervision or control. We explained in *Lee* that the "preservation and transmission of religious beliefs and worship is a responsibility and a choice committed to the private sphere." The two student elections authorized by the policy, coupled with the debates that presumably must precede each, impermissibly invade that private sphere. . . .

The District further argues that attendance at the commencement ceremonies at issue in *Lee* "differs dramatically" from attendance at high school football games, which it contends "are of no more than passing interest to many students" and are "decidedly extracurricular," thus dissipating any coercion. Attendance at a high school football game, unlike showing up for class, is certainly not required in order to receive a diploma.

There are some students, however, such as cheerleaders, members of the band, and, of course, the team members themselves, for whom seasonal commitments mandate their attendance, sometimes for class credit. The District also minimizes the importance to many students of attending and participating in extracurricular activities as part of a complete educational experience. As we noted in *Lee*, "[l]aw reaches past formalism." To assert that high school students do not feel immense social pressure, or have a truly genuine desire, to be involved in the extracurricular event that is American high school football is "formalistic in the extreme." . . .

Under the *Lemon* [*v. Kurtzman*, 403 U.S. 602 (1971)] standard, a court must invalidate a statute if it lacks "a secular legislative purpose." It is therefore proper, as part of this facial challenge, for us to examine the purpose of the October policy.

As discussed, . . . the plain language of the policy clearly spells out the extent of school involvement in both the election of the speaker and the content of the message. Additionally, the text of the October policy specifies only one, clearly preferred message—that of Santa Fe's traditional religious "invocation." Finally, the extremely selective access of the policy and other content restrictions confirm that it is not a content-neutral regulation that creates a limited public forum for the expression of student speech. . . .

The judgment of the Court of Appeals is, accordingly, affirmed. It is so ordered.

Chief Justice REHNQUIST, with whom Justice SCALIA and Justice THOMAS join, dissenting.

The Court distorts existing precedent to conclude that the school district's student-message program is invalid on its face under the Establishment Clause. But even more disturbing than its holding is the tone of the Court's opinion; it bristles with hostility to all things religious in public life. Neither the holding nor the tone of the opinion is faithful to the meaning of the Establishment Clause, when it is recalled that George Washington himself, at the request of the very Congress which passed the Bill of Rights, proclaimed a day of "public thanksgiving and prayer, to be observed by acknowledging with grateful hearts the many and signal favors of Almighty God."

The Court . . . invalidates the District's policy on its face. To do so, it applies the most rigid version of the oft-criticized test of *Lemon v. Kurtzman*, 403 U.S. 602 (1971).

Lemon has had a checkered career in the decisional law of this Court. [But, even] if it were appropriate to apply the *Lemon* test here, the district's student-message policy should not be invalidated on its face. The Court applies *Lemon* and holds that the "policy is invalid on its face because it establishes an improper majoritarian election on religion, and unquestionably has the purpose and creates the perception of encouraging the delivery of prayer at a series of important school events." The Court's reliance on each of these conclusions misses the mark.

First, the Court misconstrues the nature of the "majoritarian election" permitted by the policy as being an election on "prayer" and "religion." To the contrary, the election . . . could become one in which student candidates campaign on platforms that focus on whether or not they will pray if elected. It is also conceivable that the election could lead to a Christian prayer before 90 percent of the football games. If, upon implementation, the policy operated in this fashion, we would have a record before us to review whether the policy, as applied, violated the Establishment Clause or unduly suppressed minority viewpoints. But it is possible that the students might vote not to have a pregame speaker, in which case there would be no threat of a constitutional violation. . . .

Second, with respect to the policy's purpose, the Court holds that "the simple enactment of this policy, with the purpose and perception of school endorsement of student prayer, was a constitutional violation." But the policy itself has plausible secular purposes: "[T]o solemnize the event, to promote good sportsmanship and student safety, and to establish the appropriate environment for the competition." Where a governmental body "expresses a plausible secular purpose" for an enactment, "courts should generally defer to that stated intent." *Wallace.*

The Court also relies on our decision in *Lee v. Weisman*, 505 U.S. 577 (1992), to support its conclusion. In *Lee*, we concluded that the content of the speech at issue, a graduation prayer given by a rabbi, was "directed and controlled" by a school official. In other words, at issue in *Lee* was government speech. Here, by contrast, the potential speech at issue, if the policy had been allowed to proceed, would be a message or invocation selected or created by a student. That is, if there were speech at issue here, it would be private speech.

Finally, the Court seems to demand that a government policy be completely neutral as to content or be considered one that endorses religion. This is undoubtedly a new requirement, as our Establishment Clause jurisprudence simply does not mandate "content neutrality." That concept is found in our First Amendment speech cases and is used as a guide for determining when we apply strict scrutiny. For example, we look to "content neutrality" in reviewing loudness restrictions imposed on speech in public forums, see *Ward v. Rock Against Racism*, 491 U.S. 781 (1989), and regulations against picketing, see *Boos v. Barry*, 485 U.S. 312 (1988). The Court seems to think that the fact that the policy is not content neutral somehow controls the Establishment Clause inquiry.

But even our speech jurisprudence would not require that all public school actions with respect to student speech be content neutral. See, e.g., *Bethel School Dist. No. 403 v. Fraser*, 478 U.S. 675 (1986) (allowing the imposition of sanctions against a student speaker who, in nominating a fellow student for elective office during an assembly, referred to his candidate in terms of an elaborate sexually explicit metaphor). Schools do not violate the First Amendment every time they restrict student speech to certain categories. But under the Court's view, a school policy under which the student body president is to solemnize the graduation ceremony by giving a favorable introduction to the guest speaker would be facially unconstitutional. Solemnization "invites and encourages" prayer and the policy's content limitations prohibit the student body president from giving a solemn, yet non-religious, message like "commentary on United States foreign policy."

The policy at issue here may be applied in an unconstitutional manner, but it will be time enough to invalidate it if that is found to be the case. I would reverse the judgment of the Court of Appeals.

Mitchell v. Helms
530 U.S. 793, 120 S.Ct. 2530 (2000)

Chapter 2 of the Education Consolidation and Improvement Act of 1981 authorizes federal funds for state and local educational agencies, which in turn may lend educational materials and equipment—such as library and media materials, as well as computer software and hardware—to public and private elementary and secondary schools to implement "secular, neutral, and nonideological" programs. In an average year, Jefferson Parish, Louisiana, allocated about 30 percent of its Chapter 2 funds to private schools, most of which are Catholic or otherwise religiously affiliated. That practice was challenged as a violation of the First Amendment (dis)Establishment

Clause. A federal district court agreed, relying on *Meek v. Pittenger*, 421 U.S. 349 (1975), and *Wolman v. Walter*, 433 U.S. 229 (1997), which struck down programs providing many of the same kinds of materials and equipment. But after the presiding district court judge retired, another judge reversed the decision on the basis of *Zobrest v. Catalina Foothills Schools District*, 509 U.S. 1 (1993), which allowed, under a federal program for the disabled, a public school to provide a sign-language interpreter for a deaf student in a Catholic high school. While that decision was appealed, the Supreme Court handed down *Agostini v. Felton*, 521 U.S. 203 (1997), which approved a program, under Title I of the Elementary and Secondary Education Act of 1965, providing public school teachers for remedial classes at religious and other private schools. Subsequently, in reversing the district court's decision allowing Chapter 2 funds to go to Catholic schools, the Court of Appeals for the Fifth Circuit concluded that the ruling in *Agostini* neither overruled *Meek* and *Wolman* nor rejected their distinction between loaning textbooks and other kinds of materials and equipment that might be diverted for religious purposes to private religious schools. That decision was appealed, and the Supreme Court granted review.

The appellate court's decision was reversed in a six to three decision, with the opinion of the Court delivered by Justice Thomas. Justice O'Connor filed a concurring opinion. Justice Souter filed a dissenting opinion, which Justices Stevens and Ginsburg joined.

Justice THOMAS announced the judgment of the Court and delivered an opinion in which the Chief Justice REHNQUIST, Justice SCALIA, and Justice KENNEDY join.

The question is whether Chapter 2, as applied in Jefferson Parish, Louisiana, is a law respecting an establishment of religion, because many of the private schools receiving Chapter 2 aid in that parish are religiously affiliated. We hold that Chapter 2 is not such a law.

The Establishment Clause of the First Amendment dictates that "Congress shall make no law respecting an establishment of religion." In the over 50 years since *Everson* [*v. Bd. of Education*, 330 U.S. 1 (1947)], we have consistently struggled to apply these simple words in the context of governmental aid to religious schools.

In *Agostini* [*v. Felton*, 521 U.S. 203 (1997)], however, we brought some clarity to our case law by overruling two anomalous precedents (one in whole, the other in part) and by consolidating some of our previously disparate considerations under a revised test. Whereas in *Lemon* [*v. Kurtzman*, 403 U.S. 602 (1971)], we had considered whether a statute (1) has a secular purpose, (2) has a primary effect of advancing or inhibiting religion, or (3) creates an excessive entanglement between government and religion, in *Agostini* we modified *Lemon* for purposes of evaluating aid to schools and examined only the first and second factors. We acknowledged that our cases discussing excessive entanglement had applied many of the same considerations as had our cases discussing primary effect, and we therefore recast *Lemon*'s entanglement inquiry as simply one criterion relevant to determining a statute's effect. We also acknowledged that our cases had pared somewhat the factors that could justify a finding of excessive entanglement. We then set out revised criteria for determining the effect of a statute: "To summarize, New York City's Title I program does not run afoul of any of three primary criteria we currently use to evaluate whether government aid has the effect of advancing religion: It does not result in governmental indoctrination; define its recipients by reference to religion; or create an excessive entanglement."

In this case, our inquiry under *Agostini*'s purpose and effect test is a narrow one. Because respondents do not challenge the District Court's holding that Chapter 2 has a secular purpose, and because the Fifth Circuit also did not question that holding, we will consider only Chapter 2's effect. Further, in determining that effect, we will consider only the first two *Agostini* criteria, since neither respondents nor the Fifth Circuit has questioned the District Court's holding that Chapter 2 does not create an excessive entanglement. Considering Chapter 2 in light of our more recent case law, we conclude that it neither results in religious indoctrination by the government nor defines its recipients by reference to religion. We therefore hold that Chapter 2 is not a "law respecting an establishment of religion." In so holding, we acknowledge what both the Ninth and Fifth Circuits saw was inescapable—*Meek* [*v. Pittenger*, 421 U.S. 349 (1975)] and *Wolman* [*v. Walter*, 433 U.S. 229 (1977)], are anomalies in our case law. We therefore conclude that they are no longer good law.

As we indicated in *Agostini*, and have indicated elsewhere, the question whether governmental aid to religious schools results in governmental indoctrination is ultimately a question whether any religious indoctrination that occurs in those schools could reasonably be attributed to governmental action. We have also indicated that the answer to the question of indoctrination will resolve the question whether a program of educational aid "subsidizes" religion, as our religion cases use that term.

In distinguishing between indoctrination that is attributable to the State and indoctrination that is not, we have consistently turned to the principle of neutrality, upholding aid that is offered to a broad range of groups or persons without regard to their religion. If the religious, irreligious, and areligious are all alike eligible for governmental aid, no one would conclude that any indoctrination that any particular recipient conducts has been done at the behest of the government. . . .

As a way of assuring neutrality, we have repeatedly considered whether any governmental aid that goes to a religious institution does so "only as a result of the genuinely independent and private choices of individuals." *Agostini*. We have viewed as significant whether the "private choices of individual parents," as opposed to the "unmediated" will of government, [*School District of Grand Rapids v.*] *Ball*, [473 U.S. 373 (1985)], determine what schools ultimately benefit from the governmental aid, and how much. For if numerous private choices, rather than the single choice of a government, determine the distribution of aid pursuant to neutral eligibility criteria, then a government cannot, or at least cannot easily, grant special favors that might lead to a religious establishment. Private choice also helps guarantee neutrality by mitigating the preference for pre-existing recipients that is arguably inherent in any governmental aid program, and that could lead to a program inadvertently favoring one religion or favoring religious private schools in general over nonreligious ones.

The principles of neutrality and private choice, and their relationship to each other, were prominent not only in *Agostini*, but also in *Zobrest* [*v. Catalina Foothills School District*, 509 U.S. 1 (1993); *Witters* [*v. Washington Dept. of Services for the Blind*, 474 U.S. 481 (1986)]; and *Mueller* [*v. Allen*, 463 U.S. 388 (1983)]. . . .

Agostini's second primary criterion for determining the effect of governmental aid is closely related to the first. The second criterion requires a court to consider whether an aid program "define[s] its recipients by reference to religion." As we briefly explained in *Agostini*, this second criterion looks to the same set of facts as does our focus, under the first criterion, on neutrality, but the second criterion uses those facts to answer a somewhat different question—whether the criteria for allocating the aid "creat[e] a financial incentive to undertake religious indoctrination." In *Agostini* we set out the following rule for answering this question: "This incentive is not present, however, where the aid is allocated on the basis of neutral, secular criteria that neither favor nor disfavor religion, and is made available to both religious and secular beneficiaries on a nondiscriminatory basis. Under such circumstances, the aid is less likely to have the effect of advancing religion." The cases on which *Agostini* relied for this rule, and *Agostini* itself, make clear the close relationship between this rule, incentives, and private choice. For to say that a program does not create an incentive to choose religious schools is to say that the private choice is truly "independent," *Witters*. When such an incentive does exist, there is a greater risk that one could attribute to the government any indoctrination by the religious schools. See *Zobrest*.

We hasten to add, what should be obvious from the rule itself, that simply because an aid program offers private schools, and thus religious schools, a benefit that they did not previously receive does not mean that the program, by reducing the cost of securing a religious education, creates, under *Agostini*'s second criterion, an "incentive" for parents to choose such an education for their children. For any aid will have some such effect. . . .

Respondents also contend that the Establishment Clause requires that aid to religious schools not be impermissibly religious in nature or be divertible to religious use. We agree with the first part of this argument but not the second. Respondents' "no divertibility" rule is inconsistent with our more recent case law and is unworkable. So long as the governmental aid is not itself "unsuitable for use in the public schools because of religious content," *Allen*, and eligibility for aid is determined in a constitutionally permissible manner, any use of that aid to indoctrinate cannot be attributed to the government and is thus not of constitutional concern. And, of course, the use to which the aid is put does not affect the criteria governing the aid's allocation and thus does not create any impermissible incentive under *Agostini*'s second criterion. . . .

Respondents appear to rely on *Meek* and *Wolman* to establish their rule against "divertible" aid. But those cases offer little, if any, support for respondents. *Meek* mentioned divertibility only briefly in a concluding footnote, and that mention was, at most, peripheral to the Court's reasoning in striking down the lending of instructional materials and equipment. The aid program in *Wolman* explicitly barred divertible aid, so a concern for divertibility could not have been part of our reason for finding that program invalid. The issue is not divertibility of aid but rather whether the aid itself has an impermissible content.

Where the aid would be suitable for use in a public school, it is also suitable for use in any private school. Similarly, the prohibition against the government providing impermissible content resolves the Establishment Clause concerns that exist if aid is actually diverted to religious uses. In *Agostini*, we explained *Zobrest* by making just this distinction between the content of aid and the use of that aid: "Because the only government aid in *Zobrest* was the interpreter, who was herself not inculcating any religious messages, no government indoctrination took place." *Agostini* also acknowledged that what the dissenters in *Zobrest* had charged was essentially true: *Zobrest* did effect a "shift in our Establishment Clause law." The interpreter herself, assuming that she fulfilled her assigned duties, had "no inherent religious significance," *Allen*, and so it did not matter (given the neutrality and private choice involved in the program) that she "would be a mouthpiece for religious instruction," *Agostini*. And just as a government interpreter does not herself inculcate a religious message—even when she is conveying one—so also a government computer or overhead projector does not itself inculcate a religious message, even when it is conveying one.

In *Agostini* itself, we approved the provision of public employees to teach secular remedial classes in private schools partly because we concluded that there was no reason to suspect that indoctrinating content would be part of such governmental aid. Relying on *Zobrest*, we refused to presume that the public teachers would "inject religious content" into their classes, especially given certain safeguards that existed; we also saw no evidence that they had done so. . . .

In short, nothing in the Establishment Clause requires the exclusion of pervasively sectarian schools from otherwise permissible aid programs, and other doctrines of this Court bar it. This doctrine, born of bigotry, should be buried now.

Applying the two relevant *Agostini* criteria, we see no basis for concluding that Jefferson Parish's Chapter 2 program "has the effect of advancing religion." Chapter 2 does not result in governmental indoctrination, because it determines eligibility for aid neutrally, allocates that aid based on the private choices of the parents of schoolchildren, and does not provide aid that has an impermissible content. Nor does Chapter 2 define its recipients by reference to religion. . . .

There is evidence that equipment has been, or at least easily could be, diverted for use in religious classes. Justice O'CONNOR, however, finds the safeguards against diversion adequate to prevent and detect actual diversion. The safeguards on which she relies reduce to three: (1) signed assurances that Chapter 2 aid will be used only for secular, neutral, and nonideological purposes, (2) monitoring visits, and (3) the requirement that equipment be labeled as belonging to Chapter 2. . . . In any event, for reasons we discussed supra, the evidence of actual diversion and the weakness of the safeguards against actual diversion are not relevant to the constitutional inquiry, whatever relevance they may have under the statute and regulations. . . .

Chapter 2 satisfies both the first and second primary criteria of *Agostini*. It therefore does not have the effect of advancing religion. For the same reason, Chapter 2 also "cannot reasonably be viewed as an endorsement of religion." Accordingly, we hold that Chapter 2 is not a law respecting an establishment of religion. Jefferson Parish need not exclude religious schools from its Chapter 2 program. To the extent that *Meek* and *Wolman* conflict with this holding, we overrule them.

The judgment of the Fifth Circuit is reversed.

Justice O'CONNOR, with whom Justice BREYER joins, concurring in the judgment.

Three Terms ago, we held in *Agostini v. Felton* that Title I, as applied in New York City, did not violate the Establishment Clause. I believe that *Agostini* likewise controls the constitutional inquiry respecting Title II presented here, and requires the reversal of the Court of Appeals' judgment that the program is unconstitutional as applied in Jefferson Parish, Louisiana. To the extent our decisions in *Meek v. Pittenger*, and *Wolman v. Walter*, are inconsistent with the Court's judgment today, I agree that those decisions should be overruled. I therefore concur in the judgment.

I write separately because, in my view, the plurality announces a rule of unprecedented breadth for the evaluation of Establishment Clause challenges to government school-aid programs. Reduced to its essentials, the plurality's rule states that government aid to religious schools does not have the effect of advancing religion so long as the aid is offered on a neutral basis and the aid is secular in content. The plurality also rejects the distinction between direct and indirect aid, and holds that the actual diversion of secular aid by a religious school to the advancement of its religious mission is permissible. Although the expansive scope of the plurality's rule is troubling, two specific aspects of the opinion compel me to write separately. First, the plurality's treatment of neutrality comes close to assigning that factor singular importance in the future adjudication of Establishment Clause challenges to government school-aid programs. Second, the plurality's approval of actual diversion of government aid to religious indoctrination is in tension with our precedents and, in any event, unnecessary to decide the instant case. . . .

I would adhere to the rule that we have applied in the context of textbook lending programs: To establish a First Amendment violation, plaintiffs must prove that the aid in question actually is, or has been, used for religious purposes. See *Meek*, *Allen*. Just as we held in *Agostini* that our more recent cases had undermined the assumptions underlying *Ball* and *Aguilar* [*v. Felton*, 473 U.S. 402 (1985)], I would now hold that *Agostini* and the cases on which it relied have undermined the assumptions underlying *Meek* and *Wolman*. To be sure, *Agostini* only addressed the specific presumption that public-school employees teaching on the premises of religious schools would inevitably inculcate religion. Nevertheless, I believe that our definitive rejection of that presumption also stood for—or at least strongly pointed to—the broader proposition that such presumptions of religious indoctrination are normally inappropriate when evaluating neutral school-aid programs under the Establishment Clause. . . .

Given the important similarities between the Chapter 2 program here and the Title I program at issue in *Agostini*, respondents' Establishment Clause challenge must fail. As in *Agostini*, the Chapter 2 aid is allocated on the basis of neutral, secular criteria; the aid must be supplementary and cannot supplant non-Federal funds; no Chapter 2 funds ever reach the coffers of religious schools; the aid must be secular; any evidence of actual diversion is *de minimis*; and the program includes adequate safeguards. Regardless of whether these factors are constitutional requirements, they are surely sufficient to find that the program at issue here does not have the impermissible effect of advancing religion. For the same reasons, "this carefully constrained program also cannot reasonably be viewed as an endorsement of religion." *Agostini*. Accordingly, I concur in the judgment.

Justice SOUTER, with whom Justice STEVENS and Justice GINSBURG join, dissenting.

The establishment prohibition of government religious funding serves more than one end. It is meant to guarantee the right of individual conscience against compulsion, to protect the integrity of religion against the corrosion of secular support, and to preserve the unity of political society against the implied exclusion of the less favored and the antagonism of controversy over public support for religious causes.

These objectives are always in some jeopardy since the substantive principle of no aid to religion is not the only limitation on government action toward religion. Because the First Amendment also bars any prohibition of individual free exercise of religion, and because religious organizations cannot be isolated from the basic government functions that create the civil environment, it is as much necessary as it is difficult to draw lines between forbidden aid and lawful benefit. For more than 50 years, this Court has been attempting to draw these lines. Owing to the variety of factual circumstances in which the lines must be drawn, not all of the points creating the boundary have enjoyed self-evidence.

So far as the line drawn has addressed government aid to education, a few fundamental generalizations are nonetheless possible. There may be no aid supporting a sectarian school's religious exercise or the discharge of its religious mission, while aid of a secular character with no discernible benefit to such a sectarian objective is allowable. Because the religious and secular spheres largely overlap in the life of many such schools, the Court has tried to identify some facts likely to reveal the relative religious or secular intent or effect of the government benefits in particular circumstances. We have asked whether the government is acting neutrally in distributing its money, and about the form of the aid itself, its path from government to religious institution, its divertibility to religious nurture, its potential for reducing traditional expenditures of religious institutions, and its relative importance to the recipient, among other things.

In all the years of its effort, the Court has isolated no single test of constitutional sufficiency, and the question in every case addresses the substantive principle of no aid: what reasons are there to characterize this benefit as aid to the sectarian school in discharging its religious mission? Particular factual circumstances control, and the answer is a matter of judgment.

In what follows I will flesh out this summary, for this case comes at a time when our judgment requires perspective on how the Establishment Clause has come to be understood and applied. It is not just that a majority today mistakes the significance of facts that have led to conclusions of unconstitutionality in earlier cases, though I believe the Court commits error in failing to recognize the divertibility of funds to the service of religious objectives. What is more important is the view revealed in the plurality opinion, which espouses a new conception of neutrality as a practically sufficient test of constitutionality that would, if adopted by the Court, eliminate enquiry into a law's effects. The plurality position breaks fundamentally with Establishment Clause principle, and with the methodology painstakingly worked out in support of it. I mean to revisit that principle and describe the methodology at some length, lest there be any question about the rupture that the plurality view would cause. From that new view of the law, and from a majority's mistaken application of the old, I respectfully dissent. . . .

[I]n the Court's classic summation delivered in *Everson v. Board of Education*, [330 U.S. 1 (1947)], its first opinion directly addressing standards governing aid to religious schools: "The 'establishment of religion' clause of the First Amendment means at least this: Neither a state nor the Federal Government can set up a church. Neither can pass laws which aid one religion, aid all religions, or prefer one religion over another. Neither can force nor influence a person to go to or to remain away from church against his will or force him to profess a belief or disbelief in any religion. No person can be punished for entertaining or professing religious beliefs or disbeliefs, for church attendance or non-attendance. No tax in any amount, large or small, can be levied to support any religious activities or institutions, whatever they may be called, or whatever form they may adopt to teach or practice religion. Neither a state nor the Federal Government can, openly or secretly, participate in the affairs of any religious organizations or groups and vice versa. In the words of Jefferson, the clause against establishment of religion by law was intended to erect 'a wall of separation between Church and State.'" The most directly pertinent doctrinal statements here are these: no government "can pass laws which aid one religion [or] all religions. No tax in any amount can be levied to support any religious activities or institutions whatever form they may adopt to teach religion." Thus, the principle of "no aid," with which no one in *Everson* disagreed. . . .

After *Everson* and *Allen*, the state of the law applying the Establishment Clause to public expenditures producing some benefit to religious schools was this:

1. Government aid to religion is forbidden, and tax revenue may not be used to support a religious school or religious teaching.

2. Government provision of such paradigms of universally general welfare benefits as police and fire protection does not count as aid to religion.

3. Whether a law's benefit is sufficiently close to universally general welfare paradigms to be classified with them, as distinct from religious aid, is a function of the purpose and effect of the challenged law in all its particularity. The judgment is not reducible to the application of any formula. Evenhandedness of distribution as between religious and secular beneficiaries is a relevant factor, but not a sufficiency test of constitutionality. There is no rule of religious equal protection to the effect that any expenditure for the benefit of religious school students is necessarily constitutional so long as public school pupils are favored on ostensibly identical terms.

4. Government must maintain neutrality as to religion, "neutrality" being a conclusory label for the required position of government as neither aiding religion nor impeding religious exercise by believers. "Neutrality" was not the name of any test to identify permissible action, and in particular, was not synonymous with evenhandedness in conferring benefit on the secular as well as the religious.

Today, the substantive principle of no aid to religious mission remains the governing understanding of the Establishment Clause as applied to public benefits inuring to religious schools. The governing opinions on the subject in the 35 years since *Allen* have never challenged this principle. The cases have, however, recognized that in actual Establishment Clause litigation over school aid legislation, there is no pure aid to religion and no purely secular welfare benefit; the effects of the laws fall somewhere in between, with the judicial task being to make a realistic allocation between the two possibilities. The Court's decisions demonstrate its repeated attempts to isolate considerations relevant in classifying particular benefits as between those that do not discernibly support or threaten support of a school's religious mission, and those that cross or threaten to cross the line into support for religion.

The most deceptively familiar of those considerations is "neutrality," the presence or absence of which, in some sense, we have addressed from the moment of *Everson* itself. I say "some sense," for we have used the term in at least three ways in our cases, and an understanding of the term's evolution will help to explain the concept as it is understood today, as well as the limits of its significance in Establishment Clause analysis. "Neutrality" has been employed as a term to describe the requisite state of government equipoise between the forbidden encouragement and discouragement of religion; to characterize a benefit or aid as secular; and to indicate evenhandedness in distributing it. . . .

In sum, "neutrality" originally entered this field of jurisprudence as a conclusory term, a label for the required relationship between the government and religion as a state of equipoise between government as ally and government as adversary. Reexamining *Everson*'s paradigm cases to derive a prescriptive guideline, we first determined that "neutral" aid was secular, nonideological, or unrelated to religious education. Our subsequent reexamination of *Everson* and *Allen*, beginning in [*Committee for Public Education and Religious Freedom v.*] *Nyquest*, [413 U.S. 756 (1973)], and culminating in *Mueller* and most recently in *Agostini*, recast neutrality as a concept of "evenhandedness."

There is, of course, good reason for considering the generality of aid and the evenhandedness of its distribution in making close calls between benefits that in purpose or effect support a school's religious mission and those that do not. This is just what *Everson* did. Even when the disputed practice falls short of *Everson*'s paradigms, the breadth of evenhanded distribution is one pointer toward the law's purpose, since on the face of it aid distributed generally and without a religious criterion is less likely to be meant to aid religion than a benefit going only to religious institutions or people. And, depending on the breadth of distribution, looking to evenhandedness is a way of asking whether a benefit can reasonably be seen to aid religion in fact; we do not regard the postal system as aiding religion, even though parochial schools get mail. Given the legitimacy of considering evenhandedness, then, there is no reason to avoid the term "neutrality" to refer to it. But one crucial point must be borne in mind.

In the days when "neutral" was used in *Everson*'s sense of equipoise, neutrality was tantamount to constitutionality; the term was conclusory, but when it applied it meant that the government's position was constitutional under the Establishment Clause. This is not so at all, however, under the most recent use of "neutrality" to refer to generality or evenhandedness of distribution. This kind of neutrality is relevant in judging whether a benefit scheme so characterized should be seen as aiding a sectarian school's religious mission, but this neutrality is not alone sufficient to qualify the aid as constitutional. It is to be considered only along with other characteristics of aid, its administration, its recipients, or its potential that have been emphasized over the years as indicators of just how religious the intent and effect of a given aid scheme really is. Thus, the basic principle of establishment scrutiny of aid remains the principle as stated in *Everson*, that there may be no public aid to religion or support for the religious mission of any institution. . . .

[Our] doctrinal history leaves one point clear beyond peradventure: together with James Madison we have consistently understood the Establishment Clause to impose a substantive prohibition against public aid to religion and, hence, to the religious mission of sectarian schools. Evenhandedness neutrality is one, nondispositive pointer toward an intent and (to a lesser degree) probable effect on the permissible side of the line between forbidden aid and general public welfare benefit. Other pointers are facts about the religious mission and education level of benefited schools and their pupils, the pathway by which a benefit travels from public treasury to educational effect, the form and content of the aid, its adaptability to religious ends, and its effects on school budgets. The object of all enquiries into such matters is the same whatever the particular circumstances: is the benefit intended to aid in providing the religious element of the education and is it likely to do so?

The substance of the law has thus not changed since *Everson*. Emphasis on one sort of fact or another has varied depending on the perceived utility of the enquiry, but all that has been added is repeated explanation of relevant considerations, confirming that our predecessors were right in their prophecies that no simple test would emerge to allow easy application of the establishment principle.

The plurality, however, would reject that lesson. The majority misapplies it. The nub of the plurality's new position is this: "[I]f the government, seeking to further some legitimate secular purpose, offers aid on the same terms, without regard to religion, to all who adequately further that purpose, then it is fair to say that any aid going to a religious recipient only has the effect of furthering that secular purpose. The government, in crafting such an aid program, has had to conclude that a given level of aid is necessary to further that purpose among secular recipients and has provided no more than that same level to religious recipients." As a break with consistent doctrine the plurality's new criterion is unequaled in the history of Establishment Clause interpretation. Simple on its face, it appears to take evenhandedness neutrality and in practical terms promote it to a single and sufficient test for the establishment constitutionality of school aid. Even on its own terms, its errors are manifold, and attention to at least three of its mistaken assumptions will show the degree to which the plurality's proposal would replace the principle of no aid with a formula for generous religious support.

First, the plurality treats an external observer's attribution of religious support to the government as the sole impermissible effect of a government aid scheme. While perceived state endorsement of religion is undoubtedly a relevant concern under the Establishment Clause, it is certainly not the only one. *Everson* made this clear from the start: secret aid to religion by the government is also barred. State aid not attributed to the government would still violate a taxpayer's liberty of conscience, threaten to corrupt religion, and generate disputes over aid. . . .

Second, the plurality apparently assumes as a fact that equal amounts of aid to religious and nonreligious schools will have exclusively secular and equal effects, on both external perception and on incentives to attend different schools. But there is no reason to believe that this will be the case; the effects of same-terms aid may not be confined to the secular sphere at all. This is the reason that we have long recognized that unrestricted aid to religious schools will support religious teaching in addition to secular education, a fact that would be true no matter what the supposedly secular purpose of the law might be.

Third, the plurality assumes that per capita distribution rules safeguard the same principles as independent, private choices. But that is clearly not so. We approved university scholarships in *Witters* because we found them close to giving a government employee a paycheck and allowing him to spend it as he chose, but a per capita aid program is a far cry from awarding scholarships to individuals, one of whom makes an independent private choice. Not the least of the significant differences between per capita aid and aid individually determined and directed is the right and genuine opportunity of the recipient to choose not to give the aid. To hold otherwise would be to license the government to donate funds to churches based on the number of their members, on the patent fiction of independent private choice.

The plurality's mistaken assumptions explain and underscore its sharp break with the Framers' understanding of establishment and this Court's consistent interpretative course. Under the plurality's regime, little would be left of the right of conscience against compelled support for religion; the more massive the aid the more potent would be the influence of the government on the teaching mission; the more generous the support, the more divisive would be the resentments of those resisting religious support, and those religions without school systems ready to claim their fair share.

The plurality's conception of evenhandedness does not, however, control the case, whose disposition turns on the misapplication of accepted categories of school aid analysis. The facts most obviously relevant to the Chapter 2 scheme in Jefferson Parish are those showing divertibility and actual diversion in the circumstance of pervasively sectarian religious schools. The type of aid, the structure of the program, and the lack of effective safeguards clearly demonstrate the divertibility of the aid. While little is known about its use, owing to the anemic enforcement system in the parish, even the thin record before us reveals that actual diversion occurred. . . .

The plurality would break with the law. The majority misapplies it. That misapplication is, however, the only consolation in the case, which reaches an erroneous result but does not stage a doctrinal coup. But there is no mistaking the abandonment of doctrine that would occur if the plurality were to become a majority. It is beyond question that the plurality's notion of evenhandedness neutrality as a practical guarantee of the validity of aid to sectarian schools would be the end of the principle of no aid to the schools' religious mission. And if that were not so obvious it would become so after reflecting on the plurality's thoughts about diversion and about giving attention to the pervasiveness of a school's sectarian teaching.

The plurality is candid in pointing out the extent of actual diversion of Chapter 2 aid to religious use in the case before us, and equally candid in saying it does not matter. To the plurality there is nothing wrong with aiding a school's religious mission; the only question is whether religious teaching obtains its tax support under a formally evenhanded criterion of distribution. The principle of no aid to religious teaching has no independent significance.

And if this were not enough to prove that no aid in religious school aid is dead under the plurality's First Amendment, the point is nailed down in the plurality's attack on the legitimacy of considering a school's pervasively sectarian character when judging whether aid to the school is likely to aid its religious mission. The relevance of this consideration is simply a matter of common sense: where religious indoctrination pervades school activities of children and adolescents, it takes great care to be able to aid the school without supporting the doctrinal effort. This is obvious. The plurality nonetheless condemns any enquiry into the pervasiveness of doctrinal content as a remnant of anti-Catholic bigotry (as if evangelical Protestant schools and Orthodox Jewish yeshivas were never pervasively sectarian), and it equates a refusal to aid religious schools with hostility to religion (as if aid to religious teaching were not opposed in this very case by at least one religious respondent and numerous religious amici curiae in a tradition claiming descent from Roger Williams). My concern with these arguments goes not so much to their details as it does to the fact that the plurality's choice to employ imputations of bigotry and irreligion as terms in the Court's debate makes one point clear: that in rejecting the principle of no aid to a school's religious mission the plurality is attacking the most fundamental assumption underlying the Establishment Clause, that government can in fact operate with neutrality in its relation to religion. I believe that it can, and so respectfully dissent.

Good News Club v. Milford Central School
121 S.Ct. 2093 (2001)

New York state authorizes local school boards to adopt regulations governing the public use of their facilities. In 1992, Milford Central School adopted a community-use policy that permits residents to use its facilities for "instruction in any branch of education, learning or the arts" and for "social, civic and recreational meetings and entertainment events, and other uses pertaining to the welfare of the community, provided that such uses shall be nonexclusive and shall be open to the general public." Subsequently, the sponsors of the local Good News Club, a private Christian organization for children ages six to twelve, requested permission to hold weekly afternoon meetings in the school cafeteria. That request was denied on the ground that the school's policy prohibited the use of its facilities "by any individual or organization for religious purposes." The Good News Club then filed a suit in federal district court, contending that the school had violated its First and Fourteenth Amendment rights to free speech and equal protection. The district court rejected their claims and on appeal the Court of Appeals for the Second Circuit affirmed its decision.

The appellate court was reversed in a six to three decision and the opinion of the Court was delivered by Justice Thomas. Justices Scalia and Breyer filed concurring opinions. Justices Stevens and Souter filed dissenting opinions, and Justice Ginsburg joined the latter's dissent.

Justice THOMAS delivered the opinion of the Court.

This case presents two questions. The first question is whether Milford Central School violated the free speech rights of the Good News Club when it excluded the Club from meeting after hours at the school. The second question is whether any such violation is justified by Milford's concern that permitting the Club's activities would violate the Establishment Clause. We conclude that Milford's restriction violates the Club's free speech rights and that no Establishment Clause concern justifies that violation.

The standards that we apply to determine whether a State has unconstitutionally excluded a private speaker from use of a public forum depend on the nature of the forum. If the forum is a traditional or open public forum, the State's restrictions on speech are subject to stricter scrutiny than are restrictions in a limited public forum. Because the parties have agreed that Milford created a limited public forum when it opened its facilities in 1992, we need not resolve the issue here. Instead, we simply will assume that Milford operates a limited public forum.

When the State establishes a limited public forum, the State is not required to and does not allow persons to engage in every type of speech. The State may be justified "in reserving [its forum] for certain groups or for the discussion of certain topics." *Rosenberger v. Rector and Visitors of Univ. of Va.*, 515 U.S. 819 (1995); see also *Lamb's Chapel* [*v. Moriches Union Free School District*, 508 U.S. 384 (1993)]. The State's power to restrict speech, however, is not without limits. The restriction must not discriminate against speech on the basis of viewpoint, and the restriction must be "reasonable in light of the purpose served by the forum," *Cornelius v. NAACP Legal Defense & Ed. Fund, Inc.*, 473 U.S. 788 (1985).

Applying this test, we first address whether the exclusion constituted viewpoint discrimination. We are guided in our analysis by two of our prior opinions, *Lamb's Chapel* and *Rosenberger*. In *Lamb's Chapel*, we held that a school district violated the Free Speech Clause of the First Amendment when it excluded a private group from presenting films at the school based solely on the films' discussions of family values from a religious perspective. Likewise, in *Rosenberger*, we held that a university's refusal to fund a student publication because the publication addressed issues from a religious perspective violated the Free Speech Clause. Concluding that Milford's exclusion of the Good News Club based on its religious nature is indistinguishable from the exclusions in these cases, we hold that the exclusion constitutes viewpoint discrimination. Because the restriction is viewpoint discriminatory, we need not decide whether it is unreasonable in light of the purposes served by the forum.

Milford has opened its limited public forum to activities that serve a variety of purposes, including events "pertaining to the welfare of the community." Milford interprets its policy to permit discussions of subjects such as child rearing, and of "the development of character and morals from a religious perspective." For example, this policy would allow someone to use Aesop's Fables to teach children moral values. Additionally, a group could sponsor a debate on whether there should be a constitutional amendment to permit prayer in public schools, and the Boy Scouts could meet "to influence a boy's character, development and spiritual growth." In short, any group that "promote[s] the moral and character development of children" is eligible to use the school building.

Just as there is no question that teaching morals and character development to children is a permissible purpose under Milford's policy, it is clear that the Club teaches morals and character development to children. For example, no one disputes that the Club instructs children to overcome feelings of jealousy, to treat others well regardless of how they treat the children, and to be obedient, even if it does so in a nonsecular way. Nonetheless, because Milford found the Club's activities to be religious in nature—"the equivalent of religious instruction itself"—it excluded the Club from use of its facilities.

Applying *Lamb's Chapel*, we find it quite clear that Milford engaged in viewpoint discrimination when it excluded the Club from the afterschool forum. . . .

Like the church in *Lamb's Chapel*, the Club seeks to address a subject otherwise permitted under the rule, the teaching of morals and character, from a religious standpoint. Certainly, one could have characterized the film presentations in *Lamb's Chapel* as a religious use, as the Court of Appeals did. And one easily could conclude that the films' purpose to instruct that "'society's slide toward humanism . . . can only be counterbalanced by a loving home where Christian values are instilled from an early age'" was "quintessentially religious." The only apparent difference between the activity of Lamb's Chapel and the activities of the Good News Club is that the Club chooses to teach moral lessons from a Christian perspective through live storytelling and prayer, whereas Lamb's Chapel taught lessons through films. This distinction is inconsequential. Both modes of speech use a religious viewpoint. Thus, the exclusion of the Good News Club's activities, like the exclusion of Lamb's Chapel's films, constitutes unconstitutional viewpoint discrimination. . . .

Despite our holdings in *Lamb's Chapel* and *Rosenberger*, the Court of Appeals, like Milford, believed that its characterization of the Club's activities as religious in nature warranted treating the Club's activities as different in kind from the other activities permitted by the school. . . .

We disagree that something that is "quintessentially religious" or "decidedly religious in nature" cannot also be characterized properly as the teaching of morals and character development from a particular viewpoint. What matters for purposes of the Free Speech Clause is that we can see no logical difference in kind between the invocation of Christianity by the Club and the invocation of teamwork, loyalty, or patriotism by other associations to provide a foundation for their lessons. It is apparent that the unstated principle of the Court of Appeals' reasoning is its conclusion that any time religious instruction and prayer are used to discuss morals and character, the discussion is simply not a "pure" discussion of those issues. According to the Court of Appeals, reliance on Christian principles taints moral and character instruction in a way that other foundations for thought or viewpoints do not. We, however, have never reached such a conclusion. Instead, we reaffirm our holdings in *Lamb's Chapel* and *Rosenberger* that speech discussing otherwise permissible subjects cannot be excluded from a limited public forum on the ground that the subject is discussed from a religious viewpoint. Thus, we conclude that Milford's exclusion of the Club from use of the school, pursuant to its community use policy, constitutes impermissible viewpoint discrimination.

Milford argues that, even if its restriction constitutes viewpoint discrimination, its interest in not violating the Establishment Clause outweighs the Club's interest in gaining equal access to the school's facilities. In other words, according to Milford, its restriction was required to avoid violating the Establishment Clause. We disagree.

We have said that a state interest in avoiding an Establishment Clause violation "may be characterized as compelling," and therefore may justify content-based discrimination. *Widmar v. Vincent*, 454 U.S. 263 (1981). However, it is not clear whether a State's interest in avoiding an Establishment Clause violation would justify viewpoint discrimination. We need not, however, confront the issue in this case, because we conclude that the school has no valid Establishment Clause interest.

We rejected Establishment Clause defenses similar to Milford's in two previous free speech cases, *Lamb's Chapel* and *Widmar*. In particular, in *Lamb's*

Chapel, we explained that "[t]he showing of th[e] film series would not have been during school hours, would not have been sponsored by the school, and would have been open to the public, not just to church members." Accordingly, we found that "there would have been no realistic danger that the community would think that the District was endorsing religion or any particular creed." Likewise, in *Widmar*, where the university's forum was already available to other groups, this Court concluded that there was no Establishment Clause problem.

The Establishment Clause defense fares no better in this case. As in *Lamb's Chapel*, the Club's meetings were held after school hours, not sponsored by the school, and open to any student who obtained parental consent, not just to Club members. As in *Widmar*, Milford made its forum available to other organizations. The Club's activities are materially indistinguishable from those in *Lamb's Chapel* and *Widmar*. Thus, Milford's reliance on the Establishment Clause is unavailing.

Milford attempts to distinguish *Lamb's Chapel* and *Widmar* by emphasizing that Milford's policy involves elementary school children. According to Milford, children will perceive that the school is endorsing the Club and will feel coercive pressure to participate, because the Club's activities take place on school grounds, even thoughthey occur during nonschool hours. This argument is unpersuasive.

First, we have held that "a significant factor in upholding governmental programs in the face of Establishment Clause attack is their neutrality towards religion." *Rosenberger*. . . .

Second, to the extent we consider whether the community would feel coercive pressure to engage in the Club's activities. *Lee v. Weisman*, 505 U.S. 577 (1992), the relevant community would be the parents, not the elementary school children. It is the parents who choose whether their children will attend the Good News Club meetings. Because the children cannot attend without their parents' permission, they cannot be coerced into engaging in the Good News Club's religious activities. . . .

Third, whatever significance we may have assigned in the Establishment Clause context to the suggestion that elementary school children are more impressionable than adults, we have never extended our Establishment Clause jurisprudence to foreclose private religious conduct during nonschool hours merely because it takes place on school premises where elementary school children may be present. . . .

Fourth, even if we were to consider the possible misperceptions by schoolchildren in deciding whether Milford's permitting the Club's activities would violate the Establishment Clause, the facts of this case simply do not support Milford's conclusion. There is no evidence that young children are permitted to loiter outside classrooms after the schoolday has ended. Surely even young children are aware of events for which their parents must sign permission forms. The meetings were held in a combined high school resource room and middle school special education room, not in an elementary school classroom. The instructors are not schoolteachers. And the children in the group are not all the same age as in the normal classroom setting; their ages range from 6 to 12. In sum, these circumstances simply do not support the theory that small children would perceive endorsement here.

Finally, even if we were to inquire into the minds of schoolchildren in this case, we cannot say the danger that children would misperceive the endorsement of religion is any greater than the danger that they would perceive a hostility toward the religious viewpoint if the Club were excluded from the public forum. This concern is particularly acute given the reality that Milford's building is not used only for elementary school children. Students, from kindergarten through the 12th grade, all attend school in the same building. There may be as many, if not more, upperclassmen than elementary school children who occupy the school after hours. For that matter, members of the public writ large are permitted in the school after hours pursuant to the community use policy. Any bystander could conceivably be aware of the school's use policy and its exclusion of the Good News Club, and could suffer as much from viewpoint discrimination as elementary school children could suffer from perceived endorsement.

We cannot operate, as Milford would have us do, under the assumption that any risk that small children would perceive endorsement should counsel in favor of excluding the Club's religious activity. We decline to employ Establishment Clause jurisprudence using a modified heckler's veto, in which a group's religious activity can be proscribed on the basis of what the youngest members of the audience might misperceive. There are countervailing constitutional concerns related to rights of other individuals in the community. In this case, those countervailing concerns are the free speech rights of the Club and its members. And, we have already found that those rights have been violated, not merely perceived to have been violated, by the school's actions toward the Club. . . .

Accordingly, we conclude that permitting the Club to meet on the school's premises would not have violated the Establishment Clause. . . .

Justice STEVENS, dissenting.

The Milford Central School has invited the public to use its facilities for educational and recreational purposes, but not for "religious purposes." Speech for "religious purposes" may reasonably be understood to encompass three different categories. First, there is religious speech that is simply speech about a particular topic from a religious point of view. The film in *Lamb's Chapel v. Center Moriches Union Free School Dist.* illustrates this category. ([T]he film series at issue in that case "[discussed] Dr. [James] Dobson's views on the undermining influences of the media that could only be counterbalanced by returning to traditional, Christian family values instilled at an early stage"). Second, there is religious speech that amounts to worship, or its equivalent. Our decision in *Widmar v. Vincent* concerned such speech. ([T]he speech in question as involv[ed] "religious worship"). Third, there is an intermediate category that is aimed principally at proselytizing or inculcating belief in a particular religious faith.

A public entity may not generally exclude even religious worship from an open public forum. Similarly, a public entity that creates a limited public forum for the discussion of certain specified topics may not exclude a speaker simply because she approaches those topics from a religious point of view. Thus, in *Lamb's Chapel* we held that a public school that permitted its facilities to be used for the discussion of family issues and child rearing could not deny access to speakers presenting a religious point of view on those issues.

But, while a public entity may not censor speech about an authorized topic based on the point of view expressed by the speaker, it has broad discretion to "preserve the property under its control for the use to which it is lawfully dedicated." *Greer v. Spock*, 424 U.S. 828 (1976). Accordingly, "control over access to a nonpublic forum can be based on subject matter and speaker identity so long as the distinctions drawn are reasonable in light of the purpose served by the forum and are viewpoint neutral." *Cornelius v. NAACP Legal Defense & Ed. Fund, Inc.*, 473 U.S. 788 (1985). The novel question that this case presents concerns the constitutionality of a public school's attempt to limit the scope of a public forum it has created. More specifically, the question is whether a school can, consistently with the First Amendment, create a limited public forum that admits the first type of religious speech without allowing the other two.

Distinguishing speech from a religious viewpoint, on the one hand, from religious proselytizing, on the other, is comparable to distinguishing meetings to discuss political issues from meetings whose principal purpose is to recruit new members to join a political organization. If a school decides to authorize after school discussions of current events in its classrooms, it may not exclude people from expressing their views simply because it dislikes their particular political opinions. But must it therefore allow organized political groups—for example, the Democratic Party, the Libertarian Party, or the Ku Klux Klan—to hold meetings, the principal purpose of which is not to discuss the current-events topic from their own unique point of view but rather to recruit others to join their respective groups? I think not. Such recruiting meetings may introduce divisiveness and tend to separate young children into cliques that undermine the school's educational mission. *Lehman v. Shaker Heights*, 418 U.S. 298 (1974) (upholding a city's refusal to allow "political advertising" on public transportation).

School officials may reasonably believe that evangelical meetings designed to convert children to a particular religious faith pose the same risk. And, just as a school may allow meetings to discuss current events from a political perspective without also allowing organized political recruitment, so too can a school allow discussion of topics such as moral development from a religious (or nonreligious) perspective without thereby opening its forum to religious proselytizing or worship.

The particular limitation of the forum at issue in this case is one that prohibits the use of the school's facilities for "religious purposes." It is clear that, by "religious purposes," the school district did not intend to exclude all speech from a religious point of view. Instead, it sought only to exclude religious speech whose principal goal is to "promote the gospel." In other words, the school sought to allow the first type of religious speech while excluding the second and third types. As long as this is done in an even handed manner, I see no constitutional violation in such an effort. The line between the various categories of religious speech may be difficult to draw, but I think that the distinctions are valid, and that a school, particularly an elementary school, must be permitted to draw them. . . .

Accordingly, I respectfully dissent.

Justice SOUTER, with whom Justice GINSBURG joins, dissenting.

This case, like *Lamb's Chapel*, properly raises no issue about the reasonableness of Milford's criteria for restricting the scope of its designated public forum. . . . The sole question before the District Court was, therefore, whether, in refusing to allow Good News's intended use, Milford was misapplying its unchallenged restriction in a way that amounted to imposing a viewpoint-based restriction on what could be said or done by a group entitled to use the forum for an educational, civic, or other permitted purpose. The question was whether Good News was being disqualified when it merely sought to use the school property the same way that the Milford Boy and Girl Scouts and the 4–H Club did. The District Court held on the basis of undisputed facts that Good News's activity was essentially unlike the presentation of views on secular issues from a religious standpoint held to be protected in *Lamb's Chapel*, and was instead activity precluded by Milford's unchallenged policy against religious use, even under the narrowest definition of that term.

The Court of Appeals understood the issue the same way. . . . The appeals court agreed with the District Court that the undisputed facts in this case differ from those in *Lamb's Chapel*, as night from day. A sampling of those facts shows why both courts were correct.

Good News's classes open and close with prayer. In a sample lesson considered by the District Court, children are instructed that "[t]he Bible tells us how we can have our sins forgiven by receiving the Lord Jesus Christ. It tells us how to live to please Him. . . . If you have received the Lord Jesus as your Saviour from sin, you belong to God's special group—His family." The lesson plan instructs the teacher to "lead a child to Christ," and, when reading a Bible verse, to "[e]mphasize that this verse is from the Bible, God's Word" and is "important—and true—because God said it." The lesson further exhorts the teacher to "[b]e sure to give an opportunity for the 'unsaved' children in your class to respond to the Gospel" and cautions against "neglect[ing] this responsibility."

While Good News's program utilizes songs and games, the heart of the meeting is the "challenge" and "invitation," which are repeated at various times throughout the lesson. During the challenge, "saved" children who "already believe in the Lord Jesus as their Savior" are challenged to " 'stop and ask God for the strength and the "want" . . . to obey Him.' " They are instructed that "[i]f you know Jesus as your Savior, you need to place God first in your life. And if you don't know Jesus as Savior and if you would like to, then we will—we will pray with you separately, individually. . . . And the challenge would be, those of you who know Jesus as Savior, you can rely on God's strength to obey Him."

During the invitation, the teacher "invites" the "unsaved" children "to trust the Lord Jesus to be your Savior from sin," and "receiv[e] [him] as your Savior from sin." The children are then instructed that "[i]f you believe what God's Word says about your sin and how Jesus died and rose again for you, you can have His forever life today. Please bow your heads and close your eyes. If you have never believed in the Lord Jesus as your Savior and would like to do that, please show me by raising your hand. If you raised your hand to show me you want to believe in the Lord Jesus, please meet me so I can show you from God's Word how you can receive His everlasting life."

It is beyond question that Good News intends to use the public school premises not for the mere discussion of a subject from a particular, Christian point of view, but for an evangelical service of worship calling children to commit themselves in an act of Christian conversion. The majority avoids this reality only by resorting to the bland and general characterization of Good News's activity as "teaching of morals and character, from a religious standpoint." If the majority's statement ignores reality, as it surely does, then today's holding may be understood only in equally generic terms. Otherwise, indeed, this case would stand for the remarkable proposition that any public school opened for civic meetings must be opened for use as a church, synagogue, or mosque. . . .

7

THE FOURTH AMENDMENT GUARANTEE AGAINST UNREASONABLE SEARCHES AND SEIZURES

A. REQUIREMENTS FOR A WARRANT AND REASONABLE SEARCHES AND SEIZURES

In *Wilson v. Layne* (1999) (excerpted below) the Court held that police violate individuals' constitutionally protected privacy interests under the Fourth Amendment when they invite members of the media to film and photograph their execution of arrest warrants in private homes. However, writing for the Court, Chief Justice Rehnquist held that at the time this case originated—in the early 1990s—the law was unclear, and therefore police enjoyed qualified immunity from suits for damages; henceforth, though, police are liable for allowing the media to accompany them when executing arrest and search warrants in private homes. In a related decision, *Hanlon v. Berger*, 526 U.S. 603 (1999), the Court unanimously ruled in a *per curiam* opinion that federal agents had violated the Fourth Amendment's guarantees for personal privacy by allowing CNN to film the search of a ranch for evidence of the illegal possession of wildlife. But, under *Wilson*, the Court also held that here the agents enjoyed qualified immunity from suits for damages.

In its 2000–2001 term, the Court held that police, while waiting for a search warrant, may secure a dwelling and prevent the resident from entering unaccompanied, without violating the Fourth Amendment. *Illinois v. McArthur*, 531 U.S. 326 (2001), grew out of McArthur's estranged wife's telling police that there were drugs in a trailer home from which she was removing her belongings, under their protection. McArthur, however, refused to allow the police to search the trailer without a warrant, so he was detained outside by the police, while they obtained a search warrant. The search uncovered drugs and McArthur was arrested. Writing for the Court, Justice Breyer held that the search was reasonable because the officers had probable cause to believe that the trailer contained contraband and that McArthur, if unrestrained, would destroy the evidence. Justice Stevens dissented.

In its 2001–2002 term, the Court will consider whether a police officer had "reasonable suspicion" to stop a vehicle in *United States v. Arvizu* (No. 00-1519). On January 19, 1998, an officer stopped a van driven by Arvizu, who appeared "rigid and nervous," and asked Arvizu if he could "look around the van." Arvizu testified that he understood the request to mean that the officer would look outside the vehicle. But, the officer walked over to the passenger's side and opened the door, which led to his discovery of a bag containing marijuana. Arvizu moved to suppress the evidence, claiming that the officer did not have reasonable suspicion to stop the van, but the district court denied that motion. On appeal, the Court of Appeals for the Ninth Circuit reversed, concluding that reasonable suspicion did not exist and that the ten factors on which the trial court rested its decision were neither relevant nor appropriate in a reasonable suspicion analysis.

Wilson v. Layne
526, U.S. 603, 119 S.Ct. 1692 (1999)

In early 1992, the attorney general of the United States approved "Operation Gunsmoke," a national fugitive apprehension program in which U.S. marshals worked with state and local police, as well as the media, to apprehend dangerous criminals. One of the dangerous fugitives identified as a target of "Operation Gunsmoke" was Dominic Wilson, the son of petitioners Charles and Geraldine Wilson. Dominic Wilson had violated his probation on previous felony charges, and the police computer listed "caution indicators that he was likely to be armed, to resist arrest, and to assaul[t] police." The computer also listed his address as 909 North StoneStreet Avenue in Rockville, Maryland. Unknown to the police, however, this was actually the home of his parents. In April 1992 a state court issued three arrest warrants for Dominic Wilson. Subsequently, in the early morning hours of April 16, 1992, a Gunsmoke team, along with a reporter and a photographer from the *Washington Post* who had been invited to accompany them, drove to Wilson's alleged address. At 6:45 A.M., the officers, with media representatives in tow, entered the dwelling at 909 North StoneStreet Avenue, where the petitioners were still in bed when they heard the officers enter. Charles Wilson, dressed only in a pair of briefs, ran into the living room to investigate and discovered at least five men in street clothes with guns in his living room. He angrily demanded that they state their business and repeatedly cursed the officers. Believing him to be an angry Dominic Wilson, the officers quickly subdued him on the floor. Once their protective sweep was completed, the officers learned that Dominic Wilson was not in the house and they departed. But, during the time that the officers were in the home, the *Washington Post* photographer took numerous pictures, including of the confrontation between the police and Charles Wilson; however, none were published. Wilson later sued the police for money damages under *Bivens v. Six Unknown Fed. Narcotics Agents*, 403 U.S. 388 (1971), and Section 1983 of the U.S. Code, which authorizes suits for damages when officials violate individuals' constitutional rights. Attorneys for the police countered that the officers enjoyed qualified immunity because they had not knowingly violated any constitutional rights by allowing members of the media to accompany them. A district court rejected the latter argument but an appellate court reversed. Wilson appealed to the Supreme Court, which granted review and affirmed the appellate court's ruling.

The Court's decision was eight to one, and its opinion was delivered by Chief Justice Rehnquist. Justice Stevens issued a separate opinion in part concurring and dissenting.

Chief Justice REHNQUIST delivered the opinion of the Court.

While executing an arrest warrant in a private home, police officers invited representatives of the media to accompany them. We hold that such a "media ride along" does violate the Fourth Amendment, but that because the state of the law was not clearly established at the time the search in this case took place, the officers are entitled to the defense of qualified immunity. . . .

The petitioners sued the federal officials under *Bivens* and the state officials under Section 1983. Both *Bivens* and Section 1983 allow a plaintiff to seek money damages from government officials who have violated his Fourth Amendment rights. But government officials performing discretionary functions generally are granted a qualified immunity and are "shielded from liability for civil damages insofar as their conduct does not violate clearly established statutory or constitutional rights of which a reasonable person would have known." *Harlow v. Fitzgerald*, 457 U.S. 800 (1982).

Although this case involves suits under both Section 1983 and *Bivens*, the qualified immunity analysis is identical under either cause of action. A court evaluating a claim of qualified immunity "must first determine whether the plaintiff has alleged the deprivation of an actual constitutional right at all, and if so, proceed to determine whether that right was clearly established at the time of the alleged violation." *Conn. v. Gabbert*, [526 U.S. 286] (1999). . . .

The Fourth Amendment embodies [a] centuries-old principle of respect for the privacy of the home: "The right of the people to be secure in their persons, houses, papers, and effects, against unreasonable searches and seizures, shall not be violated, and no Warrants shall issue, but upon probable cause, supported by

Oath or affirmation, and particularly describing the place to be searched, and the persons or things to be seized."

Our decisions have applied these basic principles of the Fourth Amendment to situations, like those in this case, in which police enter a home under the authority of an arrest warrant in order to take into custody the suspect named in the warrant. In *Payton v. New York*, 445 U.S. 573 (1980), we noted that although clear in its protection of the home, the common-law tradition at the time of the drafting of the Fourth Amendment was ambivalent on the question of whether police could enter a home without a warrant. We were ultimately persuaded that the "overriding respect for the sanctity of the home that has been embedded in our traditions since the origins of the Republic" meant that absent a warrant or exigent circumstances, police could not enter a home to make an arrest. We decided that "an arrest warrant founded on probable cause implicitly carries with it the limited authority to enter a dwelling in which the suspect lives when there is reason to believe the suspect is within."

Here, of course, the officers had such a warrant, and they were undoubtedly entitled to enter the Wilson home in order to execute the arrest warrant for Dominic Wilson. But it does not necessarily follow that they were entitled to bring a newspaper reporter and a photographer with them. . . .

Respondents argue that the presence of the *Washington Post* reporters in the Wilsons' home nonetheless served a number of legitimate law enforcement purposes. They first assert that officers should be able to exercise reasonable discretion about when it would "further their law enforcement mission to permit members of the news media to accompany them in executing a warrant." But this claim ignores the importance of the right of residential privacy at the core of the Fourth Amendment. It may well be that media ride-alongs further the law enforcement objectives of the police in a general sense, but that is not the same as furthering the purposes of the search. Were such generalized "law enforcement objectives" themselves sufficient to trump the Fourth Amendment, the protections guaranteed by that Amendment's text would be significantly watered down.

Respondents next argue that the presence of third parties could serve the law enforcement purpose of publicizing the government's efforts to combat crime, and facilitate accurate reporting on law enforcement activities. There is certainly language in our opinions interpreting the First Amendment which points to the importance of "the press" in informing the general public about the administration of criminal justice. . . . But the Fourth Amendment also protects a very important right, and in the present case it is in terms of that right that the media ride-alongs must be judged.

Finally, respondents argue that the presence of third parties could serve in some situations to minimize police abuses and protect suspects, and also to protect the safety of the officers. While it might be reasonable for police officers to themselves videotape home entries as part of a "quality control" effort to ensure that the rights of homeowners are being respected, or even to preserve evidence, such a situation is significantly different from the media presence in this case. The *Washington Post* reporters in the Wilsons' home were working on a story for their own purposes. They were not present for the purpose of protecting the officers, much less the Wilsons. A private photographer was acting for private purposes, as evidenced in part by the fact that the newspaper and not the police retained the photographs. Thus, although the presence of third parties during the execution of a warrant may in some circumstances be constitutionally permissible, the presence of these third parties was not. . . .

Since the police action in this case violated the petitioners' Fourth Amendment right, we now must decide whether this right was clearly established at the time of the search. As noted above, government officials performing discretionary functions generally are granted a qualified immunity and are "shielded from liability for civil damages insofar as their conduct does not violate clearly established statutory or constitutional rights of which a reasonable person would have known." *Harlow v. Fitzgerald.* What this means in practice is that "whether an official protected by qualified immunity may be held personally liable for an allegedly unlawful official action generally turns on the 'objective legal reasonableness' of the action, assessed in light of the legal rules that were 'clearly established' at the time it was taken." *Anderson v. Creighton,* 483 U.S. 635 (1987).

In *Anderson,* we explained that what "clearly established" means in this context depends largely "upon the level of generality at which the relevant 'legal rule' is to be established." . . .

We hold that it was not unreasonable for a police officer in April 1992 to have believed that bringing media observers along during the execution of an arrest warrant (even in a home) was lawful. First, the constitutional question presented by this case is by no means open and shut. . . .

Second, although media ride-alongs of one sort or another had apparently become a common police practice, in 1992 there were no judicial opinions holding that this practice became unlawful when it entered a home. . . .

Finally, important to our conclusion was the reliance by the United States marshals in this case on a Marshal's Service ride-along policy which explicitly contemplated that media who engaged in ride-alongs might enter private homes with their cameras as part of fugitive apprehension arrests. . . . Such a policy, of course, could not make reasonable a belief that was contrary to a decided body of case law. But here the state of the law as to third parties accompanying police on home entries was at best undeveloped, and it was not unreasonable for law enforcement officers to look and rely on their formal ride-along policies. . . .

For the foregoing reasons, the judgment of the Court of Appeals is affirmed.

Justice STEVENS, concurring in part and dissenting in part.

In my view, . . . the homeowner's right to protection against this type of trespass was clearly established long before April 16, 1992. My sincere respect for the competence of the typical member of the law enforcement profession precludes my assent to the suggestion that "a reasonable officer could have believed that bringing members of the media into a home during the execution of an arrest warrant was lawful." I therefore disagree with the Court's resolution of the conflict in the Circuits on the qualified immunity issue. The clarity of the constitutional rule, a federal statute, common-law decisions, and the testimony of the senior law enforcement officer all support my position that it has long been clearly established that officers may not bring third parties into private homes to witness the execution of a warrant. . . .

I respectfully dissent.

B. EXCEPTIONS TO THE WARRANT REQUIREMENT

In a brief *per curiam* opinion in *Maryland v. Dyson*, 527 U.S. 465 (1999), the Court underscored that the automobile exception to the Fourth Amendment's warrant requirement does not require police to obtain a warrant to search a car when they have probable cause to believe that it contains contraband. In doing so, the Court reversed a state court ruling that, unless exigent circumstances justify a warrantless search, police must obtain a warrant before conducting a search, even though they have probable cause to believe that the automobile contains contraband. As in *Pennsylvania v. Labron*, 518 U.S. 938 (1996), the Court repeated that "the automobile exception does not have a separate exigency requirement: 'If a car is readily mobile and probable cause exists to believe it contains contraband, the Fourth Amendment permits police to search the vehicle without more.'" Justice Breyer dissented and would have granted oral arguments in the case.

In another brief *per curiam* opinion, in *Flippo v. West Virginia*, 528 U.S. 11 (1999), the Court unanimously overturned a state court decision that upheld warrantless police searches of murder crime scenes. In rejecting that court's "murder crime scene" exception for warrantless searches, the Court reaffirmed the holding in *Mincey v. Arizona*, 437 U.S. 385 (1978).

In another unanimous decision, the Court refused to extend the scope of permissible stopping and frisking of individuals by police, as set forth in *Terry v. Ohio*, 392 U.S. 1 (1968), and *Adams v. Williams*, 407 U.S. 590 (1972). *Adams* had extended *Terry*'s exception to the Fourth Amendment in upholding the stopping and frisking of an individual by an officer based on a tip from a known informant that he was carrying a gun. However, in *Florida v. J.L.*, 120 S.Ct. 1375 (2000), the Court held unconstitutional the stopping and frisking of an individual for a gun based on a police officer's receiving an anonymous tip that a young black male wearing a plaid shirt at a bus stop was carrying a gun. Writing for the Court, Justice Ginsburg ruled that anonymous tips, unless accompanied by other specific indicators of reliability, fall short of providing a basis for reasonable suspicion to justify officers' stopping and frisking of individuals.

In its 1999–2000 term the Court also considered, in *Illinois v. Wardlow* (excerpted below), whether an individual's flight from police justifies their stopping the individual under the important stop-and-frisk ruling in *Terry v. Ohio*, 392 U.S. 1 (1968) (excerpted in Vol. 2, Ch. 7). In *Bond v. United States* (excerpted below) the Court also drew the line on suspicionless searches by police of luggage on public transportation in an opinion by Chief Justice Rehnquist; Justices Breyer and Scalia dissented.

In its 2001–2002 term, the Court will consider the constitutionality of requiring consent to warrantless searches as a condition of probation, in *United States v. Knights* (No. 00-1260). Knights was suspected of vandalism of the property of Pacific Gas and Electric (PG&E). At the time, he was on probation after a conviction for a drug offense. And a term of his probation required him to allow searches of his "person, property, place of residence, vehicle, and personal effects" at any time, "with or without a search warrant, warrant of arrest or reasonable cause by any probation officer or law enforcement officer." Based on that condition of probation, a police detective conducted a warrantless search of Knights's home and found a detonation cord, ammunition, liquid chemicals, and manuals on chemical and electrical circuitry, bolt cutters, drug paraphernalia, blueprints stolen from the burglarized building, and a brass padlock stamped "PG&E." Knights was arrested and indicted, but his lawyer moved to suppress the evidence obtained in the search on the ground that the search violated the protections of the Fourth Amendment. Subsequently, the Court of Appeals for the Ninth Circuit held that search violated the Fourth Amendment because it was not a genuine attempt to enforce probation but instead motivated by law enforcement interests in avoiding the Fourth Amendment's requirements in pursuing criminal investigations.

Illinois v. Wardlow
528 U.S. 119, 120 S.Ct. 673 (2000)

Around noon in an area of Chicago known for drug trafficking, two uniformed police officers were riding in the last of a four-car police caravan when they noticed William Wardlow holding an opaque bag. After looking in their direction, Wardlow fled down an alley and the officers followed, eventually cornering him. During a pat-down search for weapons, one of the officers squeezed the bag and felt a heavy object, which turned out to be a .38-caliber handgun. At his trial, Wardlow's attorney moved to suppress the use of the gun as evidence on the ground that the officer did not have a "reasonable suspicion" to justify the search and seizure under *Terry v. Ohio*, 392 U.S. 1 (1968). The trial court disagreed, but a state appellate court reversed Wardlow's conviction and the Illinois Supreme Court affirmed, concluding that a sudden flight from police, even in a high crime area, does not create a "reasonable suspicion" to justify a *Terry* stop. The state appealed and the Supreme Court granted review.

The state supreme court's decision was reversed in a five to four decision, with the opinion delivered by Chief Justice Rehnquist. Justice Stevens filed an opinion in part concurring and dissenting, which Justices Breyer, Ginsburg, and Souter joined.

Chief Justice REHNQUIST delivered the opinion of the Court.

This case, involving a brief encounter between a citizen and a police officer on a public street, is governed by the analysis we first applied in *Terry* [*v. Ohio*].

In *Terry*, we held that an officer may, consistent with the Fourth Amendment, conduct a brief, investigatory stop when the officer has a reasonable, articulable suspicion that criminal activity is afoot. While "reasonable suspicion" is a less demanding standard than probable cause and requires a showing considerably less than preponderance of the evidence, the Fourth Amendment requires at least a minimal level of objective justification for making the stop.

An individual's presence in an area of expected criminal activity, standing alone, is not enough to support a reasonable, particularized suspicion that the person is committing a crime. But officers are not required to ignore the relevant characteristics of a location in determining whether the circumstances are sufficiently suspicious to warrant further investigation. . . .

In this case, moreover, it was not merely respondent's presence in an area of heavy narcotics trafficking that aroused the officers' suspicion but his unprovoked flight upon noticing the police. Our cases have also recognized that nervous, evasive behavior is a pertinent factor in determining reasonable suspicion. Headlong flight—wherever it occurs—is the consummate act of evasion: it is not necessarily indicative of wrongdoing, but it is certainly suggestive of such. In reviewing the propriety of an officer's conduct, courts do not have available empirical studies dealing with inferences drawn from suspicious behavior, and we cannot reasonably demand scientific certainty from judges or law enforcement officers where none exists. Thus, the determination of reasonable suspicion must be based on commonsense judgments and inferences about human behavior. We conclude Officer Nolan was justified in suspecting that Wardlow was involved in criminal activity, and, therefore, in investigating further. . . .

Justice STEVENS, with whom Justice SOUTER, Justice GINSBURG, and Justice BREYER join, concurring in part and dissenting in part.

Guided by that totality-of-the-circumstances test, the Court concludes that Officer Nolan had reasonable suspicion to stop respondent. In this respect, my view differs from the Court's. The entire justification for the stop is articulated in the brief testimony of Officer Nolan. Some facts are perfectly clear; others are not. This factual insufficiency leads me to conclude that the Court's judgment is mistaken.

Nolan was part of an eight-officer, four-car caravan patrol team. The officers were headed for "one of the areas in the 11th District [of Chicago] that's high [in] narcotics traffic." The reason why four cars were in the caravan was that "[n]ormally in these different areas there's an enormous amount of people, sometimes lookouts, customers." Officer Nolan testified that he was in uniform on that day, but he did not recall whether he was driving a marked or an unmarked car.

Officer Nolan and his partner were in the last of the four patrol cars that "were all caravaning eastbound down Van Buren." Nolan first observed respondent "in front of 4035 West Van Buren." Wardlow "looked in our direction and began fleeing." Nolan then "began driving southbound down the street observing [respondent] running through the gangway and the alley southbound," and observed that Wardlow was carrying a white, opaque bag under his arm. After the car turned south and intercepted respondent as he "ran right towards us,"

Officer Nolan stopped him and conducted a "protective search," which revealed that the bag under respondent's arm contained a loaded handgun.

This terse testimony is most noticeable for what it fails to reveal. Though asked whether he was in a marked or unmarked car, Officer Nolan could not recall the answer. He was not asked whether any of the other three cars in the caravan were marked, or whether any of the other seven officers were in uniform. Though he explained that the size of the caravan was because "[n]ormally in these different areas there's an enormous amount of people, sometimes lookouts, customers," Officer Nolan did not testify as to whether anyone besides Wardlow was nearby 4035 West Van Buren. Nor is it clear that that address was the intended destination of the caravan. As the Appellate Court of Illinois interpreted the record, "it appears that the officers were simply driving by, on their way to some unidentified location, when they noticed defendant standing at 4035 West Van Buren." Officer Nolan's testimony also does not reveal how fast the officers were driving. It does not indicate whether he saw respondent notice the other patrol cars. And it does not say whether the caravan, or any part of it, had already passed Wardlow by before he began to run. . . .

No other factors sufficiently support a finding of reasonable suspicion. . . . Officer Nolan did testify that he expected to find "an enormous amount of people," including drug customers or lookouts, and the Court points out that "[i]t was in this context that Officer Nolan decided to investigate Wardlow after observing him flee." This observation, in my view, lends insufficient weight to the reasonable suspicion analysis; indeed, in light of the absence of testimony that anyone else was nearby when respondent began to run, this observation points in the opposite direction. . . .

It is the State's burden to articulate facts sufficient to support reasonable suspicion. In my judgment, Illinois has failed to discharge that burden. I am not persuaded that the mere fact that someone standing on a sidewalk looked in the direction of a passing car before starting to run is sufficient to justify a forcible stop and frisk.

Bond v. United States
529 U.S. 334, 120 S.Ct. 1462 (2000)

The facts are stated by Chief Justice Rehnquist in the opinion of the Court, reversing the appellate court's decision. Justice Breyer filed a dissenting opinion, which Justice Scalia joined.

Chief Justice REHNQUIST delivered the opinion of the Court.

Petitioner Steven Dewayne Bond was a passenger on a Greyhound bus that left California bound for Little Rock, Arkansas. The bus stopped, as it was required to do, at the permanent Border Patrol checkpoint in Sierra Blanca, Texas. Border Patrol Agent Cesar Cantu boarded the bus to check the immigration status of its passengers. After reaching the back of the bus, having satisfied himself that the passengers were lawfully in the United States, Agent Cantu began walking toward the front. Along the way, he squeezed the soft luggage which passengers had placed in the overhead storage space above the seats.

As Agent Cantu inspected the luggage in the compartment above petitioner's seat, he squeezed a green canvas bag and noticed that it contained a "brick-like" object. Petitioner admitted that the bag was his and agreed to allow Agent Cantu to open it. Upon opening the bag, Agent Cantu discovered a "brick" of methamphetamine. The brick had been wrapped in duct tape until it was oval-shaped and then rolled in a pair of pants.

Petitioner was indicted for conspiracy to possess, and possession with intent to distribute, methamphetamine. He moved to suppress the drugs, arguing that Agent Cantu conducted an illegal search of his bag. Petitioner's motion was denied, and the District Court found him guilty on both counts and sentenced him to 57 months in prison. On appeal, he conceded that other passengers had access to his bag, but contended that Agent Cantu manipulated the bag in a way that other passengers would not. The Court of Appeals rejected this argument. . . . We granted *certiorari*, and now reverse.

[T]he Government asserts that by exposing his bag to the public, petitioner lost a reasonable expectation that his bag would not be physically manipulated. The Government relies on our decisions in *California v. Ciraolo*, [476 U.S. 207 (1986)], and *Florida v. Riley*, 488 U.S. 445 (1989), for the proposition that matters open to public observation are not protected by the Fourth Amendment. In *Ciraolo*, we held that police observation of a backyard from a plane flying at an altitude of 1,000 feet did not violate a reasonable expectation of privacy. Similarly, in *Riley*, we relied on *Ciraolo* to hold that police observation of a greenhouse in a home's curtilage from a helicopter passing at an altitude of 400 feet did not violate the Fourth Amendment. We reasoned that the property was "not necessarily protected from inspection that involves no physical invasion," and determined that because any member of the public could have lawfully observed the defendants' property by flying overhead, the defendants' expectation of privacy was "not reasonable and not one 'that society is prepared to honor.'"

But *Ciraolo* and *Riley* are different from this case because they involved only visual, as opposed to tactile, observation. Physically invasive inspection is simply more intrusive than purely visual inspection. For example, in *Terry v. Ohio*, 392 U.S. 1 (1968), we stated that a "careful [tactile] exploration of the outer surfaces of a person's clothing all over his or her body" is a "serious intrusion upon the sanctity of the person, which may inflict great indignity and arouse strong resentment, and is not to be undertaken lightly." Although Agent Cantu did not "frisk" petitioner's person, he did conduct a probing tactile examination of petitioner's carry-on luggage. Obviously, petitioner's bag was not part of his person. But travelers are particularly concerned about their carry-on luggage; they generally use it to transport personal items that, for whatever reason, they prefer to keep close at hand. . . .

Our Fourth Amendment analysis embraces two questions. First, we ask whether the individual, by his conduct, has exhibited an actual expectation of privacy; that is, whether he has shown that "he [sought] to preserve [something] as private." Here, petitioner sought to preserve privacy by using an opaque bag and placing that bag directly above his seat. Second, we inquire whether the individual's expectation of privacy is "one that society is prepared to recognize as reasonable." When a bus passenger places a bag in an overhead bin, he expects that other passengers or bus employees may move it for one reason or another. Thus, a bus passenger clearly expects that his bag may be handled. He does not expect that other passengers or bus employees will, as a matter of course, feel the bag in an exploratory manner. But this is exactly what the agent did here. We therefore hold that the agent's physical manipulation of petitioner's bag violated the Fourth Amendment.

Justice BREYER, with whom Justice SCALIA joins, dissenting.

Does a traveler who places a soft-sided bag in the shared overhead storage compartment of a bus have a "reasonable expectation" that strangers will not push, pull, prod, squeeze, or otherwise manipulate his luggage? Unlike the majority, I believe that he does not. . . .
[A]n individual cannot reasonably expect privacy in respect to objects or activities that he "knowingly exposes to the public." Indeed, the Court has said that it is not objectively reasonable to expect privacy if "[a]ny member of the public could have" used his senses to detect "everything that th[e] officers observed." *California v. Ciraolo*. Thus, it has held that the fact that strangers may look down at fenced-in property from an aircraft or sift through garbage bags on a public street can justify a similar police intrusion. Consider, too, the accepted police practice of using dogs to sniff for drugs hidden inside luggage. . . .
Of course, the agent's purpose here—searching for drugs—differs dramatically from the intention of a driver or fellow passenger who squeezes a bag in the process of making more room for another parcel. But in determining whether an expectation of privacy is reasonable, it is the effect, not the purpose, that matters. . . .
If we are to depart from established legal principles, we should not begin here. At best, this decision will lead to a constitutional jurisprudence of "squeezes," thereby complicating further already complex Fourth Amendment law, increasing the difficulty of deciding ordinary criminal matters, and hindering the administrative guidance (with its potential for control of unreasonable police practices) that a less complicated jurisprudence might provide. . . .

C. THE SPECIAL PROBLEMS OF AUTOMOBILES IN A MOBILE SOCIETY

In *Wyoming v. Houghton* (excerpted below) the Court held that police may without a warrant search the belongings of passengers in cars if they have probable cause for doing so. And in *Florida v. White* (excerpted below), the Court held that the Fourth Amendment does not require police to obtain a warrant before seizing an automobile from a public place when they have probable cause to believe that it is forfeitable contraband. However, in *Indianapolis v. Edmond* (excerpted below) the Court drew a line at checkpoint roadblocks of cars for the purpose of interdicting unlawful drugs, determining that such roadblocks violate the Fourth Amendment requirement for individualized suspicion of illegal activities as a basis for stopping cars. Yet, a bare majority ruled, in *Atwater v. Lago Vista* (excerpted below), that police may arrest and jail drivers whom they stop for routine misdemeanor traffic violations, which are punishable only by fines.

Wyoming v. Houghton
526 U.S. 295, 119 S.Ct. 1297 (1999)

In the early morning hours of July 23, 1995, a highway patrol officer stopped a car for speeding and having a faulty brake light. After noticing a syringe in the driver's shirt pocket, the officer instructed the driver and passengers to get out of the car and proceeded to search the car. The officer found the purse of one of the passengers, Sandra Houghton, on the back seat of the car and discovered inside it drugs and another syringe. Ms. Houghton was charged with felony drug possession, and at her trial, she moved to suppress the introduction of the evidence against her. The trial court dismissed her motion and she was convicted, but on appeal the Wyoming State Supreme Court reversed on the ground that the officer did not have probable cause to search the passengers' possessions. The state appealed, and the Supreme Court overruled the state supreme court's decision.

The Court's decision was six to three, and its opinion was delivered by Justice Scalia. Justice Breyer filed a concurring opinion, and Justice Stevens issued a dissenting opinion, which was joined by Justices Ginsburg and Souter.

Justice SCALIA delivered the opinion of the Court.

The Fourth Amendment protects "[t]he right of the people to be secure in their persons, houses, papers, and effects, against unreasonable searches and seizures." In determining whether a particular governmental action violates this provision, we inquire first whether the action was regarded as an unlawful search or seizure under the common law when the Amendment was framed. Where that inquiry yields no answer, we must evaluate the search or seizure under traditional standards of reasonableness by assessing, on the one hand, the degree to which it intrudes upon an individual's privacy and, on the other, the degree to which it is needed for the promotion of legitimate governmental interests.

It is uncontested in the present case that the police had probable cause to believe there were illegal drugs in the car. *Carroll v. United States*, 267 U.S. 132 (1925), similarly involved the warrantless search of a car that law enforcement officials had probable cause to believe contained contraband—in that case, bootleg liquor. The Court concluded that the Framers would have regarded such a search as reasonable in light of legislation enacted by Congress from 1789 through 1799—as well as subsequent legislation from the Founding era and beyond—that empowered customs officials to search any ship or vessel without a warrant if they had probable cause to believe that it contained goods subject to a duty. See also *United States v. Ross*, 456 U.S. 798 (1982). Thus, the Court held that "contraband goods concealed and illegally transported in an automobile or other vehicle may be searched for without a warrant" where probable cause exists.

We have furthermore read the historical evidence to show that the Framers would have regarded as reasonable (if there was probable cause) the warrantless search of containers *within* an automobile. In *Ross*, we upheld as reasonable the warrantless search of a paper bag and leather pouch found in the trunk of the defendant's car by officers who had probable cause to believe that the trunk contained drugs. . . . *Ross* summarized its holding as follows: "If probable cause justifies the search of a lawfully stopped vehicle, it justifies the search of *every part of the vehicle and its contents* that may conceal the object of the search." And our later cases describing *Ross* have characterized it as applying broadly to *all* containers within a car, without qualification as to ownership. See, e.g., *California v. Acevedo*, 500 U.S. 565 (1991). . . .

We hold that police officers with probable cause to search a car may inspect passengers' belongings found in the car that are capable of concealing the object of the search. The judgment of the Wyoming Supreme Court is reversed.

Justice STEVENS, with whom Justice SOUTER and Justice GINSBURG join, dissenting.

In all of our prior cases applying the automobile exception to the Fourth Amendment's warrant requirement, either the defendant was the operator of the vehicle and in custody of the object of the search, or no question was raised as to the defendant's ownership or custody. . . . [T]he Court's rights-restrictive approach is not dictated by precedent. For example, in *United States v. Ross*, we were concerned with the interest of the driver in the integrity of "his automobile," and we categorically rejected the notion that the scope of a warrantless search of a vehicle might be "defined by the nature of the container in which the contraband is secreted." "Rather, it is defined by the object of the search and the places in which there is probable cause to believe that it may be found." We thus disapproved of a possible container-based distinction between a man's pocket and a woman's pocketbook. Ironically, while we concluded in *Ross* that "[p]robable cause to believe that a container placed in the trunk of a taxi contains contraband or evidence does not justify a search of the entire cab," the rule the Court fashions would apparently permit a warrantless search of a passenger's briefcase if there is probable cause to believe the taxidriver had a syringe somewhere in his vehicle. . . .

Finally, in my view, the State's legitimate interest in effective law enforcement does not outweigh the privacy concerns at issue. I am as confident in a police officer's ability to apply a rule requiring a warrant or individualized probable cause to search belongings that are—as in this case—obviously owned by and in the custody of a passenger as is the Court in a "passenger-confederate[']s" ability to circumvent the rule. Certainly the ostensible clarity of the Court's rule is attractive. But that virtue is insufficient justification for its adoption. Moreover, a rule requiring a warrant or individualized probable cause to search passenger belongings is every bit as simple as the Court's rule; it simply protects more privacy.

Florida v. White
526 U.S. 559, 119 S.Ct. 1555 (1999)

The facts are discussed by Justice Thomas in the opinion for the Court, reversing a decision of the Florida State Supreme Court. The Court's decision was seven to two, with Justice Souter filing a concurring opinion and Justice Stevens filing a dissenting opinion, which Justice Ginsburg joined.

Justice THOMAS delivered the opinion of the Court.

The Florida Contraband Forfeiture Act provides that certain forms of contraband, including motor vehicles used in violation of the Act's provisions, may be seized and potentially forfeited. In this case, we must decide whether the Fourth Amendment requires the police to obtain a warrant before seizing an automobile from a public place when they have probable cause to believe that it is forfeitable contraband. We hold that it does not.

On three occasions in July and August 1993, police officers observed respondent Tyvessel Tyvorus White using his car to deliver cocaine, and thereby developed probable cause to believe that his car was subject to forfeiture under the Florida Contraband Forfeiture Act. Several months later, the police arrested respondent at his place of employment on charges unrelated to the drug transactions observed in July and August 1993. At the same time, the arresting officers, without securing a warrant, seized respondent's automobile in accordance with the provisions of the Act. They seized the vehicle solely because they believed that it was forfeitable under the Act. During a subsequent inventory search, the police found two pieces of crack cocaine in the ashtray. Based on the discovery of the cocaine, respondent was charged with possession of a controlled substance in violation of Florida law.

At his trial on the possession charge, respondent filed a motion to suppress the evidence discovered during the inventory search. He argued that the warrantless seizure of his car violated the Fourth Amendment, thereby making the cocaine the "fruit of the poisonous tree." The trial court initially reserved ruling on respondent's motion, but later denied it after the jury returned a guilty verdict. On appeal, the Florida First District Court of Appeal affirmed. . . . Because the Florida Supreme Court and this Court had not directly addressed the issue, the court certified to the Florida Supreme Court the question whether, absent exigent circumstances, the warrantless seizure of an automobile under the Act violated the Fourth Amendment.

In a divided opinion, the Florida Supreme Court answered the certified question in the affirmative, quashed the First District Court of Appeal's opinion, and remanded. The majority of the court concluded that, absent exigent circumstances, the Fourth Amendment requires the police to obtain a warrant prior to seizing property that has been used in violation of the Act. . . . We granted *certiorari* and now reverse. . . .

In deciding whether a challenged governmental action violates the Amendment, we have taken care to inquire whether the action was regarded as an unlawful search and seizure when the Amendment was framed. See *Wyoming v. Houghton*, [526 U.S. 295] (1999); *Carroll v. United States*, 267 U.S. 132 (1925).

In *Carroll*, we held that when federal officers have probable cause to believe that an automobile contains contraband, the Fourth Amendment does not require them to obtain a warrant prior to searching the car for and seizing the contraband. Our holding was rooted in federal law enforcement practice at the time of the adoption of the Fourth Amendment. Specifically, we looked to laws of the First, Second, and Fourth Congresses that authorized federal officers to conduct warrantless searches of ships and to seize concealed goods subject to duties. These enactments led us to conclude that "contemporaneously with the adoption of the Fourth Amendment," Congress distinguished "the necessity for a search warrant between goods subject to forfeiture, when concealed in a dwelling house or similar place, and like goods in course of transportation and concealed in a movable vessel where they readily could be put out of reach of a search warrant." . . .

In addition to the special considerations recognized in the context of movable items, our Fourth Amendment jurisprudence has consistently accorded law enforcement officials greater latitude in exercising their duties in public places. . . . Indeed, the facts of this case are nearly indistinguishable from those in *G. M. Leasing Corp. v. United States*, 429 U.S. 338 (1977). There, we considered whether federal agents violated the Fourth Amendment by failing to secure a warrant prior to seizing automobiles in partial satisfaction of income tax assessments. We concluded that they did not, reasoning that "[t]he seizures of the automobiles in this case took place on public streets, parking lots, or other open places, and did not involve any invasion of privacy." Here, because the police seized respondent's vehicle from a public area—respondent's employer's parking lot—the warrantless seizure also did not involve any invasion of respondent's privacy. . . .

The judgment of the Florida Supreme Court is reversed, and the case is remanded for proceedings not inconsistent with this opinion.

Justice STEVENS, with whom Justice GINSBURG joins, dissenting.

Because the Fourth Amendment plainly "protects property as well as privacy" and seizures as well as searches, I would apply to the present case our longstanding warrant presumption. In the context of property seizures by law enforcement authorities, the presumption might be overcome more easily in the absence of an accompanying privacy or liberty interest. Nevertheless, I would look to the warrant clause as a measure of reasonableness in such cases, and the circumstances of this case do not convince me that the role of a neutral magistrate was dispensable. . . .

Were we confronted with property that Florida deemed unlawful for private citizens to possess regardless of purpose, and had the State relied on the plainview doctrine, perhaps a warrantless seizure would have been defensible. But "[t]here is nothing even remotely criminal in possessing an automobile," *Austin v. United States*, 509 U.S. 602 (1993); no serious fear for officer safety or loss of evidence can be asserted in this case considering the delay and circumstances of the seizure; and only the automobile exception is at issue. . . .

Indianapolis v. Edmond
531 U.S. 32 (2000), 121 S.Ct. 447 (2000)

In 1998, Indianapolis established checkpoint roadblocks in an effort to interdict unlawful drugs. The checkpoints were identified with lighted signs reading "NARCOTICS CHECKPOINT ___ MILE AHEAD, NARCOTICS IN USE, BE PREPARED TO STOP." Once a group of cars were stopped, police conducted an open-view examination of each vehicle, while narcotics-detection dogs circled outside of each vehicle. Over a period of four months, police stopped 1,161 cars and arrested 104 motorists; 55 arrests were for drug-related crimes and 49 were for other offenses. James Edmond was one who was stopped and he sued, challenging the constitutionality of the roadblocks as a violation of the Fourth Amendment. A federal district court upheld the roadblocks but was reversed by the Court of Appeals for the Seventh Circuit.

The Court affirmed the appellate court decision by a six to three vote. Justice O'Connor delivered the opinion of the Court. Chief Justice Rehnquist filed a dissenting opinion, which was joined by Justices Scalia and Thomas, and the latter also filed a dissenting opinion.

Justice O'CONNOR delivered the opinion of the Court.

In *Michigan Dept. of State Police v. Sitz*, 496 U.S. 444 (1990), and *United States v. Martinez-Fuerte*, 428 U.S. 543 (1976), we held that brief, suspicionless seizures at highway checkpoints for the purposes of combating drunk driving and intercepting illegal immigrants were constitutional. We now consider the constitutionality of a highway checkpoint program whose primary purpose is the discovery and interdiction of illegal narcotics. . . .

The Fourth Amendment requires that searches and seizures be reasonable. A search or seizure is ordinarily unreasonable in the absence of individualized suspicion of wrongdoing. *Chandler v. Miller*, 520 U.S. 305 (1997). While such suspicion is not an "irreducible" component of reasonableness, we have recognized only limited circumstances in which the usual rule does not apply. For example, we have upheld certain regimes of suspicionless searches where the program was designed to serve "special needs, beyond the normal need for law enforcement." See, e.g., *Vernonia School Dist. 47J v. Acton*, 515 U.S. 646 (1995) (random drug testing of student-athletes); *Treasury Employees v. Von Raab*, 489 U.S. 656 (1989) (drug tests for United States Customs Service employees seeking transfer or promotion to certain positions); *Skinner v. Railway Labor Executives' Assn.*, 489 U.S. 602 (1989) (drug and alcohol tests for railway employees involved in train accidents or found to be in violation of particular safety regulations). We have also allowed searches for certain administrative purposes without articulated suspicion of misconduct, provided that those searches are appropriately limited. See, e.g., *New York v. Burger*, 482 U.S. 691 1987) (warrantless administrative inspection of premises of "closely regulated" business); *Michigan v. Tyler*, 436 U.S. 499 (1978) (administrative inspection of fire-damaged premises to determine cause of blaze); *Camara v. Municipal Court of City and County of San Francisco*, 387 U.S. 523 (1967) (administrative inspection to ensure compliance with city housing code).

We have also upheld brief, suspicionless seizures of motorists at a fixed Border Patrol checkpoint designed to intercept illegal aliens, *Martinez-Fuerte*, and at a sobriety checkpoint aimed at removing drunk drivers from the road, *Michigan Dept. of State Police v. Sitz*. In addition, in *Delaware v. Prouse*, 440 U.S. 648 (1979), we suggested that a similar type of roadblock with the purpose of verifying drivers' licenses and vehicle registrations would be permissible. In none of these cases, however, did we indicate approval of a checkpoint program whose primary purpose was to detect evidence of ordinary criminal wrongdoing. . . .

In *Sitz*, we evaluated the constitutionality of a Michigan highway sobriety checkpoint program. The *Sitz* checkpoint involved brief suspicionless stops of motorists so that police officers could detect signs of intoxication and remove impaired drivers from the road. Motorists who exhibited signs of intoxication were diverted for a license and registration check and, if warranted, further sobriety tests. This checkpoint program was clearly aimed at reducing the immediate hazard posed by the presence of drunk drivers on the highways, and there was an obvious connection between the imperative of highway safety and the law enforcement practice at issue. The gravity of the drunk driving problem and the magnitude of the State's interest in getting drunk drivers off the road weighed heavily in our determination that the program was constitutional.

In *Prouse*, we invalidated a discretionary, suspicionless stop for a spot check of a motorist's driver's license and vehicle registration. The officer's conduct in that case was unconstitutional primarily on account of his exercise of "standardless and unconstrained discretion." We nonetheless acknowledged the States' "vital interest in ensuring that only those qualified to do so are permitted to operate motor vehicles, that these vehicles are fit for safe operation, and hence that licensing, registration, and vehicle inspection requirements are being observed." Accordingly, we suggested that "[q]uestioning of all oncoming traffic at roadblock-type stops" would be a lawful means of serving this interest in highway safety. . . .

Not only does the common thread of highway safety thus run through *Sitz* and *Prouse*, but *Prouse* itself reveals a difference in the Fourth Amendment significance of highway safety interests and the general interest in crime control. . . .

We have never approved a checkpoint program whose primary purpose was to detect evidence of ordinary criminal wrongdoing. Rather, our checkpoint cases have recognized only limited exceptions to the general rule that a seizure must be accompanied by some measure of individualized suspicion. . . .

The primary purpose of the Indianapolis narcotics checkpoints is in the end to advance "the general interest in crime control," *Prouse*. We decline to suspend the usual requirement of individualized suspicion where the police seek to employ a checkpoint primarily for the ordinary enterprise of investigating crimes. We cannot sanction stops justified only by the generalized and ever-present possibility that interrogation and inspection may reveal that any given motorist has committed some crime.

Of course, there are circumstances that may justify a law enforcement checkpoint where the primary purpose would otherwise, but for some emergency, relate to ordinary crime control. For example, as the Court of Appeals noted, the Fourth Amendment would almost certainly permit an appropriately tailored roadblock set up to thwart an imminent terrorist attack or to catch a dangerous criminal who is likely to flee by way of a particular route. The exigencies created by these scenarios are far removed from the circumstances under which authorities might simply stop cars as a matter of course to see if there just happens to be a felon leaving the jurisdiction. . . .

It goes without saying that our holding today does nothing to alter the constitutional status of the sobriety and border checkpoints that we approved in *Sitz* and *Martinez-Fuerte*, or of the type of traffic checkpoint that we suggested would be lawful in *Prouse*. The constitutionality of such checkpoint programs still depends on a balancing of the competing interests at stake and the effectiveness of the program. When law enforcement authorities pursue primarily general crime control purposes at checkpoints such as here, however, stops can only be justified by some quantum of individualized suspicion. . . .

Because the primary purpose of the Indianapolis checkpoint program is ultimately indistinguishable from the general interest in crime control, the checkpoints violate the Fourth Amendment. The judgment of the Court of Appeals is accordingly affirmed.

Chief Justice REHNQUIST, with whom Justice THOMAS joins, and with whom Justice SCALIA joins as to Part I, dissenting.

This case follows naturally from *Martinez-Fuerte* and *Sitz*. . . . The use of roadblocks to look for signs of impairment was validated by *Sitz*, and the use of roadblocks to check for driver's licenses and vehicle registrations was expressly recognized in *Delaware v. Prouse*. . . .

Because of the valid reasons for conducting these roadblock seizures, it is constitutionally irrelevant that petitioners also hoped to interdict drugs. . . . [T]he roadblocks here are objectively reasonable because they serve the substantial interests of preventing drunken driving and checking for driver's licenses and vehicle registrations with minimal intrusion on motorists. . . .

The seizure is objectively reasonable as it lasts, on average, two to three minutes and does not involve a search. The subjective intrusion is likewise limited as the checkpoints are clearly marked and operated by uniformed officers who are directed to stop every vehicle in the same manner. The only difference between this case and *Sitz* is the presence of the dog. We have already held, however, that a "sniff test" by a trained narcotics dog is not a "search" within the meaning of the Fourth Amendment because it does not require physical intrusion of the object being sniffed and it does not expose anything other than the contraband items. *United States v. Place*, 462 U.S. 696 (1983). And there is nothing in the record to indicate that the dog sniff lengthens the stop. Finally, the checkpoints' success rate—49 arrests for offenses unrelated to drugs—only confirms the State's legitimate interests in preventing drunken driving and ensuring the proper licensing of drivers and registration of their vehicles.

These stops effectively serve the State's legitimate interests; they are executed in a regularized and neutral manner; and they only minimally intrude upon the privacy of the motorists. They should therefore be constitutional. . . .

Justice THOMAS, dissenting.

Taken together, our decisions in *Michigan Dept. of State Police v. Sitz*, and *United States v. Martinez-Fuerte* stand for the proposition that suspicionless roadblock seizures are constitutionally permissible if conducted according to a plan that limits the discretion of the officers conducting the stops. I am not convinced that *Sitz* and *Martinez-Fuerte* were correctly decided. Indeed, I rather doubt that the Framers of the Fourth Amendment would have considered "reasonable" a program of indiscriminate stops of individuals not suspected of wrongdoing.

Respondents did not, however, advocate the overruling of *Sitz* and *Martinez-Fuerte*, and I am reluctant to consider such a step without the benefit of briefing and argument. For the reasons given by The Chief Justice, I believe that those cases compel upholding the program at issue here. I, therefore, join his opinion.

Atwater v. Lago Vista
121 S.Ct. 1536 (2001)

In Texas, if a car is equipped with safety belts, a front-seat passenger must wear one and the driver must secure any small child riding in front. Violation of either provision is "a misdemeanor punishable by a fine not less than $25 or more than $50." Texas law expressly authorizes "[a]ny peace officer [to] arrest without warrant a person found committing a violation" of these seat belt laws, although it permits police to issue citations in lieu of arrest.

In March 1997, Gail Atwater was driving her pickup truck in Lago Vista, Texas, with her three-year-old son and five-year-old daughter in the front seat. None of them was wearing a seat belt. A Lago Vista police officer observed the seat belt violations and pulled Atwater over. According to Atwater, the officer approached the truck and "yell[ed]" something to the effect of "[w]e've met before" and "[y]ou're going to jail." He then called for backup and asked to see Atwater's driver's license and insurance documentation, which state law required her to carry. When Atwater told him that she did not have the papers because her purse had been stolen the day before, the officer said that he had "heard that story two hundred times." Atwater asked to take her "frightened, upset, and crying" children to a friend's house nearby, but the officer told her, "[y]ou're not going anywhere." As it turned out, Atwater's friend learned what was going on and soon arrived to take charge of the children. The officer then handcuffed Atwater and drove her to the local police station, where booking officers had her remove her shoes, jewelry, and eyeglasses, and empty her pockets. Officers took Atwater's "mug shot" and placed her in a jail cell for an hour, after which period she was taken before a magistrate and released on $310 bond. Atwater was charged with driving without her seat belt fastened, failing to secure her children in seat belts, driving without a license, and failing to provide proof of insurance. She pleaded no contest to the misdemeanor seat belt offenses and paid a $50 fine.

Subsequently, Atwater filed suit in a state court against the officer and the city of Lago Vista, alleging that her "right to be free from unreasonable seizure" had been violated. The city moved the suit to a federal district court, which deemed the Fourth Amendment claim "meritless." On appeal, a panel of the Court of Appeals for the Fifth Circuit reversed, concluding that "an arrest for a first-time seat belt offense" was an unreasonable seizure within the meaning of the Fourth Amendment. But sitting *en banc*, the Court of Appeals vacated that decision and affirmed the district court's judgment for the city. Atwater appealed to the Supreme Court, which granted *certiorari*.

The appellate court's decision was affirmed by a five to four vote. Justice Souter delivered the opinion for the Court. Justice O'Connor filed a dissenting opinion, which Justices Stevens, Ginsburg, and Breyer joined.

Justice SOUTER delivered the opinion of the Court.

The question is whether the Fourth Amendment forbids a warrantless arrest for a minor criminal offense, such as a misdemeanor seatbelt violation punishable only by a fine. We hold that it does not.

We begin with the state of pre-founding English common law and find that, even after making some allowance for variations in the common-law usage of the term "breach of the peace," the "founding-era common-law rules" were not nearly as clear as Atwater claims; on the contrary, the common-law commentators (as well as the sparsely reported cases) reached divergent conclusions with respect to officers' warrantless misdemeanor arrest power.

Atwater's historical argument begins with our quotation from Halsbury in *Carroll v. United States*, 267 U.S. 132 (1925), that "'[i]n cases of misdemeanor, a peace officer like a private person has at common law no power of arresting without a warrant except when a breach of the peace has been committed in his presence or there is reasonable ground for supposing that a breach of peace is about to be committed or renewed in his presence.'" But the isolated quotation tends to mislead. In *Carroll* itself we spoke of the common-law rule as only "sometimes expressed" that way and, indeed, in the very same paragraph, we conspicuously omitted any reference to a breach-of-the-peace limitation in stating that the "usual rule" at common law was that "a police officer [could] arrest without warrant . . . one guilty of a misdemeanor if committed in his presence." Thus, what *Carroll* illustrates, and what others have recognized, is that statements about the common law of warrantless misdemeanor arrest simply are not uniform. Rather, "[a]t common law there is a difference of opinion among the authorities as to whether this right to arrest [without a warrant] extends to all misdemeanors." American Law Institute, Code of Criminal Procedure. . . .

We thus find disagreement, not unanimity, among both the common-law jurists and the text-writers who sought to pull the cases together and summarize accepted practice. Having reviewed the relevant English decisions, as well as English and colonial American legal treatises, legal dictionaries, and procedure manuals, we simply are not convinced that Atwater's is the correct, or even necessarily the better, reading of the common-law history.

A second, and equally serious, problem for Atwater's historical argument is posed by the "divers Statutes," enacted by Parliament well before this Republic's founding that authorized warrantless misdemeanor arrests without reference to violence or turmoil. Quite apart from Hale and Blackstone, the legal background of any conception of reasonableness the Fourth Amendment's Framers might have entertained would have included English statutes, some centuries old, authorizing peace officers (and even private persons) to make warrantless arrests for all sorts of relatively minor offenses unaccompanied by violence. . . .

An examination of specifically American evidence is to the same effect. Neither the history of the framing era nor subsequent legal development indicates that the Fourth Amendment was originally understood, or has traditionally been read, to embrace Atwater's position.

To begin with, Atwater has cited no particular evidence that those who framed and ratified the Fourth Amendment sought to limit peace officers' warrantless misdemeanor arrest authority to instances of actual breach of the peace, and our own review of the recent and respected compilations of framing-era documentary history has likewise failed to reveal any such design. Nor have we found in any of the modern historical accounts of the Fourth Amendment's adoption any substantial indication that the Framers intended such a restriction. Indeed, to the extent the modern histories address the issue, their conclusions are to the contrary.

The evidence of actual practice also counsels against Atwater's position. During the period leading up to and surrounding the framing of the Bill of Rights, colonial and state legislatures, like Parliament before them, regularly authorized local peace officers to make warrantless misdemeanor arrests without conditioning statutory authority on breach of the peace. . . .

Nor does Atwater's argument from tradition pick up any steam from the historical record as it has unfolded since the framing, there being no indication that her claimed rule has ever become "woven . . . into the fabric" of American law. The story, on the contrary, is of two centuries of uninterrupted (and largely unchallenged) state and federal practice permitting warrantless arrests for misdemeanors not amounting to or involving breach of the peace. . . .

Small wonder, then, that today statutes in all 50 States and the District of Columbia permit warrantless misdemeanor arrests by at least some (if not all) peace officers without requiring any breach of the peace, as do a host of congressional enactments. . . .

If we were to derive a rule exclusively to address the uncontested facts of this case, Atwater might well prevail. She was a known and established resident of Lago Vista with no place to hide and no incentive to flee, and common sense says she would almost certainly have buckled up as a condition of driving off with a citation. In her case, the physical incidents of arrest were merely gratuitous humiliations imposed by a police officer who was (at best) exercising extremely poor judgment. Atwater's claim to live free of pointless indignity and confinement clearly outweighs anything the City can raise against it specific to her case.

But we have traditionally recognized that a responsible Fourth Amendment balance is not well served by standards requiring sensitive, case-by-case determinations of government need, lest every discretionary judgment in the field be converted into an occasion for constitutional review. Often enough, the Fourth Amendment has to be applied on the spur (and in the heat) of the moment, and the object in implementing its command of reasonableness is to draw standards sufficiently clear and simple to be applied with a fair prospect of surviving judicial second-guessing months and years after an arrest or search is made. Courts attempting to strike a reasonable Fourth Amendment balance thus credit the government's side with an essential interest in readily administrable rules.

At first glance, Atwater's argument may seem to respect the values of clarity and simplicity, so far as she claims that the Fourth Amendment generally forbids warrantless arrests for minor crimes not accompanied by violence or some demonstrable threat of it (whether "minor crime" be defined as a fine-only traffic offense, a fine-only offense more generally, or a misdemeanor). But the claim is not ultimately so simple, nor could it be, for complications arise the moment we begin to think about the possible applications of the several criteria Atwater proposes for drawing a line between minor crimes with limited arrest authority and others not so restricted.

One line, she suggests, might be between "jailable" and "fine-only" offenses, between those for which conviction could result in commitment and those for which it could not. The trouble with this distinction, of course, is that an officer on the street might not be able to tell. It is not merely that we cannot expect every police officer to know the details of frequently complex penalty schemes, but that penalties for ostensibly identical conduct can vary on account of facts difficult (if not impossible) to know at the scene of an arrest. Is this the first offense or is the suspect a repeat offender? Is the weight of the marijuana a gram above or a gram below the fine-only line? Where conduct could implicate more than one criminal prohibition, which one will the district attorney ultimately decide to charge? And so on. . . .

There is no need for more examples to show that Atwater's general rule and limiting proviso promise very little in the way of administrability. . . . Atwater's rule therefore would not only place police in an almost impossible spot but would guarantee increased litigation over many of the arrests that would occur. . . .

Accordingly, we confirm today what our prior cases have intimated: the standard of probable cause "applie[s] to all arrests, without the need to 'balance' the interests and circumstances involved in particular situations." *Dunaway v. New York*, 442 U.S. 200 (1979). If an officer has probable cause to believe that an individual has committed even a very minor criminal offense in his presence, he may, without violating the Fourth Amendment, arrest the offender. . . .

Justice O'CONNOR, with whom Justice STEVENS, Justice GINSBURG, and Justice BREYER join, dissenting.

A full custodial arrest, such as the one to which Ms. Atwater was subjected, is the quintessential seizure. See *Payton v. New York*, 445 U.S. 573 (1980). When a full custodial arrest is effected without a warrant, the plain language of the Fourth Amendment requires that the arrest be reasonable. It is beyond cavil that "[t]he touchstone of our analysis under the Fourth Amendment is always 'the reasonableness in all the circumstances of the particular governmental invasion of a citizen's personal security.'" *Pennsylvania v. Mimms*, 434 U.S. 106 (1977).

We have "often looked to the common law in evaluating the reasonableness, for Fourth Amendment purposes, of police activity." *Tennessee v. Garner*, 471 U.S. 1 (1985). But history is just one of the tools we use in conducting the reasonableness inquiry. And when history is inconclusive, as the majority amply demonstrates it is in this case, we will "evaluate the search or seizure under traditional standards of reasonableness by assessing, on the one hand, the degree to which it intrudes upon an individual's privacy and, on the other, the degree to which it is needed for the promotion of legitimate governmental interests." *Wyoming v. Houghton*, [526 U.S. 295 (1999)].

[W]e have held that the existence of probable cause is a necessary condition for an arrest. And in the case of felonies punishable by a term of imprisonment, we have held that the existence of probable cause is also a sufficient condition for an arrest. See *United States v. Watson*, 423 U.S. 411 (1976). In *Watson*, however, there was a clear and consistently applied common law rule permitting warrantless felony arrests. Accordingly, our inquiry ended there and we had no need to assess the reasonableness of such arrests by weighing individual liberty interests against state interests.

Here, however, we have no such luxury. The Court's thorough exegesis makes it abundantly clear that warrantless misdemeanor arrests were not the subject of a clear and consistently applied rule at common law. We therefore must engage in the balancing test required by the Fourth Amendment. While probable cause is surely a necessary condition for warrantless arrests for fine-only offenses, any realistic assessment of the interests implicated by such arrests demonstrates that probable cause alone is not a sufficient condition.

Our decision in *Whren v. United States*, 517 U.S. 806 (1996), is not to the contrary. The specific question presented there was whether, in evaluating the Fourth Amendment reasonableness of a traffic stop, the subjective intent of the police officer is a relevant consideration. We held that it is not, and stated that "[t]he making of a traffic stop . . . is governed by the usual rule that probable cause to believe the law has been broken 'outbalances' private interest in avoiding police contact."

We of course did not have occasion in *Whren* to consider the constitutional preconditions for warrantless arrests for fine-only offenses. Nor should our words be taken beyond their context. There are significant qualitative differences between a traffic stop and a full custodial arrest. . . .

A custodial arrest exacts an obvious toll on an individual's liberty and privacy, even when the period of custody is relatively brief. The arrestee is subject to a full search of her person and confiscation of her possessions. If the arrestee is the occupant of a car, the entire passenger compartment of the car, including packages therein, is subject to search as well. The arrestee may be detained for up to 48 hours without having a magistrate determine whether there in fact was probable cause for the arrest. See *County of Riverside v. McLaughlin*, 500 U.S. 44 (1991). Because people arrested for all types of violent and nonviolent offenses may be housed together awaiting such review, this detention period is potentially dangerous. And once the period of custody is over, the fact of the arrest is a permanent part of the public record. *Paul v. Davis*, 424 U.S. 693 (1976). . . .

Because a full custodial arrest is such a severe intrusion on an individual's liberty, its reasonableness hinges on "the degree to which it is needed for the promotion of legitimate governmental interests." *Wyoming v. Houghton.* In light of the availability of citations to promote a State's interests when a fine-only offense has been committed, I cannot concur in a rule which deems a full custodial arrest to be reasonable in every circumstance. Giving police officers constitutional carte blanche to effect an arrest whenever there is probable cause to believe a fine-only misdemeanor has been committed is irreconcilable with the Fourth Amendment's command that seizures be reasonable. Instead, I would require that when there is probable cause to believe that a fine-only offense has been committed, the police officer should issue a citation unless the officer is "able to point to specific and articulable facts which, taken together with rational inferences from those facts, reasonably warrant [the additional] intrusion" of a full custodial arrest. *Terry v. Ohio*, 392 U.S. [1 (1968)].

The majority insists that a bright-line rule focused on probable cause is necessary to vindicate the State's interest in easily administrable law enforcement rules. Probable cause itself, however, is not a model of precision. The rule I propose—which merely requires a legitimate reason for the decision to escalate the seizure into a full custodial arrest—thus does not undermine an otherwise "clear and simple" rule.

While clarity is certainly a value worthy of consideration in our Fourth Amendment jurisprudence, it by no means trumps the values of liberty and privacy at the heart of the Amendment's protections. What the *Terry* rule lacks in precision it makes up for in fidelity to the Fourth Amendment's command of reasonableness and sensitivity to the competing values protected by that Amendment. Over the past 30 years, it appears that the *Terry* rule has been workable and easily applied by officers on the street. . . .

The Court's error, however, does not merely affect the disposition of this case. The per se rule that the Court creates has potentially serious consequences for the everyday lives of Americans. A broad range of conduct falls into the category of fine-only misdemeanors. In Texas alone, for example, disobeying any sort of traffic warning sign is a misdemeanor punishable only by fine, as is failing to pay a highway toll, and driving with expired license plates. Nor are fine-only crimes limited to the traffic context. In several States, for example, littering is a criminal offense punishable only by fine.

To be sure, such laws are valid and wise exercises of the States' power to protect the public health and welfare. My concern lies not with the decision to enact or enforce these laws, but rather with the manner in which they may be enforced. Under today's holding, when a police officer has probable cause to believe that a fine-only misdemeanor offense has occurred, that officer may stop the suspect, issue a citation, and let the person continue on her way. Or, if a traffic violation, the officer may stop the car, arrest the driver, search the driver, search the entire passenger compartment of the car including any purse or package inside, and impound the car and inventory all of its contents. Although the Fourth Amendment expressly requires that the latter course be a reasonable and proportional response to the circumstances of the offense, the majority gives officers unfettered discretion to choose that course without articulating a single reason why such action is appropriate.

Such unbounded discretion carries with it grave potential for abuse. The majority takes comfort in the lack of evidence of "an epidemic of unnecessary minor-offense arrests." But the relatively small number of published cases dealing with such arrests proves little and should provide little solace. Indeed, as the recent debate over racial profiling demonstrates all too clearly, a relatively minor traffic infraction may often serve as an excuse for stopping and harassing an individual. After today, the arsenal available to any officer extends to a full arrest and the searches permissible concomitant to that arrest. . . .

The Court neglects the Fourth Amendment's express command in the name of administrative ease. In so doing, it cloaks the pointless indignity that Gail Atwater suffered with the mantle of reasonableness. I respectfully dissent.

D. OTHER GOVERNMENTAL SEARCHES IN THE ADMINISTRATIVE STATE

By a vote of six to three, in *Ferguson v. Charleston* (2001) (excerpted below), the Court struck down a state policy of testing pregnant women for cocaine use, without their consent, and informing police of those who tested positive. Writing for the Court, Justice Stevens refused to extend the "special needs" exception to the Fourth Amendment that had been applied in prior decisions upholding mandatory drug testing, whereas Justice Scalia, joined by Chief Justice Rehnquist and Justice Thomas, dissented.

Ferguson v. Charleston
121 S.Ct. 1281 (2001)

Staff members at the public hospital operated in the city of Charleston by the Medical University of South Carolina (MUSC) became concerned about an apparent increase in the use of cocaine by patients who were receiving prenatal treatment. In response, MUSC began ordering that drug screens be performed on urine samples from maternity patients who were suspected of using cocaine. If a patient tested positive, she was referred by MUSC staff to the county substance abuse commission for counseling and treatment. Subsequently, a nurse for the MUSC obstetrics department heard a news report that the police in Greenville, South Carolina, were arresting pregnant users of cocaine on the theory that such use harmed the fetus and was therefore child abuse. And she discussed the story with MUSC's general counsel, who in turn contacted Charleston Solicitor Charles Condon in order to offer MUSC's cooperation in prosecuting mothers whose children tested positive for drugs at birth. Condon, then, adopted a policy of prosecuting women who tested positive for cocaine while pregnant. Under the policy, patients who tested positive were promptly arrested. In 1990, however, the policy was modified to give the patient who tested positive during labor, like the patient who tested positive during a prenatal care visit, an opportunity to avoid arrest by consenting to substance abuse treatment.

Ten women who received obstetrical care at MUSC and who were arrested after testing positive for cocaine challenged the constitutionality of drug-testing policy. They challenged the validity of the policy under various theories, including the claim that warrantless and nonconsensual drug tests conducted for criminal investigatory purposes were unconstitutional searches. Attorneys for the city of Charleston countered that, (1) as a matter of fact, petitioners had consented to the searches and, (2) as a matter of law, the searches were reasonable, even absent consent, because they were justified by special non-law-enforcement purposes. A federal district court rejected the second defense because the searches in question "were not done by the medical university for independent purposes. [Instead,] the police came in and there was an agreement reached that the positive screens would be shared with the police." Accordingly, the district court submitted the factual defense to the jury with instructions that required a verdict in favor of petitioners unless the jury found consent. The jury found for the city and the women appealed. The Court of Appeals for the Fourth Circuit affirmed, finding that the searches were reasonable as a matter of law under precedents recognizing that "special needs" may, in certain exceptional circumstances, justify such searches, *Treasury Employees v. Von Raab*, 489 U.S. 656 (1989), and *Vernonia School Dist. 47J v. Acton*, 515 U.S. 646 (1995). The women appealed that decision and the Supreme Court granted *certiorari*.

The appellate court was reversed by a vote of six to three in an opinion for the Court delivered by Justice Stevens. Justice Kennedy filed a concurring opinion and Justice Scalia filed a dissenting opinion, which Chief Justice Rehnquist and Justice Thomas joined.

Justice STEVENS delivered the opinion of the Court.

In this case, we must decide whether a state hospital's performance of a diagnostic test to obtain evidence of a patient's criminal conduct for law enforcement purposes is an unreasonable search if the patient has not consented to the procedure. More narrowly, the question is whether the interest in using the threat of criminal sanctions to deter pregnant women from using cocaine can justify a departure from the general rule that an official nonconsensual search is unconstitutional if not authorized by a valid warrant. . . .

[T]he urine tests conducted by those staff members were indisputably searches within the meaning of the Fourth Amendment. Neither the District Court nor the Court of Appeals concluded that any of the . . . criteria used to identify the women to be searched provided either probable cause to believe that they were using cocaine, or even the basis for a reasonable suspicion of such use. Rather, the District Court and the Court of Appeals viewed the case as one involving MUSC's right to conduct searches without warrants or probable cause. Furthermore, given the posture in which the case comes to us, we must assume for purposes of our decision that the tests were performed without the informed consent of the patients.

Because the hospital seeks to justify its authority to conduct drug tests and to turn the results over to law enforcement agents without the knowledge or consent of the patients, this case differs from the four previous cases in which we have considered whether comparable drug tests "fit within the closely guarded category of constitutionally permissible suspicionless searches." *Chandler v. Miller*, 520 U.S. 305 (1997). In three of those cases, we sustained drug tests for railway employees involved in train accidents, *Skinner v. Railway Labor Executives' Assn.*, 489 U.S. 602 (1989), for United States Customs Service employees seeking promotion to certain sensitive positions, *Treasury Employees v. Von Raab*, 489 U.S. 656 (1989), and for high school students participating in interscholastic sports, *Vernonia School Dist. 47J v. Acton*, 515 U.S. 646 (1995). In the fourth case, we struck down such testing for candidates for designated state offices as unreasonable. *Chandler v. Miller*, 520 U.S. 305 (1997).

In each of those cases, we employed a balancing test that weighed the intrusion on the individual's interest in privacy against the "special needs" that supported the program. As an initial matter, we note that the invasion of privacy in this case is far more substantial than in those cases. In the previous four cases, there was no misunderstanding about the purpose of the test or the potential use of the test results, and there were protections against the dissemination of the results to third parties. The use of an adverse test result to disqualify one from eligibility for a particular benefit, such as a promotion or an opportunity to participate in an extracurricular activity, involves a less serious intrusion on privacy than the unauthorized dissemination of such results to third parties. The reasonable expectation of privacy enjoyed by the typical patient undergoing diagnostic tests in a hospital is that the results of those tests will not be shared with nonmedical personnel without her consent. In none of our prior cases was there any intrusion upon that kind of expectation.

The critical difference between those four drug-testing cases and this one, however, lies in the nature of the "special need" asserted as justification for the warrantless searches. In each of those earlier cases, the "special need" that was advanced as a justification for the absence of a warrant or individualized suspicion was one divorced from the State's general interest in law enforcement. In this case, however, the central and indispensable feature of the policy from its inception was the use of law enforcement to coerce the patients into substance abuse treatment. This fact distinguishes this case from circumstances in which physicians or psychologists, in the course of ordinary medical procedures aimed at helping the patient herself, come across information that under rules of law or ethics is subject to reporting requirements, which no one has challenged here.

Respondents argue in essence that their ultimate purpose—namely, protecting the health of both mother and child—is a beneficent one. In *Chandler*, however, we did not simply accept the State's invocation of a "special need." Instead, we carried out a "close review" of the scheme at issue before concluding that the need in question was not "special," as that term has been defined in our cases. In this case, a review of the M-7 policy plainly reveals that the purpose actually served by the MUSC searches "is ultimately indistinguishable from the general interest in crime control." *Indianapolis v. Edmond*, 531 U.S. 32 (2000). . . .

While the ultimate goal of the program may well have been to get the women in question into substance abuse treatment and off of drugs, the immediate objective of the searches was to generate evidence for law enforcement purposes in order to reach that goal. The threat of law enforcement may ultimately have been intended as a means to an end, but the direct and primary purpose of MUSC's policy was to ensure the use of those means. In our opinion, this distinction is critical. Because law enforcement involvement always serves some broader social purpose or objective, under respondents' view, virtually any nonconsensual suspicionless search could be immunized under the special needs doctrine by defining the search solely in terms of its ultimate, rather than immediate, purpose. Such an approach is inconsistent with the Fourth Amendment. Given the primary purpose of the Charleston program, which was to use the threat of arrest and prosecution in order to force women into treatment, and given the extensive involvement of law enforcement officials at every stage of the policy, this case simply does not fit within the closely guarded category of "special needs."

The fact that positive test results were turned over to the police does not merely provide a basis for distinguishing our prior cases applying the "special needs" balancing approach to the determination of drug use. It also provides an affirmative reason for enforcing the strictures of the Fourth Amendment. While state hospital employees, like other citizens, may have a duty to provide the police with evidence of criminal conduct that they inadvertently acquire in the course of routine treatment, when they undertake to obtain such evidence from their patients for the specific purpose of incriminating those patients, they have a special obligation to make sure that the patients are fully informed about their constitutional rights, as standards of knowing waiver require. *Miranda v. Arizona*, 384 U.S. 436 (1966).

While respondents are correct that drug abuse both was and is a serious problem, "the gravity of the threat alone cannot be dispositive of questions concerning what means law enforcement officers may employ to pursue a given purpose." *Indianapolis v. Edmond*. The Fourth Amendment's general prohibition against nonconsensual, warrantless, and suspicionless searches necessarily applies to such a policy.

Justice KENNEDY, concurring in the judgment.

In my view, it is necessary and prudent to be explicit in explaining the limitations of today's decision. The beginning point ought to be to acknowledge the legitimacy of the State's interest in fetal life and of the grave risk to the life and health of the fetus, and later the child, caused by cocaine ingestion. Infants whose mothers abuse cocaine during pregnancy are born with a wide variety of physical and neurological abnormalities. Prenatal exposure to cocaine can also result in developmental problems which persist long after birth. There can be no doubt that a mother's ingesting this drug can cause tragic injury to a fetus and a child. There should be no doubt that South Carolina can impose punishment upon an expectant mother who has so little regard for her own unborn that she risks causing him or her lifelong damage and suffering. The State, by taking special measures to give rehabilitation and training to expectant mothers with this tragic addiction or weakness, acts well within its powers and its civic obligations.

The holding of the Court, furthermore, does not call into question the validity of mandatory reporting laws such as child abuse laws which require teachers to report evidence of child abuse to the proper authorities, even if arrest and prosecution is the likely result. That in turn highlights the real difficulty. As this case comes to us, we must accept the premise that the medical profession can adopt acceptable criteria for testing expectant mothers for cocaine use in order to provide prompt and effective counseling to the mother and to take proper medical steps to protect the child. If prosecuting authorities then adopt legitimate procedures to discover this information and prosecution follows, that ought not to invalidate the testing. One of the ironies of the case, then, may be that the program now under review, which gives the cocaine user a second and third chance, might be replaced by some more rigorous system. We must, however, take the case as it comes to us; and the use of handcuffs, arrests, prosecutions, and police assistance in designing and implementing the testing and rehabilitation policy cannot be sustained under our previous cases concerning mandatory testing.

An essential, distinguishing feature of the special needs cases is that the person searched has consented, though the usual voluntariness analysis is altered because adverse consequences (e.g., dismissal from employment or disqualification from playing on a high school sports team) will follow from refusal. The person searched has given consent, as defined to take into account that the consent was not voluntary in the full sense of the word. The consent, and the circumstances in which it was given, bear upon the reasonableness of the whole special needs program. Here, on the other hand, the question of consent, even with the special connotation used in the special needs cases, has yet to be decided. . . .

Justice SCALIA, with whom THE CHIEF JUSTICE and Justice THOMAS join, dissenting.

I think it clear . . . that there is no basis for saying that obtaining of the urine sample was unconstitutional. The special-needs doctrine is thus quite irrelevant, since it operates only to validate searches and seizures that are otherwise unlawful. In the ensuing discussion, however, I shall assume (contrary to legal precedent) that the taking of the urine sample was (either because of the patients' necessitous circumstances, or because of failure to disclose that the urine would be tested for drugs, or because of failure to disclose that the results of the test would be given to the police) coerced. Indeed, I shall even assume (contrary to common sense) that the testing of the urine constituted an unconsented search of the patients' effects. On those assumptions, the special-needs doctrine would become relevant; and, properly applied, would validate what was done here. . . .

The cocaine tests started in April 1989, neither at police suggestion nor with police involvement. Expectant mothers who tested positive were referred by hospital staff for substance-abuse treatment—an obvious health benefit to both mother and child. Thus, in their origin—before the police were in any way involved—the tests had an immediate, not merely an "ultimate," purpose of improving maternal and infant health. Several months after the testing had been initiated, a nurse discovered that local police were arresting pregnant users of cocaine for child abuse, the hospital's general counsel wrote the county solicitor to ask "what, if anything, our Medical Center needs to do to assist you in this matter," the police suggested ways to avoid tainting evidence, and the hospital and police in conjunction used the testing program as a means of securing what the Court calls the "ultimate" health benefit of coercing drug-abusing mothers into drug treatment. Why would there be any reason to believe that, once this policy of using the drug tests for their "ultimate" health benefits had been adopted, use of them for their original, immediate, benefits somehow disappeared, and testing somehow became in its entirety nothing more than a "pretext" for obtaining grounds for arrest? On the face of it, this is incredible. The only evidence of the exclusively arrest-related purpose of the testing adduced by the Court is that the police-cooperation policy itself does not describe how to care for cocaine-exposed infants. But of course it does not, since that policy, adopted months after the cocaine testing was initiated, had as its only health object the "ultimate" goal of inducing drug treatment through threat of arrest. Does the Court really believe (or even hope) that, once invalidation of the program challenged here has been decreed, drug testing will cease? In sum, there can be no basis for the Court's purported ability to "distinguis[h] this case from circumstances in which physicians or psychologists, in the course of ordinary medical procedures aimed at helping the patient herself, come across information that . . . is subject to reporting requirements," unless it is this: That the addition of a law-enforcement-related purpose to a legitimate medical purpose destroys applicability of the "special-needs" doctrine. But that is quite impossible, since the special-needs doctrine was developed, and is ordinarily employed, precisely to enable searches by law enforcement officials who, of course, ordinarily have a law enforcement objective. . . .

As I indicated at the outset, it is not the function of this Court—at least not in Fourth Amendment cases—to weigh petitioners' privacy interest against the State's interest in meeting the crisis of "crack babies" that developed in the late 1980's. I cannot refrain from observing, however, that the outcome of a wise weighing of those interests is by no means clear. The initial goal of the doctors and nurses who conducted cocaine-testing in this case was to refer pregnant drug addicts to treatment centers, and to prepare for necessary treatment of their possibly affected children. When the doctors and nurses agreed to the program providing test results to the police, they did so because . . . they wanted to use the sanction of arrest as a strong incentive for their addicted patients to undertake drug-addiction treatment. And the police themselves used it for that benign purpose, as is shown by the fact that only 30 of 253 women testing positive for cocaine were ever arrested, and only 2 of those prosecuted. It would not be unreasonable to conclude that today's judgment . . . proves once again that no good deed goes unpunished. But as far as the Fourth Amendment is concerned: There was no unconsented search in this case. And if there was, it would have been validated by the special-needs doctrine. For these reasons, I respectfully dissent.

E. WIRETAPPING, BUGGING, AND POLICE SURVEILLANCE

In an unusual line-up in a five to four decision, in *Kyllo v. United States* (excerpted below), the Court held that the use by law enforcement officers of thermal imagers, in order to detect heat radiations from a house that was suspected of being used to grow marijuana, without a warrant violated the Fourth Amendment. Justice Scalia wrote for Court, while Justice Stevens, joined by Chief Justice Rehnquist and Justices O'Connor and Kennedy, dissented.

Kyllo v. United States
121 S.Ct. 2038 (2001)

In 1992, federal agents suspected Danny Kyllo of growing marijuana in his home and decided to use an Agema Thermovision 210 thermal imager to scan his house. The imagers detect infrared radiation, which virtually all objects emit, and convert the radiation into images based on their relative warmth. From the passenger's seat of their car across the street from the house, the agents scanned the house and found that the roof over the garage and a side wall of the house were relatively hot. The agents concluded that Kyllo was using high intensity halide lights to grow marijuana and on that basis, along with an informant's tip and utility bills, obtained a warrant to search the house, which revealed more than 100 marijuana plants. Kyllo sought to suppress that evidence on the ground that the use of the thermal imager constituted a warrantless search in violation of the Fourth Amendment. A federal district court rejected that motion and its decision was affirmed by an appellate court.

The appellate court's decision was reversed by a five to four vote and the opinion for the Court was delivered by Justice Scalia. Justice Stevens filed a dissenting opinion, which Chief Justice Rehnquist and Justices O'Connor and Kennedy joined.

Justice SCALIA delivered the opinion of the Court.

This case presents the question whether the use of a thermal-imaging device aimed at a private home from a public street to detect relative amounts of heat within the home constitutes a "search" within the meaning of the Fourth Amendment.

"At the very core" of the Fourth Amendment "stands the right of a man to retreat into his own home and there be free from unreasonable governmental intrusion." *Silverman v. United States*, 365 U.S. 505 (1961). . . . On the other hand, the antecedent question of whether or not a Fourth Amendment "search" has occurred is not so simple under our precedent. The permissibility of ordinary visual surveillance of a home used to be clear because, well into the 20th century, our Fourth Amendment jurisprudence was tied to common-law trespass. See, e.g., *Goldman v. United States*, 316 U.S. 129 (1942); *Olmstead v. United States*, 277 U.S. 438 (1928). Visual surveillance was unquestionably lawful because "'the eye cannot by the laws of England be guilty of a trespass.'" *Boyd v. United States*, 116 U.S. 616 1886). We have since decoupled violation of a person's Fourth Amendment rights from trespassory violation of his property, see *Rakas v. Illinois*, 439 U.S. 128 (1978), but the lawfulness of warrantless visual surveillance of a home has still been preserved. As we observed in *California v. Ciraolo*, 476 U.S. 207 (1986), "[t]he Fourth Amendment protection of the home has never been extended to require law enforcement officers to shield their eyes when passing by a home on public thoroughfares."

One might think that the new validating rationale would be that examining the portion of a house that is in plain public view, while it is a "search" despite the absence of trespass, is not an "unreasonable" one under the Fourth Amendment. But in fact we have held that visual observation is no "search" at all—perhaps in order to preserve somewhat more intact our doctrine that warrantless searches are presumptively unconstitutional. See *Dow Chemical Co. v. United States*, 476 U.S. 227 (1986). In assessing when a search is not a search, we have applied somewhat in reverse the principle first enunciated in *Katz v. United States*, 389 U.S. 347 (1967) . . . that a Fourth Amendment search does not occur—even when the explicitly protected location of a house is concerned—unless "the individual manifested a subjective expectation of privacy in the object of the challenged search," and "society [is] willing to recognize that expectation as reasonable." *Ciraolo*. . . .

The present case involves officers on a public street engaged in more than naked-eye surveillance of a home. We have previously reserved judgment as to how much technological enhancement of ordinary perception from such a vantage point, if any, is too much. While we upheld enhanced aerial photography of an industrial complex in *Dow Chemical*, we noted that we found "it important that this is not an area immediately adjacent to a private home, where privacy expectations are most heightened."

It would be foolish to contend that the degree of privacy secured to citizens by the Fourth Amendment has been entirely unaffected by the advance of technology. For example, as the cases discussed above make clear, the technology enabling human flight has exposed to public view (and hence, we have said, to official observation) uncovered portions of the house and its curtilage that once were private. The question we confront today is what limits there are upon this power of technology to shrink the realm of guaranteed privacy.

The *Katz* test—whether the individual has an expectation of privacy that society is prepared to recognize as reasonable—has often been criticized as circular, and hence subjective and unpredictable. While it may be difficult to refine *Katz* when the search of areas such as telephone booths, automobiles, or even the curtilage and uncovered portions of residences are at issue, in the case of the search of the interior of homes—the prototypical and hence most commonly litigated area of protected privacy—there is a ready criterion, with roots deep in the common law, of the minimal expectation of privacy that exists, and that is acknowledged to be reasonable. To withdraw protection of this minimum expectation would be to permit police technology to erode the privacy guaranteed by the Fourth Amendment. We think that obtaining by sense-enhancing technology any information regarding the interior of the home that could not otherwise have been obtained without physical "intrusion into a constitutionally protected area," *Silverman*, constitutes a search—at least where (as here) the technology in question is not in general public use. This assures preservation of that degree of privacy against government that existed when the Fourth Amendment was adopted. On the basis of this criterion, the information obtained by the thermal imager in this case was the product of a search.

The Government maintains, however, that the thermal imaging must be upheld because it detected "only heat radiating from the external surface of the house." The dissent makes this its leading point, contending that there is a fundamental difference between what it calls "off-the-wall" observations and "through-the-wall" surveillance." But just as a thermal imager captures only heat emanating from a house, so also a powerful directional microphone picks up only sound emanating from a house—and a satellite capable of scanning from many miles away would pick up only visible light emanating from a house. We rejected such a mechanical interpretation of the Fourth Amendment in *Katz*, where the eavesdropping device picked up only sound waves that reached the exterior of the phone booth. Reversing that approach would leave the homeowner at the mercy of advancing technology—including imaging technology that could discern all human activity in the home. While the technology used in the present case was relatively crude, the rule we adopt must take account of more sophisticated systems that are already in use or in development. . . .

We have said that the Fourth Amendment draws "a firm line at the entrance to the house," *Payton*. That line, we think, must be not only firm but also bright— which requires clear specification of those methods of surveillance that require a warrant. While it is certainly possible to conclude from the videotape of the thermal imaging that occurred in this case that no "significant" compromise of the homeowner's privacy has occurred, we must take the long view, from the original meaning of the Fourth Amendment forward. Where, as here, the Government uses a device that is not in general public use, to explore details of the home that would previously have been unknowable without physical intrusion, the surveillance is a "search" and is presumptively unreasonable without a warrant.

Since we hold the Thermovision imaging to have been an unlawful search, it will remain for the District Court to determine whether, without the evidence it provided, the search warrant issued in this case was supported by probable cause—and if not, whether there is any other basis for supporting admission of the evidence that the search pursuant to the warrant produced.

Justice STEVENS, with whom The CHIEF JUSTICE, Justice O'CONNOR, and Justice KENNEDY join, dissenting.

There is, in my judgment, a distinction of constitutional magnitude between "through-the-wall surveillance" that gives the observer or listener direct access to information in a private area, on the one hand, and the thought processes used to draw inferences from information in the public domain, on the other hand. The Court has crafted a rule that purports to deal with direct observations of the inside of the home, but the case before us merely involves indirect deductions from "off-the-wall" surveillance, that is, observations of the exterior of the home. Those observations were made with a fairly primitive thermal imager that gathered data exposed on the outside of petitioner's home but did not invade any constitutionally protected interest in privacy. Moreover, I believe that the supposedly "bright-line" rule the Court has created in response to its concerns about future technological developments is unnecessary, unwise, and inconsistent with the Fourth Amendment.

There is no need for the Court to craft a new rule to decide this case, as it is controlled by established principles from our Fourth Amendment jurisprudence. One of those core principles, of course, is that "searches and seizures inside a home without a warrant are presumptively unreasonable." *Payton v. New York*, 445 U.S. 573 (1980). But it is equally well settled that searches and seizures of property in plain view are presumptively reasonable. Whether that property is residential or commercial, the basic principle is the same: "'What a person knowingly exposes to the public, even in his own home or office, is not a subject of Fourth Amendment protection.'" *California v. Ciraolo*, 476 U.S. 207 (1986).

[T]he notion that heat emissions from the outside of a dwelling is a private matter implicating the protections of the Fourth Amendment is not only unprecedented but also quite difficult to take seriously. Heat waves, like aromas that are generated in a kitchen, or in a laboratory or opium den, enter the public domain if and when they leave a building. A subjective expectation that they would remain private is not only implausible but also surely not "one that society is prepared to recognize as 'reasonable.'" *Katz* (HARLAN, J., concurring).

To be sure, the homeowner has a reasonable expectation of privacy concerning what takes place within the home, and the Fourth Amendment's protection against physical invasions of the home should apply to their functional equivalent. But the equipment in this case did not penetrate the walls of petitioner's home, and while it did pick up "details of the home" that were exposed to the public, it did not obtain "any information regarding the interior of the home." In the Court's own words, based on what the thermal imager "showed" regarding the outside of petitioner's home, the officers "concluded" that petitioner was engaging in illegal activity inside the home. It would be quite absurd to characterize their thought processes as "searches," regardless of whether they inferred (rightly) that petitioner was growing marijuana in his house, or (wrongly) that "the lady of the house [was taking] her daily sauna and bath." In either case, the only conclusions the officers reached concerning the interior of the home were at least as indirect as those that might have been inferred from the contents of discarded garbage, see *California v. Greenwood*, 486 U.S. 35 (1988), or pen register data, see *Smith v. Maryland*, 442 U.S. 735 (1979). . . .

Since what was involved in this case was nothing more than drawing inferences from "off-the-wall" surveillance, rather than any "through-the-wall" surveillance, the officers' conduct did not amount to a search and was perfectly reasonable. . . .

Despite the Court's attempt to draw a line that is "not only firm but also bright," the contours of its new rule are uncertain because its protection apparently dissipates as soon as the relevant technology is "in general public use." Yet how much use is general public use is not even hinted at by the Court's opinion, which makes the somewhat doubtful assumption that the thermal imager used in this case does not satisfy that criterion. In any event, putting aside its lack of clarity, this criterion is somewhat perverse because it seems likely that the threat to privacy will grow, rather than recede, as the use of intrusive equipment becomes more readily available. . . .

The two reasons advanced by the Court as justifications for the adoption of its new rule are both unpersuasive. First, the Court suggests that its rule is compelled by our holding in *Katz*, because in that case, as in this, the surveillance consisted of nothing more than the monitoring of waves emanating from a private area into the public domain. Yet there are critical differences between the cases. In *Katz*, the electronic listening device attached to the outside of the phone booth allowed the officers to pick up the content of the conversation inside the booth, making them the functional equivalent of intruders because they gathered information that was otherwise available only to someone inside the private area; it would be as if, in this case, the thermal imager presented a view of the heat-generating activity inside petitioner's home. By contrast, the thermal imager here disclosed only the relative amounts of heat radiating from the house; it would be as if, in *Katz*, the listening device disclosed only the relative volume of sound leaving the booth, which presumably was discernible in the public domain. Surely, there is a significant difference between the general and well-settled expectation that strangers will not have direct access to the contents of private communications, on the one hand, and the rather theoretical expectation that an occasional homeowner would even care if anybody noticed the relative amounts of heat emanating from the walls of his house, on the other. It is pure hyperbole for the Court to suggest that refusing to extend the holding of *Katz* to this case would leave the homeowner at the mercy of "technology that could discern all human activity in the home."

Second, the Court argues that the permissibility of "through-the-wall surveillance" cannot depend on a distinction between observing "intimate details" such as "the lady of the house [taking] her daily sauna and bath," and noticing only "the nonintimate rug on the vestibule floor" or "objects no smaller than 36 by 36 inches." This entire argument assumes, of course, that the thermal imager in this case could or did perform "through-the-wall surveillance" that could identify any detail "that would previously have been unknowable without physical intrusion." In fact, the device could not and did not enable its user to identify either the lady of the house, the rug on the vestibule floor, or anything else inside the house. . . .

Although the Court is properly and commendably concerned about the threats to privacy that may flow from advances in the technology available to the law enforcement profession, it has unfortunately failed to heed the tried and true counsel of judicial restraint. Instead of concentrating on the rather mundane issue that is actually presented by the case before it, the Court has endeavored to craft an all-encompassing rule for the future. It would be far wiser to give legislators an unimpeded opportunity to grapple with these emerging issues rather than to shackle them with prematurely devised constitutional constraints. I respectfully dissent.

8

THE FIFTH AMENDMENT
GUARANTEE AGAINST
SELF-ACCUSATION

In its 2001–2002 term, the Court will consider whether requiring a prisoner to disclose his sexual history as a condition of participating in a treatment program violates the Fifth Amendment guarantee against self-incrimination, in *McKune v. Lile* (No. 00-11187). Lile was convicted in Kansas state court of aggravated kidnapping, rape, and sodomy. The state department of corrections recommended that he participate in the Sexual Abuse Treatment Program (SATP). Under the program, however, prisoners must disclose their sexual history, including any crimes of which they have been convicted and any uncharged sexual offenses. Lile refused to make such admissions and filed a lawsuit alleging that the SATP violated the Fifth Amendment right against self-incrimination. Subsequently, the Court of Appeals for the Tenth Circuit held that the SATP sought information that could incriminate prisoners and subject them to further criminal charges, as well as required prisoners to choose between making personal disclosures and forfeiting their right against self-incrimination, and therefore violated the Fifth Amendment.

A. COERCED CONFESSIONS AND
POLICE INTERROGATIONS

In its 2000–2001 term, a bare majority reaffirmed and extended the holding in *McNeil v. Wisconsin* (1991) (excerpted in Vol. 2, Ch. 8), that the Sixth Amendment right to counsel is independent of the right to counsel recognized in *Miranda*, in *Texas v. Cobb*, 121 S.Ct. 1335 (2001). Cobb was arrested on burglary charges and confessed to that crime in 1994, but denied any knowledge of the disappearance of the mother and child at the residence. Counsel was appointed to represent him on that charge. But subsequently, in 1995, while in custody in response to police questioning,

Cobb waived his *Miranda* rights and confessed to the murders. He was later convicted and sentenced to death. On appeal, however, the Texas court for criminal appeals ruled that confession to the murders should have been suppressed because his right to counsel had come into play when counsel was appointed in the burglary case. Reversing that decision in his opinion for the Court, Chief Justice Rehnquist held that, pursuant to *McNeil*, the Sixth Amendment right to counsel is offense specific and cannot be invoked for all future prosecutions. In addition, Chief Justice Rehnquist reasoned that because burglary and murder are separate offenses, the Sixth Amendment did not bar the police from interrogating Cobb about the murders, and therefore, his confession was admissible. Justices Stevens, Souter, Ginsburg, and Breyer dissented.

In a widely watched case, *Dickerson v. United States* (excerpted below), the Court reaffirmed the constitutionality of its ruling in *Miranda v. Arizona*, 384 U.S. 436 (1966) (in Vol. 2, Ch. 8), in holding that Congress could not override the decision by statute.

Dickerson v. United States
530 U.S. 428 (2000), 120 S.Ct. 2326 (2000)

In *Miranda v. Arizona*, 384 U.S. 436 (1966) (see Vol. 2, Ch. 8), the Supreme Court held that, before police question criminal suspects, they must warn them of their Fifth and Sixth Amendment rights to remain silent and to have an attorney present; otherwise, any incriminating statements are considered involuntary and excluded at trial. That decision applied to all state courts and remains controversial. Two years later, Congress enacted the Crime Control and Safe Streets Act of 1968, in which Section 3501 specified that the pre-*Miranda* standard of "the totality of circumstances" for determining the voluntariness of a confession would apply in federal courts, not whether a defendant had been given the *Miranda* warnings. Subsequently, the Department of Justice, in both Republican and Democratic administrations, except in a couple of cases during the administration of Republican President Ronald Reagan, maintained the position that *Miranda* governed in both state and federal criminal prosecutions.

In 1997, Thomas Dickerson was arrested and indicted for bank robbery. At a pretrial hearing, his attorney moved to suppress an incriminating statement made at a Federal Bureau of Investigation office on the ground that the agents failed to read Dickerson his *Miranda* rights. A federal district court agreed that *Miranda* applied, but the Court of Appeals for the Fourth Circuit reversed, holding that *Miranda* was not a constitutional ruling and therefore Congress could determine the standard for voluntary confessions admitted into evidence in federal courts. That decision was appealed, and the Supreme Court granted review.

The appellate court's decision was reversed in a seven to two decision, and opinion for the Court was delivered by Chief Justice Rehnquist. Justice Scalia filed a dissenting opinion, which Justice Thomas joined.

Chief Justice REHNQUIST delivered the opinion of the Court.

We hold that *Miranda*, being a constitutional decision of this Court, may not be in effect overruled by an Act of Congress, and we decline to overrule *Miranda* ourselves. We therefore hold that *Miranda* and its progeny in this Court govern the admissibility of statements made during custodial interrogation in both state and federal courts. . . .

In *Miranda*, we noted that the advent of modern custodial police interrogation brought with it an increased concern about confessions obtained by coercion. Because custodial police interrogation, by its very nature, isolates and pressures the individual, we stated that "[e]ven without employing brutality, the 'third degree' or [other] specific stratagems, custodial interrogation exacts a heavy toll on individual liberty and trades on the weakness of individuals." We concluded that the coercion inherent in custodial interrogation blurs the line between voluntary and involuntary statements, and thus heightens the risk that an individual will not be "accorded his privilege under the Fifth Amendment not to be compelled to incriminate himself." Accordingly, we laid down "concrete constitutional guidelines for law enforcement agencies and courts to follow." Those guidelines established that the admissibility in evidence of any statement given during custodial interrogation of a suspect would depend on whether the police provided the suspect with four warnings. These warnings (which have come to be known colloquially as *Miranda* rights") are: a suspect "has the right to remain silent, that anything he says can be used against him in a court of law, that he has the right to the presence of an attorney, and that if he cannot afford an attorney one will be appointed for him prior to any questioning if he so desires."

Two years after *Miranda* was decided, Congress enacted Section 3501. Given Section 3501's express designation of voluntariness as the touchstone of admissibility, its omission of any warning requirement, and the instruction for trial courts to consider a nonexclusive list of factors relevant to the circumstances of a confession, we agree with the Court of Appeals that Congress intended by its enactment to overrule *Miranda*. Because of the obvious conflict between our decision in *Miranda* and Section 3501, we must address whether Congress has constitutional authority to thus supersede *Miranda*. If Congress has such authority, Section 3501's totality-of-the-circumstances approach must prevail over *Miranda*'s requirement of warnings; if not, that section must yield to *Miranda*'s more specific requirements.

The law in this area is clear. This Court has supervisory authority over the federal courts, and we may use that authority to prescribe rules of evidence and procedure that are binding in those tribunals. However, the power to judicially create and enforce nonconstitutional "rules of procedure and evidence for the federal courts exists only in the absence of a relevant Act of Congress." Congress retains the ultimate authority to modify or set aside any judicially created rules of evidence and procedure that are not required by the Constitution.

But Congress may not legislatively supersede our decisions interpreting and applying the Constitution. See, e.g., *City of Boerne v. Flores*, 521 U.S. 507 (1997). This case therefore turns on whether the *Miranda* Court announced a constitutional rule or merely exercised its supervisory authority to regulate evidence in the absence of congressional direction. Recognizing this point, the Court of Appeals surveyed *Miranda* and its progeny to determine the constitutional status of the *Miranda* decision. Relying on the fact that we have created several exceptions to *Miranda*'s warnings requirement and that we have repeatedly referred to the *Miranda* warnings as "prophylactic," *New York v. Quarles*, 467 U.S. 649 (1984), and "not themselves rights protected by the Constitution," *Michigan v. Tucker*, 417 U.S. 433 (1974), the Court of Appeals concluded that the protections announced in *Miranda* are not constitutionally required.

We disagree with the Court of Appeals' conclusion, although we concede that there is language in some of our opinions that supports the view taken by that court. But first and foremost of the factors on the other side—that *Miranda* is a constitutional decision—is that both *Miranda* and two of its companion cases applied the rule to proceedings in state courts—to wit, Arizona, California, and New York. Since that time, we have consistently applied *Miranda*'s rule to prosecutions arising in state courts. It is beyond dispute that we do not hold a supervisory power over the courts of the several States.

The *Miranda* opinion itself begins by stating that the Court granted *certiorari* "to explore some facets of the problems of applying the privilege against self-incrimination to in-custody interrogation, and to give concrete constitutional guidelines for law enforcement agencies and courts to follow." In fact, the majority opinion is replete with statements indicating that the majority thought it was announcing a constitutional rule. Indeed, the Court's ultimate conclusion was that the unwarned confessions obtained in the four cases before the Court in *Miranda* "were obtained from the defendant under circumstances that did not meet constitutional standards for protection of the privilege." . . .

Whether or not we would agree with *Miranda*'s reasoning and its resulting rule, were we addressing the issue in the first instance, the principles of *stare decisis* weigh heavily against overruling it now.

We do not think there is such justification for overruling *Miranda*. *Miranda* has become embedded in routine police practice to the point where the warnings have become part of our national culture. See *Mitchell v. United States*, 526 U.S. 314 (1999) (SCALIA, J., dissenting) (stating that the fact that a rule has found "wide acceptance in the legal culture" is "adequate reason not to overrule" it). While we have overruled our precedents when subsequent cases have undermined their doctrinal underpinnings, we do not believe that this has happened to the *Miranda* decision. If anything, our subsequent cases have reduced the impact of the *Miranda* rule on legitimate law enforcement while reaffirming the decision's core ruling that unwarned statements may not be used as evidence in the prosecution's case in chief. . . .

In sum, we conclude that *Miranda* announced a constitutional rule that Congress may not supersede legislatively. Following the rule of *stare decisis*, we decline to overrule *Miranda* ourselves. The judgment of the Court of Appeals is therefore Reversed.

Justice SCALIA, with whom Justice THOMAS joins, dissenting.

Those to whom judicial decisions are an unconnected series of judgments that produce either favored or disfavored results will doubtless greet today's decision as a paragon of moderation, since it declines to overrule *Miranda v. Arizona.* Those who understand the judicial process will appreciate that today's decision is not a reaffirmation of *Miranda,* but a radical revision of the most significant element of *Miranda* (as of all cases): the rationale that gives it a permanent place in our jurisprudence.

Marbury v. Madison, 1 Cranch 137 (1803), held that an Act of Congress will not be enforced by the courts if what it prescribes violates the Constitution of the United States. That was the basis on which *Miranda* was decided. One will search today's opinion in vain, however, for a statement (surely simple enough to make) that what Section 3501 prescribes—the use at trial of a voluntary confession, even when a *Miranda* warning or its equivalent has failed to be given—violates the Constitution. The reason the statement does not appear is not only (and perhaps not so much) that it would be absurd, inasmuch as Section 3501 excludes from trial precisely what the Constitution excludes from trial, viz., compelled confessions; but also that Justices whose votes are needed to compose today's majority are on record as believing that a violation of *Miranda* is not a violation of the Constitution. And so, to justify today's agreed-upon result, the Court must adopt a significant new, if not entirely comprehensible, principle of constitutional law. As the Court chooses to describe that principle, statutes of Congress can be disregarded, not only when what they prescribe violates the Constitution, but when what they prescribe contradicts a decision of this Court that "announced a constitutional rule." As I shall discuss in some detail, the only thing that can possibly mean in the context of this case is that this Court has the power, not merely to apply the Constitution but to expand it, imposing what it regards as useful "prophylactic" restrictions upon Congress and the States. That is an immense and frightening antidemocratic power, and it does not exist.

It takes only a small step to bring today's opinion out of the realm of power-judging and into the mainstream of legal reasoning: The Court need only go beyond its carefully couched iterations that "*Miranda* is a constitutional decision," that "*Miranda* is constitutionally based," that *Miranda* has "constitutional underpinnings," and come out and say quite clearly: "We reaffirm today that custodial interrogation that is not preceded by *Miranda* warnings or their equivalent violates the Constitution of the United States." It cannot say that, because a majority of the Court does not believe it. The Court therefore acts in plain violation of the Constitution when it denies effect to this Act of Congress.

It was once possible to characterize the so-called *Miranda* rule as resting (however implausibly) upon the proposition that what the statute here before us permits—the admission at trial of un-Mirandized confessions—violates the Constitution. That is the fairest reading of the *Miranda* case itself. The Court began by announcing that the Fifth Amendment privilege against self-incrimination applied in the context of extrajudicial custodial interrogation—itself a doubtful proposition as a matter both of history and precedent. Having extended the privilege into the confines of the station house, the Court liberally sprinkled throughout its sprawling 60-page opinion suggestions that, because of the compulsion inherent in custodial interrogation, the privilege was violated by any statement thus obtained that did not conform to the rules set forth in *Miranda*, or some functional equivalent. . . .

Miranda was objectionable for innumerable reasons, not least the fact that cases spanning more than 70 years had rejected its core premise that, absent the warnings and an effective waiver of the right to remain silent and of the (thith-erto unknown) right to have an attorney present, a statement obtained pursuant to custodial interrogation was necessarily the product of compulsion. Moreover, history and precedent aside, the decision in *Miranda*, if read as an explication of what the Constitution requires, is preposterous. There is, for example, simply no basis in reason for concluding that a response to the very first question asked, by a suspect who already knows all of the rights described in the *Miranda* warning, is anything other than a volitional act. And even if one assumes that the elimi-nation of compulsion absolutely requires informing even the most knowledge-able suspect of his right to remain silent, it cannot conceivably require the right to have counsel present. There is a world of difference, which the Court recog-nized under the traditional voluntariness test but ignored in *Miranda*, between compelling a suspect to incriminate himself and preventing him from foolishly doing so of his own accord. Only the latter (which is not required by the Constitution) could explain the Court's inclusion of a right to counsel and the requirement that it, too, be knowingly and intelligently waived. Counsel's pres-ence is not required to tell the suspect that he need not speak; the interrogators can do that. The only good reason for having counsel there is that he can be counted on to advise the suspect that he should not speak.

Preventing foolish (rather than compelled) confessions is likewise the only conceivable basis for the rules that courts must exclude any confession elicited by questioning conducted, without interruption, after the suspect has indicated a desire to stand on his right to remain silent, see *Michigan v. Mosley*, 423 U.S. 96 (1975), or initiated by police after the suspect has expressed a desire to have counsel present, see *Edwards v. Arizona*, 451 U.S. 477 (1981). Nonthreatening attempts to persuade the suspect to reconsider that initial decision are not, with-out more, enough to render a change of heart the product of anything other than the suspect's free will. Thus, what is most remarkable about the *Miranda* deci-sion—and what made it unacceptable as a matter of straightforward consti-tutional interpretation in the *Marbury* tradition—is its palpable hostility toward the act of confession per se, rather than toward what the Constitution abhors, compelled confession.

For these reasons, and others more than adequately developed in the *Miranda* dissents and in the subsequent works of the decision's many critics, any conclu-sion that a violation of the *Miranda* rules necessarily amounts to a violation of the privilege against compelled self-incrimination can claim no support in his-tory, precedent, or common sense, and as a result would at least presumptively be worth reconsidering even at this late date. But that is unnecessary, since the Court has (thankfully) long since abandoned the notion that failure to comply with *Miranda*'s rules is itself a violation of the Constitution.

As the Court today acknowledges, since *Miranda* we have explicitly, and repeatedly, interpreted that decision as having announced, not the circumstances in which custodial interrogation runs afoul of the Fifth or Fourteenth Amend-ment, but rather only "prophylactic" rules that go beyond the right against compelled self-incrimination. Of course the seeds of this "prophylactic" interpretation of *Miranda* were present in the decision itself. In subsequent cases, the seeds have sprouted and borne fruit: The Court has squarely concluded that it is possible—indeed not uncommon—for the police to violate *Miranda* without also violating the Constitution. [See *Michigan v. Tucker*, 417 U.S. 433 (1974); *Oregon v. Hass*, 420 U.S. 714 (1975); *New York v. Quarles*, 467 U.S. 649 (1984); and *Oregon v. Elstad*, 470 U.S. 298 (1985).]

In light of these cases, and our statements to the same effect in others, it is simply no longer possible for the Court to conclude, even if it wanted to, that a violation of *Miranda*'s rules is a violation of the Constitution. But as I explained at the outset, that is what is required before the Court may disregard a law of Congress governing the admissibility of evidence in federal court. The Court today insists that the decision in *Miranda* is a "constitutional" one; that it has "constitutional underpinnings"; "constitutional basis" and a "constitutional origin"; that it was "constitutionally based"; and that it announced a "constitutional rule." It is fine to play these word games; but what makes a decision "constitutional" in the only sense relevant here—in the sense that renders it impervious to supersession by congressional legislation such as Section 3501—is the determination that the Constitution requires the result that the decision announces and the statute ignores. By disregarding congressional action that concededly does not violate the Constitution, the Court flagrantly offends fundamental principles of separation of powers, and arrogates to itself prerogatives reserved to the representatives of the people. . . .

Finally, I am not convinced by petitioner's argument that *Miranda* should be preserved because the decision occupies a special place in the "public's consciousness." As far as I am aware, the public is not under the illusion that we are infallible. I see little harm in admitting that we made a mistake in taking away from the people the ability to decide for themselves what protections (beyond those required by the Constitution) are reasonably affordable in the criminal investigatory process. And I see much to be gained by reaffirming for the people the wonderful reality that they govern themselves—which means that "[t]he powers not delegated to the United States by the Constitution" that the people adopted, "nor prohibited to the States" by that Constitution, "are reserved to the States respectively, or to the people," U.S. Const., Amdt. 10. . . .

I dissent from today's decision, and, until Section 3501 is repealed, will continue to apply it in all cases where there has been a sustainable finding that the defendant's confession was voluntary.

9

THE RIGHTS TO COUNSEL AND OTHER PROCEDURAL GUARANTEES

A. THE RIGHT TO COUNSEL

In *Martinez v. Court of Appeal of California*, 528 U.S. 152 (2000), the Court held that the Sixth Amendment right to waive the benefits of counsel and to self-representation at trials, recognized in *Faretta v. California*, 422 U.S. 806 (1975), does not extend to direct appeals of criminal convictions. In writing for the Court, Justice Stevens reaffirmed that the Sixth Amendment right to self-representation does not apply to appellate proceedings.

B. PLEA BARGAINING AND THE RIGHT TO EFFECTIVE COUNSEL

THE DEVELOPMENT OF LAW

Rulings on Plea Bargaining and Effective Counsel

Case	Vote	Ruling
Roe v. Flores-Ortega, 528 U.S. 470 (2000)	6:3	Writing for the Court, Justice O'Connor reaffirmed the holding, in *Strickland v. Washington*, 466 U.S. 668 (1984), that a defendant claiming ineffective counsel must show (1) that the counsel's representation fell below an objective standard of reasonableness and (2) that the deficient performance prejudiced the defendant. It was further held that counsel has a constitutionally imposed duty to consult with the defendant about an appeal when there is reason to think either that a rational defendant would want to appeal or that the defendant indicated an interest in appealing.

Williams v. Taylor, 529 U.S. 362 (2000)	6:3 and 5:4	Writing for the Court, Jus- tice Stevens held that Terry Williams was denied his con-

stitutionally guaranteed right to effective counsel, as defined in *Strickland v. Washington*, 466 U.S. 668 (1984), because his attorney failed to investigate and to present substantial mitigating evidence to the jury, and thus he was entitled to appeal his death sentence under the Antiterrorism and Effective Death Penalty Act of 1996 (AEDPA). Justices O'Connor, Kennedy, Souter, Ginsburg, and Breyer joined portions of the opinion. Justice O'Connor delivered the opinion of the Court, holding that the AEDPA places a new constraint on federal courts in granting writs of *habeas corpus* review; they may grant review only if the state court's adjudication was "contrary to" or "involved an unreasonable application of clearly established federal law." Chief Justice Rehnquist and Justices Kennedy, Scalia, and Thomas joined that opinion.

10

CRUEL AND UNUSUAL PUNISHMENT

B. CAPITAL PUNISHMENT

In its 2001–2002 term, the Court will revisit the question of whether executing mentally retarded convicts violates the Eighth Amendment ban on cruel and unusual punishment. In *Penry v. Lynaugh*, 492 U.S. 302 (1989) (excerpted in Vol. 2, Ch. 10), a bare majority held that such executions do not necessarily violate the Eighth Amendment. At the time *Penry* was decided only two states forbid such executions, whereas in 2001, of the 37 states that impose capital punishment, 12 bar the execution of the mentally retarded; thus, when those states are combined with the 13 states that do not have the death penalty, half of the total number of states bar executing mentally retarded individuals, as does federal law. The case the Court will decide is *McCarver v. North Carolina* (No. 00-8727).

THE DEVELOPMENT OF LAW

Post-*Furman* Rulings
on Capital Punishment

Case	Vote	Ruling
Williams v. Taylor, 595 U.S. 420 (2000)	9:0	Justice Kennedy held that, under the Antiterrorism and Effective Death Penalty Act

of 1996, which limits federal court *habeas* review, Michael Williams and other death row inmates may raise issues in federal appeals for which they were unable to develop enough information to bring up during state court proceedings, if they were diligent in seeking the information.

Williams v. Taylor, 529   6:3 and   Writing for the Court, Jus-
U.S. 362 (2000)   5:4   tice Stevens held that Terry
                                               Williams was denied his
constitutionally guaranteed right to effective counsel, as defined in *Strickland v. Washington*, 466 U.S. 668 (1984), because his attorney failed to
investigate and to present substantial mitigating evidence to the jury, and thus
he was entitled to appeal his death sentence under the Antiterrorism and
Effective Death Penalty Act of 1996 (AEDPA). Justices O'Connor, Kennedy,
Souter, Ginsburg, and Breyer joined portions of the opinion. Justice O'Connor delivered the opinion of the Court, holding that the AEDPA places a new
constraint on federal courts in granting writs of *habeas corpus* review; they
may grant review only if the state court's adjudication was "contrary to" or
"involved an unreasonable application of clearly established federal law."
Chief Justice Rehnquist and Justices Kennedy, Scalia, and Thomas joined
that opinion.

Ramdass v. Angelone,   5:4   Justice Kennedy held that
530 U.S. 156 (2000)   the failure to inform the sen-
                                              tencing jury in a capital case
that the defendant was not entitled to parole under Virginia's "three strikes
and you're out" law, which denies parole for those convicted of three separate felonies, did not run afoul of constitutional requirements. Justices
Stevens, Souter, Ginsburg, and Breyer dissented.

Shafer v. South Carolina,   7:2   Writing for the Court, Justice
121 S.Ct. 1263 (2001)   Ginsburg held that whenever
                                              future dangerousness of the
defendant in a capital case is an issue, the defendant has a right to have the sentencing jury informed that he would not be eligible for parole if sentenced
to life imprisonment. Justices Scalia and Thomas dissented.

Penry v. Johnson,   6:3   Overturning the death sen-
121 S.Ct. 1910 (2001)   tence of Johnny Penry for a
                                              second time, the Court held
that the judge's instructions to the sentencing jury were unconstitutional
under *Penry I, Penry v. Lynaugh*, 492 U.S. 302 (1989) (excerpted in Vol. 2,
Ch.9). Writing for the Court, Justice O'Connor found that the instructions
were not broad enough for the jury to give mitigative effect to evidence of
Penry's mental retardation and childhood abuse.

11

THE RIGHT OF PRIVACY

A. PRIVACY AND REPRODUCTIVE FREEDOM

For the first time since *Planned Parenthood of Southeastern Pennsylvania v. Casey*, 505 U.S. 833 (1992) (excerpted in Vol. 2, Ch. 11), the Court handed down a ruling on abortion in *Stenberg v. Carhart* (excerpted below). By a five to four vote, the Court struck down Nebraska's ban on "partial birth abortions" as an "undue burden" on women.

Stenberg v. Carhart
530 U.S. 914, 120 S.Ct. 2597 (2000)

The Court's decision was five to four in affirming the federal appellate court's decision invalidating Nebraska's "partial birth abortion" law. The facts are discussed in the opinion for the Court delivered by Justice Breyer. Justices Ginsburg and Stevens filed concurring opinions. Chief Justice Rehnquist and Justices Kennedy, Scalia, and Thomas each filed dissenting opinions.

Justice BREYER delivered the opinion of the Court.

We again consider the right to an abortion. We understand the controversial nature of the problem. Millions of Americans believe that life begins at conception and consequently that an abortion is akin to causing the death of an innocent child; they recoil at the thought of a law that would permit it. Other millions fear that a law that forbids abortion would condemn many American women to lives that lack dignity, depriving them of equal liberty and leading those with least resources to undergo illegal abortions with the attendant risks of death and suffering. Taking account of these virtually irreconcilable points of view, aware that constitutional law must govern a society whose different members sincerely hold directly opposing views, and considering the matter in light of the Constitution's guarantees of fundamental individual liberty, this Court, in the course of a generation, has determined and then redetermined that the Constitution offers basic protection to the woman's right to choose. *Roe v. Wade*, 410 U.S. 113 (1973); *Planned Parenthood of Southeastern Pa. v. Casey*, 505 U.S. 833 (1992). We shall not revisit those legal principles. Rather, we apply them to the circumstances of this case.

Three established principles determine the issue before us. We shall set them forth in the language of the joint opinion in *Casey*. First, before "viability the woman has a right to choose to terminate her pregnancy."

Second, "a law designed to further the State's interest in fetal life which imposes an undue burden on the woman's decision before fetal viability" is unconstitutional. An "undue burden is shorthand for the conclusion that a state regulation has the purpose or effect of placing a substantial obstacle in the path of a woman seeking an abortion of a nonviable fetus."

Third, "subsequent to viability, the State in promoting its interest in the potentiality of human life may, if it chooses, regulate, and even proscribe, abortion except where it is necessary, in appropriate medical judgment, for the preservation of the life or health of the mother."

We apply these principles to a Nebraska law banning "partial birth abortion." The statute reads as follows: "No partial birth abortion shall be performed in this state, unless such procedure is necessary to save the life of the mother whose life is endangered by a physical disorder, physical illness, or physical injury, including a life-endangering physical condition caused by or arising from the pregnancy itself." The statute defines "partial birth abortion" as: "an abortion procedure in which the person performing the abortion partially delivers vaginally a living unborn child before killing the unborn child and completing the delivery." It further defines "partially delivers vaginally a living unborn child before killing the unborn child" to mean "deliberately and intentionally delivering into the vagina a living unborn child, or a substantial portion thereof, for the purpose of performing a procedure that the person performing such procedure knows will kill the unborn child and does kill the unborn child." The law classifies violation of the statute as a "Class III felony" carrying a prison term of up to 20 years, and a fine of up to $25,000. It also provides for the automatic revocation of a doctor's license to practice medicine in Nebraska.

We hold that this statute violates the Constitution. . . .

The evidence before the trial court, as supported or supplemented in the literature, indicates the following:

1. About 90% of all abortions performed in the United States take place during the first trimester of pregnancy, before 12 weeks of gestational age. During the first trimester, the predominant abortion method is "vacuum aspiration," which involves insertion of a vacuum tube (cannula) into the uterus to evacuate the contents. Such an abortion is typically performed on an outpatient basis under local anesthesia. The procedure's mortality rates for first trimester abortion are, for example, 5 to 10 times lower than those associated with carrying the fetus to term. Complication rates are also low. As the fetus grows in size, however, the vacuum aspiration method becomes increasingly difficult to use.

2. Approximately 10% of all abortions are performed during the second trimester of pregnancy (12 to 24 weeks). In the early 1970's, inducing labor through the injection of saline into the uterus was the predominant method of second trimester abortion. Today, however, the medical profession has switched from medical induction of labor to surgical procedures for most second trimester

abortions. The most commonly used procedure is called "dilation and evacuation" (D&E). That procedure (together with a modified form of vacuum aspiration used in the early second trimester) accounts for about 95% of all abortions performed from 12 to 20 weeks of gestational age.

3. D&E "refers generically to transcervical procedures performed at 13 weeks gestation or later." . . . There are variations in D&E operative strategy. However, the common points are that D&E involves (1) dilation of the cervix; (2) removal of at least some fetal tissue using nonvacuum instruments; and (3) (after the 15th week) the potential need for instrumental disarticulation or dismemberment of the fetus or the collapse of fetal parts to facilitate evacuation from the uterus.

4. When instrumental disarticulation incident to D&E is necessary, it typically occurs as the doctor pulls a portion of the fetus through the cervix into the birth canal. . . .

5. The D&E procedure carries certain risks. The use of instruments within the uterus creates a danger of accidental perforation and damage to neighboring organs. Sharp fetal bone fragments create similar dangers. And fetal tissue accidentally left behind can cause infection and various other complications. Nonetheless studies show that the risks of mortality and complication that accompany the D&E procedure between the 12th and 20th weeks of gestation are significantly lower than those accompanying induced labor procedures (the next safest midsecond trimester procedures).

6. At trial, Dr. Carhart and Dr. Stubblefield described a variation of the D&E procedure, which they referred to as an "intact D&E." Like other versions of the D&E technique, it begins with induced dilation of the cervix. The procedure then involves removing the fetus from the uterus through the cervix "intact," i.e., in one pass, rather than in several passes. It is used after 16 weeks at the earliest, as vacuum aspiration becomes ineffective and the fetal skull becomes too large to pass through the cervix. . . .

7. The intact D&E procedure can also be found described in certain obstetric and abortion clinical textbooks, where two variations are recognized. The first, as just described, calls for the physician to adapt his method for extracting the intact fetus depending on fetal presentation. A slightly different version of the intact D&E procedure, associated with Dr. Martin Haskell, calls for conversion to a breech presentation in all cases.

8. The American College of Obstetricians and Gynecologists describes the D&X procedure in a manner corresponding to a breech-conversion intact D&E, including the following steps: "1. deliberate dilation of the cervix, usually over a sequence of days; 2. instrumental conversion of the fetus to a footling breech; 3. breech extraction of the body excepting the head; and 4. partial evacuation of the intracranial contents of a living fetus to effect vaginal delivery of a dead but otherwise intact fetus." Despite the technical differences we have just described, intact D&E and D&X are sufficiently similar for us to use the terms interchangeably.

9. Dr. Carhart testified he attempts to use the intact D&E procedure during weeks 16 to 20 because (1) it reduces the dangers from sharp bone fragments passing through the cervix, (2) minimizes the number of instrument passes needed for extraction and lessens the likelihood of uterine perforations caused by those instruments, (3) reduces the likelihood of leaving infection-causing fetal and placental tissue in the uterus, and (4) could help to prevent potentially fatal absorption of fetal tissue into the maternal circulation. The District Court

made no findings about the D&X procedure's overall safety. The District Court concluded, however, that "the evidence is both clear and convincing that Carhart's D&X procedure is superior to, and safer than, the other abortion procedures used during the relevant gestational period in the 10 to 20 cases a year that present to Dr. Carhart."

10. The materials presented at trial referred to the potential benefits of the D&X procedure in circumstances involving nonviable fetuses, such as fetuses with abnormal fluid accumulation in the brain (hydrocephaly).

11. There are no reliable data on the number of D&X abortions performed annually. Estimates have ranged between 640 and 5,000 per year.

The question before us is whether Nebraska's statute, making criminal the performance of a "partial birth abortion," violates the Federal Constitution, as interpreted in *Planned Parenthood of Southeastern Pa. v. Casey*, and *Roe v. Wade*. We conclude that it does for at least two independent reasons. First, the law lacks any exception "for the preservation of the health of the mother." Second, it "imposes an undue burden on a woman's ability" to choose a D&E abortion, thereby unduly burdening the right to choose abortion itself. We shall discuss each of these reasons in turn. . . .

The fact that Nebraska's law applies both pre- and postviability aggravates the constitutional problem presented. The State's interest in regulating abortion previability is considerably weaker than postviability. Since the law requires a health exception in order to validate even a postviability abortion regulation, it at a minimum requires the same in respect to previability regulation.

The quoted standard also depends on the state regulations "promoting [the State's] interest in the potentiality of human life." The Nebraska law, of course, does not directly further an interest "in the potentiality of human life" by saving the fetus in question from destruction, as it regulates only a method of performing abortion. Nebraska describes its interests differently. It says the law "show[s] concern for the life of the unborn," "prevent[s] cruelty to partially born children," and "preserve[s] the integrity of the medical profession." But we cannot see how the interest-related differences could make any difference to the question at hand, namely, the application of the "health" requirement.

Consequently, the governing standard requires an exception "where it is necessary, in appropriate medical judgment for the preservation of the life or health of the mother," for this Court has made clear that a State may promote but not endanger a woman's health when it regulates the methods of abortion. *Thornburgh v. American College of Obstetricians and Gynecologists*, 476 U.S. 747 (1986); *Colautti v. Franklin*, 439 U.S. 379 (1979); *Doe v. Bolton*, 410 U.S. 179 (1973). Justice THOMAS says that the cases just cited limit this principle to situations where the pregnancy itself creates a threat to health. He is wrong. The cited cases, reaffirmed in *Casey*, recognize that a State cannot subject women's health to significant risks both in that context, and also where state regulations force women to use riskier methods of abortion. Our cases have repeatedly invalidated statutes that in the process of regulating the methods of abortion, imposed significant health risks. They make clear that a risk to a women's health is the same whether it happens to arise from regulating a particular method of abortion, or from barring abortion entirely. Our holding does not go beyond those cases, as ratified in *Casey*. . . .

Nebraska responds that the law does not require a health exception unless there is a need for such an exception. . . . Nebraska, along with supporting *amici*, replies that these findings are irrelevant, wrong, or applicable only in a tiny number of instances. It says (1) that the D&X procedure is "little-used," (2) by only "a handful of doctors." It argues (3) that D&E and labor induction are at all times "safe alternative procedures." It refers to the testimony of petitioners' medical expert, who testified (4) that the ban would not increase a woman's risk of several rare abortion complications (disseminated intravascular coagulopathy and amniotic fluid embolus).

The Association of American Physicians and Surgeons et al., *amici* supporting Nebraska, argue (5) that elements of the D&X procedure may create special risks, including cervical incompetence caused by overdilitation, injury caused by conversion of the fetal presentation, and dangers arising from the "blind" use of instrumentation to pierce the fetal skull while lodged in the birth canal.

Nebraska further emphasizes (6) that there are no medical studies "establishing the safety of the partial-birth abortion/D&X procedure," and "no medical studies comparing the safety of partial-birth abortion/D&X to other abortion procedures," (7) an American Medical Association policy statement that "there does not appear to be any identified situation in which intact D&X is the only appropriate procedure to induce abortion." And it points out (8) that the American College of Obstetricians and Gynecologists qualified its statement that D&X "may be the best or most appropriate procedure," by adding that the panel "could identify no circumstances under which [the D&X] procedure would be the only option to save the life or preserve the health of the woman."

We find these eight arguments insufficient to demonstrate that Nebraska's law needs no health exception. For one thing, certain of the arguments are beside the point. The D&X procedure's relative rarity (argument (1)) is not highly relevant. The D&X is an infrequently used abortion procedure; but the health exception question is whether protecting women's health requires an exception for those infrequent occasions. A rarely used treatment might be necessary to treat a rarely occurring disease that could strike anyone—the State cannot prohibit a person from obtaining treatment simply by pointing out that most people do not need it. Nor can we know whether the fact that only a "handful" of doctors use the procedure (argument (2)) reflects the comparative rarity of late second term abortions, the procedure's recent development, the controversy surrounding it, or, as Nebraska suggests, the procedure's lack of utility.

For another thing, the record responds to Nebraska's (and *amici*'s) medically based arguments. In respect to argument (3), for example, the District Court agreed that alternatives, such as D&E and induced labor, are "safe" but found that the D&X method was significantly safer in certain circumstances. In respect to argument (4), the District Court simply relied on different expert testimony—testimony stating that "[a]nother advantage of the Intact D&E is that it eliminates the risk of embolism of cerebral tissue into the woman's blood stream."

In response to *amici*'s argument (5), the American College of Obstetricians and Gynecologists, in its own *amici* brief, denies that D&X generally poses risks greater than the alternatives. It says that the suggested alternative procedures involve similar or greater risks of cervical and uterine injury, for "D&E procedures, involve similar amounts of dilitation" and "of course childbirth involves even greater cervical dilitation." The College points out that Dr. Carhart does not reposition the fetus thereby avoiding any risks stemming from conversion to breech presentation, and that, as compared with D&X, D&E involves the same, if not greater, "blind" use of sharp instruments in the uterine cavity.

We do not quarrel with Nebraska's argument (6), for Nebraska is right. There are no general medical studies documenting comparative safety. Neither do we deny the import of the American Medical Association's statement (argument (7))—even though the State does omit the remainder of that statement: "The AMA recommends that the procedure not be used unless alternative procedures pose materially greater risk to the woman."

We cannot, however, read the American College of Obstetricians and Gynecologists panel's qualification (that it could not "identify" a circumstance where D&X was the "only" life- or health-preserving option) as if, according to Nebraska's argument (8), it denied the potential health-related need for D&X. That is because the College writes the following in its *amici* brief: "Depending on the physician's skill and experience, the D&X procedure can be the most appropriate abortion procedure for some women in some circumstances. D&X presents a variety of potential safety advantages over other abortion procedures used during the same gestational period." . . .

The upshot is a District Court finding that D&X significantly obviates health risks in certain circumstances, a highly plausible record-based explanation of why that might be so, a division of opinion among some medical experts over whether D&X is generally safer, and an absence of controlled medical studies that would help answer these medical questions. Given these medically related evidentiary circumstances, we believe the law requires a health exception. . . .

The Eighth Circuit found the Nebraska statute unconstitutional because, in *Casey*'s words, it has the "effect of placing a substantial obstacle in the path of a woman seeking an abortion of a nonviable fetus." It thereby places an "undue burden" upon a woman's right to terminate her pregnancy before viability. Nebraska does not deny that the statute imposes an "undue burden" if it applies to the more commonly used D&E procedure as well as to D&X. And we agree with the Eighth Circuit that it does so apply. . . .

The judgment of the Court of Appeals is affirmed.

Justice O'CONNOR, concurring.

I write separately to emphasize the following points.

First, the Nebraska statute is inconsistent with *Casey* because it lacks an exception for those instances when the banned procedure is necessary to preserve the health of the mother. . . . Contrary to the assertions of Justice KENNEDY and Justice THOMAS, the need for a health exception does not arise from "the individual views of Dr. Carhart and his supporters." Rather, as the majority explains, where, as here, "a significant body of medical opinion believes a procedure may bring with it greater safety for some patients and explains the medical reasons supporting that view," then Nebraska cannot say that the procedure will not, in some circumstances, be "necessary to preserve the life or health of the mother." Accordingly, our precedent requires that the statute include a health exception.

Second, Nebraska's statute is unconstitutional on the alternative and independent ground that it imposes an undue burden on a woman's right to choose to terminate her pregnancy before viability. Nebraska's ban covers not just the dilation and extraction (D&X) procedure, but also the dilation and evacuation

(D&E) procedure, "the most commonly used method for performing previability second trimester abortions." . . . Thus, it is not possible to interpret the statute's language as applying only to the D&X procedure. Moreover, it is significant that both the District Court and the Court of Appeals interpreted the statute as prohibiting abortions performed using the D&E method as well as the D&X method. . . . Indeed, Nebraska conceded at oral argument that "the State could not prohibit the D&E procedure." By proscribing the most commonly used method for previability second trimester abortions, the statute creates a "substantial obstacle to a woman seeking an abortion," and therefore imposes an undue burden on a woman's right to terminate her pregnancy prior to viability.

It is important to note that, unlike Nebraska, some other States have enacted statutes more narrowly tailored to proscribing the D&X procedure alone. Some of those statutes have done so by specifically excluding from their coverage the most common methods of abortion, such as the D&E and vacuum aspiration procedures. . . . By restricting their prohibitions to the D&X procedure exclusively, the Kansas, Utah, and Montana statutes avoid a principal defect of the Nebraska law. . . .

Nebraska's statute, however, does not meet these criteria. It contains no exception for when the procedure, in appropriate medical judgment, is necessary to preserve the health of the mother; and it proscribes not only the D&X procedure but also the D&E procedure, the most commonly used method for previability second trimester abortions, thus making it an undue burden on a woman's right to terminate her pregnancy. For these reasons, I agree with the Court that Nebraska's law is unconstitutional.

Justice GINSBURG, with whom Justice STEVENS joins, concurring.

I write separately only to stress that amidst all the emotional uproar caused by an abortion case, we should not lose sight of the character of Nebraska's "partial birth abortion" law. As the Court observes, this law does not save any fetus from destruction, for it targets only "a method of performing abortion." Nor does the statute seek to protect the lives or health of pregnant women. Moreover, as Justice STEVENS points out, the most common method of performing previability second trimester abortions is no less distressing or susceptible to gruesome description. . . .

A state regulation that "has the purpose or effect of placing a substantial obstacle in the path of a woman seeking an abortion of a nonviable fetus" violates the Constitution. *Casey.*

Justice STEVENS, with whom Justice GINSBURG joins, concurring.

[D]uring the past 27 years, the central holding of *Roe v. Wade* has been endorsed by all but 4 of the 17 Justices who have addressed the issue. That holding—that the word "liberty" in the Fourteenth Amendment includes a woman's right to make this difficult and extremely personal decision—makes it impossible for me to understand how a State has any legitimate interest in requiring a doctor to follow any procedure other than the one that he or she reasonably believes will best protect the woman in her exercise of this constitutional liberty.

But one need not even approach this view today to conclude that Nebraska's law must fall. For the notion that either of these two equally gruesome procedures performed at this late stage of gestation is more akin to infanticide than the other, or that the State furthers any legitimate interest by banning one but not the other, is simply irrational.

Justice SCALIA, dissenting.

I have joined Justice THOMAS's dissent because I agree that today's decision is an "unprecedented expansio[n]" of our prior cases, "is not mandated" by *Casey*'s "undue burden" test, and can even be called (though this pushes me to the limit of my belief) "obviously irreconcilable with *Casey*'s explication of what its undue-burden standard requires." But I never put much stock in *Casey*'s explication of the inexplicable. In the last analysis, my judgment that *Casey* does not support today's tragic result can be traced to the fact that what I consider to be an "undue burden" is different from what the majority considers to be an "undue burden"—a conclusion that can not be demonstrated true or false by factual inquiry or legal reasoning. It is a value judgment, dependent upon how much one respects (or believes society ought to respect) the life of a partially delivered fetus, and how much one respects (or believes society ought to respect) the freedom of the woman who gave it life to kill it. . . .

While I am in an I-told-you-so mood, I must recall my bemusement, in *Casey*, at the joint opinion's expressed belief that *Roe v. Wade* had "call[ed] the contending sides of a national controversy to end their national division by accepting a common mandate rooted in the Constitution," and that the decision in *Casey* would ratify that happy truce. It seemed to me, quite to the contrary, that "*Roe* fanned into life an issue that has inflamed our national politics in general, and has obscured with its smoke the selection of Justices to this Court in particular, ever since"; and that, "by keeping us in the abortion-umpiring business, it is the perpetuation of that disruption, rather than of any Pax Roeana, that the Court's new majority decrees." Today's decision, that the Constitution of the United States prevents the prohibition of a horrible mode of abortion, will be greeted by a firestorm of criticism—as well it should. I cannot understand why those who acknowledge that, in the opening words of Justice O'CONNOR's concurrence, "[t]he issue of abortion is one of the most contentious and controversial in contemporary American society," persist in the belief that this Court, armed with neither constitutional text nor accepted tradition, can resolve that contention and controversy rather than be consumed by it. If only for the sake of its own preservation, the Court should return this matter to the people—where the Constitution, by its silence on the subject, left it—and let them decide, State by State, whether this practice should be allowed. *Casey* must be overruled.

Justice KENNEDY, with whom Chief Justice REHNQUIST joins, dissenting.

For close to two decades after *Roe v. Wade*, the Court gave but slight weight to the interests of the separate States when their legislatures sought to address persisting concerns raised by the existence of a woman's right to elect an abortion in defined circumstances. When the Court reaffirmed the essential holding of *Roe*, a central premise was that the States retain a critical and legitimate role in legislating on the subject of abortion, as limited by the woman's right the Court restated and again guaranteed. *Planned Parenthood of Southeastern Pa. v. Casey.* The political processes of the State are not to be foreclosed from enacting laws to promote the life of the unborn and to ensure respect for all human life and its potential. The State's constitutional authority is a vital means for citizens to address these grave and serious issues, as they must if we are to progress in knowledge and understanding and in the attainment of some degree of consensus.

The Court's decision today, in my submission, repudiates this understanding by invalidating a statute advancing critical state interests, even though the law denies no woman the right to choose an abortion and places no undue burden upon the right. The legislation is well within the State's competence to enact. Having concluded Nebraska's law survives the scrutiny dictated by a proper understanding of *Casey*, I dissent from the judgment invalidating it. . . .

Justice THOMAS, with whom Chief Justice REHNQUIST and Justice SCALIA join, dissenting.

Today's decision is so obviously irreconcilable with *Casey*'s explication of what its undue-burden standard requires, let alone the Constitution, that it should be seen for what it is, a reinstitution of the pre-*Webster* abortion-on-demand era in which the mere invocation of "abortion rights" trumps any contrary societal interest. If this statute is unconstitutional under *Casey*, then *Casey* meant nothing at all, and the Court should candidly admit it.

To reach its decision, the majority must take a series of indefensible steps. The majority must first disregard the principles that this Court follows in every context but abortion: We interpret statutes according to their plain meaning and we do not strike down statutes susceptible of a narrowing construction. The majority also must disregard the very constitutional standard it purports to employ, and then displace the considered judgment of the people of Nebraska and 29 other States. The majority's decision is lamentable, because of the result the majority reaches, the illogical steps the majority takes to reach it, and because it portends a return to an era I had thought we had at last abandoned. . . .

[Because I interpret] Nebraska's partial birth abortion statute [to] permi[t] doctors to perform D&E abortions, the question remains whether a State can constitutionally prohibit the partial birth abortion procedure without a health exception. Although the majority and Justice O'CONNOR purport to rely on the standard articulated in the *Casey* joint opinion in concluding that a State may not, they in fact disregard it entirely.

Though Justices O'CONNOR, KENNEDY, and SOUTER declined in *Casey*, on the ground of *stare decisis*, to reconsider whether abortion enjoys any constitutional protection, *Casey* professed to be, in part, a repudiation of *Roe* and its progeny. The *Casey* joint opinion expressly noted that prior case law had undervalued the State's interest in potential life, and had invalidated regulations of abortion that "in no real sense deprived women of the ultimate decision." The joint opinion repeatedly recognized the States' weighty interest in this area.

The *Casey* joint opinion therefore adopted the standard: "Only where state regulation imposes an undue burden on a woman's ability to make this decision does the power of the State reach into the heart of the liberty protected by the Due Process Clause." A regulation imposes an "undue burden" only if it "has the effect of placing a substantial obstacle in the path of a woman's choice."

There is no question that the State of Nebraska has a valid interest—one not designed to strike at the right itself—in prohibiting partial birth abortion. *Casey* itself noted that States may "express profound respect for the life of the unborn."

The next question, therefore, is whether the Nebraska statute is unconstitutional because it does not contain an exception that would allow use of the procedure whenever "necessary in appropriate medical judgment, for the preservation of the health of the mother." According to the majority, such a health exception is required here because there is a "division of opinion among some medical experts over whether D&X is generally safer [than D&E], and an absence of controlled medical studies that would help answer these medical questions." The rule set forth by the majority and Justice O'CONNOR dramatically expands on our prior abortion cases and threatens to undo any state regulation of abortion procedures.

The majority and Justice O'CONNOR suggest that their rule is dictated by a straightforward application of *Roe* and *Casey*. But that is simply not true. In *Roe* and *Casey*, the Court stated that the State may "regulate, and even proscribe, abortion except where it is necessary, in appropriate medical judgment, for the preservation of the life or health of the mother." *Casey* said that a health exception must be available if "continuing her pregnancy would constitute a threat" to the woman. Under these cases, if a State seeks to prohibit abortion, even if only temporarily or under particular circumstances, as *Casey* says that it may, the State must make an exception for cases in which the life or health of the mother is endangered by continuing the pregnancy. These cases addressed only the situation in which a woman must obtain an abortion because of some threat to her health from continued pregnancy. But *Roe* and *Casey* say nothing at all about cases in which a physician considers one prohibited method of abortion to be preferable to permissible methods. Today's majority and Justice O'CONNOR twist *Roe* and *Casey* to apply to the situation in which a woman desires—for whatever reason—an abortion and wishes to obtain the abortion by some particular method. In other words, the majority and Justice O'CONNOR fail to distinguish between cases in which health concerns require a woman to obtain an abortion and cases in which health concerns cause a woman who desires an abortion (for whatever reason) to prefer one method over another. . . .

We were reassured repeatedly in *Casey* that not all regulations of abortion are unwarranted and that the States may express profound respect for fetal life. Under *Casey*, the regulation before us today should easily pass constitutional muster. But the Court's abortion jurisprudence is a particularly virulent strain of constitutional exegesis. And so today we are told that 30 States are prohibited from banning one rarely used form of abortion that they believe to border on infanticide. It is clear that the Constitution does not compel this result.

12

THE EQUAL PROTECTION
OF THE LAWS

A. RACIAL DISCRIMINATION AND STATE ACTION

THE DEVELOPMENT OF LAW

Other Rulings on State Action

Case	Vote	Ruling
Brentwood Academy v. Tennessee Secondary School Athletic Association, 531 U.S. 288 (2001)	5:4	The Court held that the Tennessee Secondary School Athletic Association is a "state actor" because of its pervasive

entwinement with state school officials. The association regulates interscholastic sports among Tennessee public and private high schools. Its staff, although not classified as state employees, may join the state retirement system, and the association sets membership standards and student eligibility rules, as well as has the power to penalize schools that violate its rules. When the association penalized Brentwood Academy for violating its recruitment rules, Brentwood Academy sued, claiming that enforcement of the rules constituted state action that violated the First and Fourteenth Amendments. Writing for the Court, Justice Souter reaffirmed that state action may be found when there exists a "close nexus between the state and the challenged action" and when seemingly private behavior "may be fairly treated as that of the state itself," citing *Jackson v. Metropolitan Edison Co.*, 419 U.S. 345 (1974). Chief Justice Rehnquist and Justices Kennedy, Scalia, and Thomas dissented.

C. AFFIRMATIVE ACTION AND
REVERSE DISCRIMINATION

In its 2001–2002 term, the Court will revisit the issue of constitutionality of affirmative-action programs in *Adarand Constructors, Inc. v. Mineta*

(No. 00-730) (*Adarand II*). In *Adarand Constructors, Inc. v. Pena* (1995) (*Adarand I*) (excerpted in Vol. 2, Ch. 12), a bare majority of the Court invalidated federal affirmative-action programs that are not narrowly tailored to remedying past discrimination. Subsequently, the Court of Appeals for the Tenth Circuit upheld a revised version of the federal subcontracting affirmative-action program that was challenged in *Adarand I*. It found that Congress had provided strong evidence of intentional discrimination against minority-owned businesses in highway construction and concluded that the program survived "strict scrutiny," 228 F.3d 1147 (10th Cir., 2001). Adarand Constructors, a white-owned guardrail installer, appealed that decision to the Court, which granted review.

D. NONRACIAL CLASSIFICATIONS AND THE EQUAL PROTECTION OF THE LAWS

(1) Gender-Based Discrimination

THE DEVELOPMENT OF LAW

Other Rulings Upholding Gender-Based Distinctions under the Constitution

Case	Vote	Ruling
Tuan Anh Nguyen v. Immigration and Naturalization Service, 121 S.Ct. 2053 (2001)	5:4	The Court rejected a challenge to a federal statute that makes it more difficult for children born out of wedlock

to fathers who are U.S. citizens, in contrast to mothers who are U.S. citizens, to become citizens. Children born of mothers who are U.S. citizens are almost automatically made U.S. citizens, whereas those born out of wedlock to mothers who are foreign nationals and to fathers who are U.S. citizens must apply for citizenship before they are 18 years old and must present evidence of their paternity. Writing for the Court, Justice Kennedy deemed the law rational and not based on stereotypes, whereas Justice O'Connor, in dissent, countered that the majority's decision rested on stereotypes of male versus female irresponsibility and violated the Fourteenth Amendment. Justices Souter, Ginsburg, and Breyer joined her dissent.

---

(3) Wealth, Poverty, and Illegitimacy

In *Saenz v. Roe* (1999) (excerpted below) the Court struck down California's limiting the welfare benefits of new residents to that paid by the state in which they previously resided. In doing so, Justice Stevens reaffirmed the ruling in *Shapiro v. Thompson*, 394 U.S. 618 (1969) (excerpted in Vol. 2, Ch. 12), and held that the state, in penalizing new residents, had run afoul of their constitutional right to travel. Chief Justice Rehnquist and Justice Thomas dissented.

Saenz v. Roe

526 U.S. 489, 119 S.Ct. 1518 (1999)

California, which has the sixth highest welfare benefits budget in the country, amended Section 11450.03 of its Aid to Families with Dependent Children (AFDC) program in 1992 so as to limit new residents, for the first year that they live in the state, to the benefits they would have received in the state of their prior residence. Although the secretary of the Department of Health and Human Services (HHS) approved the change, which was a requirement for its going into effect, a federal district court enjoined its implementation upon finding that, under *Shapiro v. Thompson*, 394 U.S. 618 (1969) (excerpted in Vol. 2, Ch. 12), it penalized new residents and infringed on their constitutional right to travel. Subsequently, in a separate proceeding the Court of Appeals for the Ninth Circuit invalidated the HHS's approval of Section 11450.03. However, in 1996 Congress enacted the Personal Responsibility and Work Opportunity Reconciliation Act (PRWORA), which replaced AFDC with Temporary Assistance to Needy Families (TANF). PRWORA expressly authorized any state receiving a TANF grant to pay the benefit amount of another state's TANF program to residents who lived in the state for less than one year. Whereupon, California announced that it would now enforce Section 11450.03 beginning on April 1, 1997. On that date, a class action lawsuit was filed, challenging the constitutionality of Section 11450.03's residency requirement and PRWORA's approval of that requirement. The district court found that PRWORA did not affect its earlier decision and issued a preliminary injunction against the enforcement of Section 11450.03, which the Ninth Circuit affirmed. An appeal was then made to the Supreme Court, which granted review.

The Court's decision, affirming the appellate court, was seven to two, and its opinion was delivered by Justice Stevens. Chief Justice Rehnquist and Justice Thomas each filed dissenting opinions.

Justice STEVENS delivered the opinion of the Court.

The word "travel" is not found in the text of the Constitution. Yet the "constitutional right to travel from one State to another" is firmly embedded in our jurisprudence. *United States v. Guest*, 383 U.S. 745 (1966). Indeed, as Justice

STEWART reminded us in *Shapiro v. Thompson*, 394 U.S. 618 (1969), the right is so important that it is "assertable against private interference as well as governmental action—a virtually unconditional personal right, guaranteed by the Constitution to us all."

In *Shapiro*, we reviewed the constitutionality of three statutory provisions that denied welfare assistance to residents of Connecticut, the District of Columbia, and Pennsylvania, who had resided within those respective jurisdictions less than one year immediately preceding their applications for assistance. Without pausing to identify the specific source of the right, we . . . squarely held that it was "constitutionally impermissible" for a State to enact durational residency requirements for the purpose of inhibiting the migration by needy persons into the State. We further held that a classification that had the effect of imposing a penalty on the exercise of the right to travel violated the Equal Protection Clause "unless shown to be necessary to promote a compelling governmental interest," and that no such showing had been made. . . .

The "right to travel" discussed in our cases embraces at least three different components. It protects the right of a citizen of one State to enter and to leave another State, the right to be treated as a welcome visitor rather than an unfriendly alien when temporarily present in the second State, and, for those travelers who elect to become permanent residents, the right to be treated like other citizens of that State.

It was the right to go from one place to another, including the right to cross state borders while en route, that was vindicated in *Edwards v. California*, 314 U.S. 160 (1941), which invalidated a state law that impeded the free interstate passage of the indigent. We reaffirmed that right in *United States v. Guest*, 383 U.S. 745 (1966), which afforded protection to the "right to travel freely to and from the State of Georgia and to use highway facilities and other instrumentalities of interstate commerce within the State of Georgia." Given that Section 11450.03 imposed no obstacle to respondents' entry into California, we think the State is correct when it argues that the statute does not directly impair the exercise of the right to free interstate movement. For the purposes of this case, therefore, we need not identify the source of that particular right in the text of the Constitution. . . .

The second component of the right to travel is, however, expressly protected by the text of the Constitution. The first sentence of Article IV, Sec. 2, provides: "The Citizens of each State shall be entitled to all Privileges and Immunities of Citizens in the several States." Thus, by virtue of a person's state citizenship, a citizen of one State who travels in other States, intending to return home at the end of his journey, is entitled to enjoy the "Privileges and Immunities of Citizens in the several States" that he visits. This provision removes "from the citizens of each State the disabilities of alienage in the other States." *Paul v. Virginia*, 8 Wall. 168 (1869). It provides important protections for nonresidents who enter a State whether to obtain employment, *Hicklin v. Orbeck*, 437 U.S. 518 (1978), to procure medical services, *Doe v. Bolton*, 410 U.S. 179 (1973), or even to engage in commercial shrimp fishing, *Toomer v. Witsell*, 334 U.S. 385 (1948). Those protections are not "absolute," but the Clause "does bar discrimination against citizens of other States where there is no substantial reason for the discrimination beyond the mere fact that they are citizens of other States." There may be a substantial reason for requiring the nonresident to pay more than the resident for a hunting license, or to enroll in the state university, see *Vlandis v. Kline*, 412

U.S. 441 (1973), but our cases have not identified any acceptable reason for qualifying the protection afforded by the Clause for "the 'citizen of State A who ventures into State B' to settle there and establish a home." Permissible justifications for discrimination between residents and nonresidents are simply inapplicable to a nonresident's exercise of the right to move into another State and become a resident of that State.

What is at issue in this case, then, is this third aspect of the right to travel—the right of the newly arrived citizen to the same privileges and immunities enjoyed by other citizens of the same State. That right is protected not only by the new arrival's status as a state citizen, but also by her status as a citizen of the United States. That additional source of protection is plainly identified in the opening words of the Fourteenth Amendment: "All persons born or naturalized in the United States, and subject to the jurisdiction thereof, are citizens of the United States and of the State wherein they reside. No State shall make or enforce any law which shall abridge the privileges or immunities of citizens of the United States." Despite fundamentally differing views concerning the coverage of the Privileges or Immunities Clause of the Fourteenth Amendment, most notably expressed in the majority and dissenting opinions in the *Slaughter-House Cases*, 16 Wall. 36 (1873), it has always been common ground that this Clause protects the third component of the right to travel. . . .

The classifications challenged in this case—and there are many—are defined entirely by (a) the period of residency in California and (b) the location of the prior residences of the disfavored class members. The favored class of beneficiaries includes all eligible California citizens who have resided there for at least one year, plus those new arrivals who last resided in another country or in a State that provides benefits at least as generous as California's. Thus, within the broad category of citizens who resided in California for less than a year, there are many who are treated like lifetime residents. And within the broad sub-category of new arrivals who are treated less favorably, there are many smaller classes whose benefit levels are determined by the law of the States from whence they came. To justify Section 11450.03, California must therefore explain not only why it is sound fiscal policy to discriminate against those who have been citizens for less than a year, but also why it is permissible to apply such a variety of rules within that class. . . .

Disavowing any desire to fence out the indigent, California has instead advanced an entirely fiscal justification for its multitiered scheme. The enforcement of Section 11450.03 will save the State approximately $10.9 million a year. The question is not whether such saving is a legitimate purpose but whether the State may accomplish that end by the discriminatory means it has chosen. An evenhanded, across-the-board reduction of about 72 cents per month for every beneficiary would produce the same result. But our negative answer to the question does not rest on the weakness of the State's purported fiscal justification. It rests on the fact that the Citizenship Clause of the Fourteenth Amendment expressly equates citizenship with residence: "That Clause does not provide for, and does not allow for, degrees of citizenship based on length of residence." It is equally clear that the Clause does not tolerate a hierarchy of 45 subclasses of similarly situated citizens based on the location of their prior residence. Thus Section 11450.03 is doubly vulnerable: Neither the duration of respondents' California residence, nor the identity of their prior States of residence, has any relevance to their need for benefits. Nor do those factors bear any relationship to the State's interest in making an equitable allocation of the funds to be distributed among its needy citizens. As in *Shapiro*, we reject any contributory rationale for the denial of benefits to new residents. . . .

The question that remains is whether congressional approval of durational residency requirements in the 1996 amendment to the Social Security Act somehow resuscitates the constitutionality of Section 11450.03. That question is readily answered, for we have consistently held that Congress may not authorize the States to violate the Fourteenth Amendment. Moreover, the protection afforded to the citizen by the Citizenship Clause of that Amendment is a limitation on the powers of the National Government as well as the States. . . .

The judgment of the Court of Appeals is affirmed.

Chief Justice REHNQUIST, with whom Justice THOMAS joins, dissenting.

The Court today breathes new life into the previously dormant Privileges or Immunities Clause of the Fourteenth Amendment—a Clause relied upon by this Court in only one other decision, *Colgate v. Harvey*, 296 U.S. 404 (1935), overruled five years later by *Madden v. Kentucky*, 309 U.S. 83 (1940). It uses this Clause to strike down what I believe is a reasonable measure falling under the head of a "good-faith residency requirement." Because I do not think any provision of the Constitution—and surely not a provision relied upon for only the second time since its enactment 130 years ago—requires this result, I dissent. . . .

In unearthing from its tomb the right to become a state citizen and to be treated equally in the new State of residence, . . . the Court ignores a State's need to assure that only persons who establish a bona fide residence receive the benefits provided to current residents of the State. . . .

States employ objective criteria such as durational residence requirements to test a new resident's resolve to remain before these new citizens can enjoy certain in-state benefits. Recognizing the practical appeal of such criteria, this Court has repeatedly sanctioned the State's use of durational residence requirements before new residents receive in-state tuition rates at state universities. *Starns v. Malkerson*, 401 U.S. 985 (1971) (upholding 1-year residence requirement for in-state tuition); *Sturgis v. Washington*, 414 U.S. 1057 (1973) (same). . . . The Court has done the same in upholding a 1-year residence requirement for eligibility to obtain a divorce in state courts, see *Sosna v. Iowa*, 419 U.S. 393 (1975), and in upholding political party registration restrictions that amounted to a durational residency requirement for voting in primary elections, see *Rosario v. Rockefeller*, 410 U.S. 752 (1973).

If States can require individuals to reside in-state for a year before exercising the right to educational benefits, the right to terminate a marriage, or the right to vote in primary elections that all other state citizens enjoy, then States may surely do the same for welfare benefits. Indeed, there is no material difference between a 1-year residence requirement applied to the level of welfare benefits given out by a State, and the same requirement applied to the level of tuition subsidies at a state university. . . .

I therefore believe that the durational residence requirement challenged here is a permissible exercise of the State's power to "assur[e] that services provided for its residents are enjoyed only by residents." . . .

(4) Alienage and Age

THE DEVELOPMENT OF LAW

Recent Rulings on Age Discrimination

Case	Vote	Ruling
Kimel v. Florida Board of Regents, 528 U.S. 62 (2000)	5:4	Writing for the Court, Justice O'Connor held that Congress exceeded its powers under

Section 5 of the Fourteenth Amendment and violated states' sovereign immunity under the Eleventh Amendment in extending provisions of the Age Discrimination in Employment Act to state employees and ruled that state employees may not bring suits in federal courts to enforce those provisions. In reaffirming that age discrimination is not a suspect classification under the Fourteenth Amendment, Justice O'Connor emphasized that "[o]ld age also does not define a discrete and insular minority because all persons, if they live out normal life spans, will experience it." Justices Stevens, Breyer, Ginsburg, and Souter dissented.

Reeves v. Sanderson Plumbing Products, Inc., 530 U.S. 133 (2000)	9:0	Writing for the Court, Justice O'Connor ruled that workers need not provide direct evidence that their employers

intentionally discriminated against them in hiring and promotion decisions, in a suit brought under the Age Discrimination in Employment Act. Employees need only prove that the employer's stated reason for their dismissal was false, and juries may infer from the evidence presented whether the employer's true motive was discriminatory.

INDEX OF CASES

Cases printed in boldface are excerpted on the page(s) printed in boldface.

Other Books by David M. O'Brien

STORM CENTER:
THE SUPREME COURT IN AMERICAN POLITICS
FIFTH EDITION

CONSTITUTIONAL LAW AND POLITICS:
Vol. 1, STRUGGLES FOR POWER AND GOVERNMENTAL
ACCOUNTABILITY

Vol. 2, CIVIL RIGHTS AND CIVIL LIBERTIES
FOURTH EDITION

ABORTION AND AMERICAN POLITICS
(co-authored)

JUDICIAL ROULETTE

WHAT PROCESS IS DUE?
COURTS AND SCIENCE-POLICY DISPUTES

VIEWS FROM THE BENCH:
THE JUDICIARY AND CONSTITUTIONAL POLITICS
(co-authored)

THE POLITICS OF TECHNOLOGY ASSESSMENT:
INSTITUTIONS, PROCESSES, AND POLICY DISPUTES
(co-authored)

THE PUBLIC'S RIGHT TO KNOW:
THE SUPREME COURT AND THE FIRST AMENDMENT

PRIVACY, LAW, AND PUBLIC POLICY

THE POLITICS OF AMERICAN GOVERNMENT
THIRD EDITION
(co-authored)

TO DREAM OF DREAMS:
RELIGIOUS FREEDOM AND CONSTITUTIONAL POLITICS
IN POSTWAR JAPAN

JUDGES ON JUDGING

LANAHAN READINGS IN CIVIL RIGHTS AND
CIVIL LIBERTIES

JUDICIAL INDEPENDENCE IN THE AGE OF DEMOCRACY:
CRITICAL PERSPECTIVES FROM AROUND THE WORLD
(co-edited)

GOVERNMENT BY THE PEOPLE
NINETEENTH EDITION
(co-authored)